THE OCEANIC FEELING

THE OCEANIC FEELING

ON THE NEED FOR A NEW NARRATIVE

ISABELLA LÖVIN

PARAGON PUBLISHING

© Isabella Lövin, 2024

Publishing partner: Paragon Publishing

Originally published as *Oceankänslan - Om behovet av en ny berättelse*, in Swedish by Natur & Kultur Förlag, 2022

Translation to English by Melissa Bowes

Cover design by Sigge Kühlhorn

Also by Isabella Lövin: *Silent Seas - the Fish Race to the Bottom*, Paragon Publishing 2012

ISBN 978-1-78792-038-5

Book design, layout and production management by Into Print
www.intoprint.net
+44 (0)1604 832149

The printer is committed to its Chain of Custody program under the regulatory standards and social responsibility goals established by SFI®, FSC®, or PEFC™

FOR LASSE

"I dissolved in the sea, became white sails and flying spray, became beauty and rhythm, became moonlight and the ship and the high dim-starred sky! I belonged, without past or future, within peace and unity and a wild joy, within something greater than my own life, or the life of Man, to Life itself!"

EUGENE O'NEILL, *Long Days Journey Into Night*, 1956

"A human being is a part of the whole, called by us the 'Universe', a part limited in time and space. He experiences himself, his thoughts and feelings as something separated from the rest, a kind of optical delusion of his consciousness. This delusion is a kind of prison for us, restricting us to our personal desires and to affection for a few persons nearest to us. Our task must be to free ourselves from this prison by widening our circle of compassion to embrace all living creatures and the whole of nature in its beauty."

ALBERT EINSTEIN, *Mathematical Circles Adieu*, Howard Eves, 1977

"We do not own the fish, the trees or the Earth. We have a relationship with them."

FRANK ETTAWAGESHIK, United Tribes of Michigan, COP25, 2019

CONTENTS

Foreword

I AM WRITING this new foreword a little more than a year after the publication in Sweden of my book *The Oceanic Feeling – on the Need for a New narrative*. It has been a year of quite extraordinary response from the readers particularly to one of the themes I introduce – admittedly quite briefly – in the book: that of the concept of the "Oceanic Feeling". It has attracted a lot of interest, much more than I expected, and has started to crop up in many different contexts in a rapidly expanding discussion on what we need to do to change the course of our global society as it heads towards disaster. More and more people are saying, and more and more have concluded, separately, following different tracks, that to save this planet from the worst effects of the climate crisis and the overexploitation of nature, we need neither more money, nor more facts nor more science – we need to redefine our relationship with nature. We need a more grounded and realistic world view, recognising that we, as humans, are not rulers or distant observers of this living planet, but a part of it ourselves. Which in turn means that when we destroy our planet, we destroy ourselves.

This is a negative way of describing this deep knowledge that so many of us sense intuitively, and that today often expresses itself in depression, eco-anxiety, aggressive denial, cynicism or existential doubts about the meaning of life and especially the role of humanity.

The positive way of expressing this is to recognise that we, as humans, are part of a miraculously beautiful, living and vibrant planet in which we are uniquely able to express, register, praise and care for the wonders before us, and that we all have the ability to let those wonders permeate us when we are in contact with nature. We can be standing on the shore gazing out to the ocean and for a moment forgetting ourselves, letting our own boundaries dissolve and feeling we are part of the whole. We can be under an infinitely starry sky at night, or looking into an animal's eyes and sensing it has a soul that touches ours. The oceanic feeling is a source of joy, of energy and reverence that we all can tap into, and that almost doesn't need to be explained, but needs to be recognised and accorded importance in our lives and cultures if we are to be able to turn scientific facts and arguments into widely accepted actions that will halt the worst effects of climate change and let our planet recover.

But this book didn't start with the title, or the concept of the oceanic feeling (which I owe to the French author Romain Rolland who first wrote about it in a letter to Sigmund Freud in 1927). It started with my need after twelve years at the highest level in the political world, dealing particularly with global ocean and climate policies, to report back to my voters on the political dynamics that sometimes allow, but all too often stop us doing the things that we all know we need to do. I needed to disentangle my thoughts and find some perspective to look at all the narratives and current justifications that are making voters in all too many countries say 'no' to policies that could actually lead to a much more sustainable, peaceful and resilient world. My background as a journalist for more than twenty years before coming into politics has of course influenced me. Some people have described the book as an undercover report on international politics, and there is some truth to that. But it is even more true that it is a reflection from me as a person, or as a global citizen, as someone who has been given the responsibility by their fellow citizens to witness and engage in EU negotiations and global climate negotiations on an inside track. And someone who has also served as a minister for international development, and through that role has been able to travel to places hardly anyone one gets to go to – especially conflict-affected countries, remote small island states and the so called least developed countries (LDC:s) – and meet and listen to so many people, a fact that has given me a much deeper understanding of the global challenges the world is facing than I could otherwise have had. I do think therefore this book has a great relevance to an international audience and I want to express my deep gratitude to my Swedish publishers Natur och Kultur, who believed in a worldwide publication, and have very generously supported the English translation.

This book spans over many years, travels, meetings and themes. It's about oil company lobbying, fake news, the media climate that fosters shallow populists. It's about science, international cooperation, the EU, Donald Trump, Greta Thunberg, the Swedish climate law, the high seas treaty, activists, psychology, threats to democracy and much more. You might say it has a somewhat oceanic approach, but the messages I want to convey can be distilled into two simple ones. The first is that we should not give up on democracy just because it is not always perfect. There are strong forces out there trying to convince us that democratic systems are not capable of solving the problems of our time, but my message is that democracy works. The rule of law works. With free media, independent courts and an open and transparent political system based on elected

THE OCEANIC FEELING

representatives of the citizens, we already have the tools necessary to bring about change through reforms, legislation and international agreements – and it's not too late to do that. My experience after years in politics is that the system can take you almost anywhere, depending on who is in power. There are huge differences between ideologies and political parties, yet too many young people – not least climate activists – believe that all politicians are the same and do practically nothing. This is absolutely not true. Those of us that really want to make a change just need more support.

The other message is about us. All of us. Wherever I have travelled – to Somalia, South Sudan, Bangladesh, Kiribati, Bolivia, Liberia or Norway – people are just people. Borders are as man-made as are the cultures and stories that define them. We very soon understand, when we get to know people from other cultures, that much more unites us than divides us, yet humanity as a whole seems to be in denial about the fact that we need to cooperate in order to halt the worst effects of climate change, stop wars and create a sustainable global society for all. The now-dominant neo-liberal narrative rests on the conviction that competition, self-interest, material wealth and selfishness not only run the world, but *should* run the world. But what would happen if instead we insisted on another narrative? One of collaboration, empathy and solidarity? Inner values rather than wealth accumulation? An oceanic rather than an egocentric feeling?

I think it is possible. Societies have changed their values, cultures and systems so many times before. The present societal logic where economic profit is allowed to take precedence over forests, oceans, entire species, indigenous communities and young people's futures *can* change. But for change to happen we will have start by changing the way we think about ourselves and the world. The world is not a machine we can manage or fix. It is a living whole. Humans are not the centre of the universe. We are a part of an amazing web of interconnected life. Humans are not just egoistic creatures who can't help destroying our planet. We can help ourselves. We can change – if only we can change the way we see the world. In the words of the Sufi poet Rumi: "Why this prison, when the door is open?"

Isabella Lövin, Stockholm, October 2023

CHAPTER I

The Ocean

I'M STANDING WITH researcher Sam Dupont in his windowless laboratory at the Kristineberg Center for Marine Research and Innovation in Lysekil, Sweden. The air is cool in here, the humidity high and the lighting spare. It smells like sea and basement, and the sound of a multitude of small whirring and bubbling pumps fills the room.

In front of us is a whole wall of aquariums, all with different small, juvenile aquatic animals and all with different pH levels in the water. In the aquariums with the same pH as the sea off Sweden's west coast – around 8.1 – we see the little larvae and fry energetically swimming around, presumably doing what these animals normally do. With each one-tenth-unit increase in the acidity of the water, we see the animals doing worse. Getting smaller and smaller, paler and less active. At a pH of 7.9, the brittle stars die; at 7.8 the mussels die. At 7.6 we reach a threshold, Sam tells me, where suddenly a huge number of the snails and calcareous-shelled animals die. The sea urchins are hardier; they can survive at 7.5. The sea hasn't been that acidic in 55 million years. The sea will be that acidic a hundred years from now – if we don't meet the goals of the Paris Agreement.

"But not very many people care about brittle stars, or mussels," Sam sighs and shrugs. "Not even if we explain how everything in the ecosystem is interconnected. That's why

I started looking at shrimps instead. I thought maybe that would get people's attention."

Sam and his research team set up blind tests in which people tasted a variety of shrimps, not knowing that some had been kept for a period of time in the acidic seawater of the future, while others were raised in the pH of today. The results were astonishingly clear. The Swedes, who love shrimp in all forms, especially on heavily laden sandwiches with mayonnaise and dill, did not like the acidic shrimps. They had less flavor, and the flesh was pulpy in texture.

"When will this change happen?" I ask.

"Pretty soon," Sam says. "The end of this century, or sooner, it depends. By the way, we also saw a dramatic increase in mortality in the acidic shrimp. And we know that many other species won't survive past 2050 because of the acidification we're expecting," he adds.

"2050?

He nods.

"You mean that it is already irreversible, because of the acidification pace?"

He nods ruefully again and shrugs.

"Unfortunately, yes."

I'm speechless. I stare blankly at his aquariums as I gather my thoughts.

"Depressing, isn't it?" he asks and gives me a searching look. "I'm just a researcher. I just try to do my part, then someone else has to take care of the results. But what about you, as a politician? How are you going to take care of this now?"

*

I'm looking out over the Baltic Sea as I write this. Yesterday the bay glimmered in the sun like a silver sequined dress; today it's gray in the rain, like concrete.

It occurs to me that the sea is hard to compare with anything else. It's not really "like" anything. It's bigger than anything else we can relate to, completely different in its essence, ever-changing. It's not even like outer space. The sea has a physical form; we can touch it. It rolls, dips, swells, freezes, melts, sprays, evaporates, rains, swirls, surrounds. Its coordinates may be constant, but you cannot step into the same sea twice. The water moves, changes form, shifts constantly. Everything flows.

In Sanskrit the sea is called Samudra, which means "the gathering together of waters." All water, every drop, belongs to it: the water in the clouds, in the lakes and rivers, the morning dew, even the tears in our eyes.

Seventy-one percent of the Earth's surface is covered by ocean. An astounding 99 percent of the planet's living space exists there. The ocean is an average of 4,000 meters deep and contains 1.37 billion cubic kilometers of water.

That sounds infinite, but is it really? If you put all the water of the ocean into one single drop and placed it next to Earth, it would be no bigger than a very small grape next to a soccer ball. Imagine then that this tiny, fragile blue drop sustains all life we know of in the universe, that it is the most important climate regulator of our planet, that it produces half of all the oxygen that animals, including humans breathe, that it is in itself a living system of everything from plankton to whales, and that it also absorbs and handles all the carbon dioxide, pollutants and all the trash we've ever released.

Three and a half million years ago, the very first single-celled organism on the planet evolved in the ocean. Today, the microscopic throng of life in the ocean is almost inconceivable, and the role of all of those organisms in the planet's carbon cycle is impossible to overstate; a single liter of coastal water contains around one billion microbes and ten billion viruses. The amount of viruses in the sea is unfathomable. Researchers have estimated that if we placed all the viruses in the ocean in one long, microscopic thread, it would be over ten million light years long. That is to say, a thread longer than a hundred galaxies the size of the Milky Way.

Where does the water come from? No one can say for sure. Either it was already inside the earth and was ejected from the Earth's crust through volcanic craters, or it was brought here by frozen comets in cosmic snowball attacks, or both. What we know is that today's ocean is the result of millions of years of rain as the water cycle slowly, slowly cooled the smoldering magma planet. Water's three forms – liquid water, ice, and water vapor – incessantly did the job. It evaporated, rose, cooled down, rained, evaporated, rose, cooled, rained, until the water slowly, slowly began to fill the planet's deep holes and low plains.

And it became ocean.

Water is the prerequisite for all life on earth. Astronomers who search for life in outer space search first and foremost for water. No water, no life.

On our planet, ocean is the rule and land the exception. That's why we can get that dizzying feeling when we gaze at the vastness of the ocean, because intuitively we know that we're just living on islands of land, and that the sea is so much bigger than the crust we stand on, and that it envelops everything. We think therefore that a drop in the ocean dilutes down to nothing, and that what sinks to the bottom vanishes forever. The ocean's ability to swallow, conceal, wash, purify and flush away is our security; the ocean is a last resort where we've always been able to rid ourselves of what we don't want. The ocean has covered the tracks, swallowed the poisons, and very few of us have been able to conceive that this borderless, all-encompassing given outpost of our world could be negatively affected – or even destroyed. If the ocean didn't serve as our dumping ground, where would we then throw away what we don't want? Can we even imagine a world where "away" no longer exists?

In 1947, Norwegian adventurer Thor Heyerdahl crossed the Pacific Ocean from Peru to Polynesia on his balsa raft, *Kon-Tiki*. It was a journey of 101 days, in an attempt to prove his controversial thesis that the islands of the South Pacific had been populated by people from South America, who would have gotten there on rafts using the Humboldt Current. Heyerdahl's best-selling book about this adventure is a spirited read, typical of its time. But it's also a unique account of what the ocean looked like mid 20th century from the perspective of a quiet raft, close to the surface of the sea, far from land. In the book sharks are constantly circling, schools of fish are leaping and splashing, whales, dolphins, turtles and flying fish are visiting the raft day and night. The cans of food the crew had packed never needed to be opened – fresh fish even presented themselves to the men by jumping onto the deck of the raft! The ocean seemed to boil with life.

Some fifty years later, in 2006, Thor Heyerdahl's grandson Olav decided to repeat his grandfather's feat. The expedition went very well, all according to the plan, and, just like *Kon-Tiki*, the grandson's balsa raft, *Tangaroa*, received constant help from ocean currents as it made its way across the Pacific. The crew even landed earlier than expected at their final destination in Polynesia.

But, the ocean Olav traversed was a totally different one. While the grandfather's colorful tales of ocean fauna seemed inexhaustible, the grandson chronicled a journey of over 90 days spent in almost haunting solitude. Sure, the crew got the occasional bite, but the whales and sharks that were constantly seen fifty years earlier were now conspicuous by their absence. In fact, fifty-four days passed on *Tangaroa* before they saw their first shark: a starving creature that took one bite of the bait dragging behind the raft, then quickly went on its way. For the rest of the journey, the filmmakers saw no other marine life of any interest.

The grandfather, Thor, died in 2002 and never got to see the film about his grandson's voyage. But he expressed his views on humans and the ocean in a speech at a conference of the United Nations Environmental Programme (UNEP) in London in 1982. "We are sweeping the floor and throwing it all under the carpet," he said, "and this carpet, the ocean, is the most important part of the planet." "I am convinced," he added, "that man today overestimates the size of the oceans and underestimates the importance of life on the planet."

I read about the ocean currents, the ones that encircle the planet in the so-called thermohaline conveyor belt, and my mind boggles. Is it really possible to overestimate the size of the ocean? The ocean currents in the conveyor belt are many times larger than all the world's land-based water-courses combined. They are planetary rivers, rushing sometimes thousands of meters deep, sometimes at the ocean's surface, driven by trade winds, temperature, differences in salinity, and the rotation of the planet on its own axis, known as the Coriolis effect. The polar regions are home to the planet's great pumping heart muscles, or polar convection areas, where warm water from the equator is cooled and becomes heavier and sinks. The amount of water gushing down to the deep each second is the equivalent of at least 5,000 out of sight Niagara Falls. Once the water is down there, its high density slows it to a flow rate no higher than three kilometers per hour as it slowly turns back toward the equator. Hundreds, or even up to a thousand years can pass before it rises to the surface again.

Most of these so-called upwelling areas are near the west

coasts of continents, such as off the coast of Peru, California, Namibia, and Western Australia. The fact that the water wells up on western coasts has to do with the shape of the oceanic basins and the trade winds, but also with how the Earth rotates eastward on its axis. The water that rises to the surface is cold and nutrient-rich. The nutrients come from organic matter that has fallen to the deep-sea floor and then been brought back into circulation by the conveyor belt to become food for fish – fish that in turn feed us humans.

But the great underwater rivers don't just bring nutrients; they also pump oxygen, carbon dioxide, and all other water-soluble materials up and down through the ocean. And, not least, they redistribute energy. At any given moment, ocean currents are transporting three quadrillion watts (three petawatts) of heat from the planet's warmer oceans to the cooler ones – 600 times more than all the power plants in the world combined.

The ocean's immense, pulsating, salty bloodstream moves slowly, in a cosmic rhythm. The thermohaline conveyor belt continuously transports heat, nutrients, oxygen and organisms in a cycle that has evolved over billions of years on our blue planet. The moon's gravitational pull controls the ebb and flow of the tides. Earth's rotation controls the ocean currents and is a result of the Big Bang itself. To think that humans can come anywhere close to being able to affect this planetary pulse seems almost laughable.

But – we can.

When my first book *Silent Seas – the Fish Race to the Bottom* came out in 2007 in the wake of the International Panel on Climate Change (IPCC) Fourth Assessment Report, I was often asked if there was a connection between climate change and the book's theme, overfishing. There wasn't much research on this at the time, but many indications pointed to a link. Many researchers suggested that the radical, global-scale decimation of fish and marine mammals in what has been, evolutionarily speaking, a very short time in the planet's history would prove to weaken the ocean's resilience to climate change.

It is estimated that between 70 and 90 percent of all predatory fish have been removed from the ocean since the 1950s through increasingly efficient industrial fishing. As a result, marine ecosystems have been forced to adapt very rapidly and, in many cases, have "flipped," which means the ecosystems have passed a tipping point and locked into an alternative state. This means that when there gets to be too few of, for example, a particular fish, other species – usually those the fish used to eat – take its place and prevent the fish from reclaiming its earlier dominant position. For example, this has happened on Canada's east coast, where the world's largest stocks of cod collapsed due to overfishing in the early 1990s and still haven't recovered, despite thirty years of a near-total ban on cod fishing. This is most likely because the shellfish that had been the cod's prey are now instead feeding on cod larvae and competing for the larvae's food. Marine biologists call this an "ecosystem flip."

Unpredictable changes have resulted from these flips in sea area after sea area. Where cod were plentiful, now cyano-bacteria are plentiful instead. Where there were dolphins, sharks, and tuna in abundance, jellyfish bloom instead. The result has been a lower trophic level in in the food web, that is, fewer predatory fish and more of the predatory fishes' prey, which now lack a natural enemy. And the fewer species that interact, the poorer an ecosystem's resilience, which is bad news for oceans, which are threatened not only by overfishing but also by eutrophication, acidification, invasive species, environmental pollutants, plastic waste, noise pollution, coastal development, and global warming.

That alone would be bad enough. But overfishing has also

contributed to changing the ocean's fundamental biochemistry, which reduces the ocean's ability to function as a carbon sink – researchers' term for the natural processes that capture the carbon humans release into the atmosphere. The 2009 UNEP report "Blue Carbon" was early to point out that the ocean's ability to store carbon dioxide has decreased significantly due to the ongoing destruction of coastal ecosystems such as mangrove forests, salt marshes, kelp forests, and seagrass meadows – and it estimated that restoring these ecosystems would mean more for the climate than ending half of the deforestation of the earth's rainforests.

But it's taken longer for researchers to dare estimate the loss of carbon sinks in the form of fish and marine mammals. Only in recent years have multiple studies pointed to the fact that decimated whale and fish populations have led to major degradation of the ocean's function as a carbon sink. This is partly because we've hauled up billions of tons of fish, sharks, and whales that otherwise would have stayed in the ocean and not contributed to emissions in the atmosphere, and partly because all the organic matter these animals would have eaten, which would have sunk to the seabed in the form of waste and stayed there for hundreds, perhaps thousands of years, has instead remained at the surface and impaired the ocean's ability to handle new carbon dioxide.

The scale of this biochemical transformation is "insane," according to the researchers. We're talking about decreases of 50 percent in the global fish population and up to 90 percent in the whale population; the total impact on the climate could be massive. A single great whale binds more carbon than 1,000 trees, according to an analysis by the International Monetary Fund, which also estimates the value of the ecosystem services provided by an average whale, including as a carbon sink, at $2 million.

Another contributor to climate change wasn't highlighted until 2021, when a study published in the journal *Nature* showed that bottom trawling further exacerbates the situation, not only through the direct diesel emissions from fishing vessels, but also from the bottom trawling itself, which churns up organic matter that would otherwise be stored in the seafloor. The full extent of this contribution to carbon emissions is still under investigation.

Climate change is not only about warming of the planet, it also contributes to another problem of planetary proportions – by some called "the evil twin of global warming" – namely the acidification of the ocean. The IPCC estimates that around 30 percent of all the carbon dioxide humans have emitted since preindustrial times has dissolved in ocean water, which has already lowered the ocean's pH by 0.1 – equivalent to a 30 percent increase in acidity (the pH scale is logarithmic, not linear, which means each step on the scale is multiplied by a specific value). Depending on how successful we are in decreasing carbon dioxide emissions, the pH of the world's oceans will decrease by an additional 0.3–0.4 by as early as the end of this century, which corresponds to an increase in acidity of 100–150 percent. The last time the oceans were that acidic was 55 million years ago.

So, practically speaking, what does it mean that the ocean's acidity has increased at this astronomical rate? The first victims are the coral reefs, because the calcium in their skeletons can't tolerate acidic environments. According to the IPCC, 90 percent of coral reefs will die at a global warming of 1.5 degrees Celsius, and more than 99 percent at 2 degrees. Shellfish will have thinner shells and will grow more slowly, if they even reach adulthood. And perhaps worst of all is that calcareous marine algae will be affected, that is, plankton with calcareous shells or skeletons such as foraminifera and coccoliths, which account for a large part of the ocean's primary production – which means the base of the ocean's food pyramid might change. Pteropods, small snails with translucent shells that are a foundation of the polar food webs, are already being affected in the sea north of Canada. Researchers predict that they will soon also be affected in the Southern Ocean surrounding Antarctica, where krill nourishes all other life.

Given that life on the planet will have enormous difficulty surviving without a functioning ocean, the research on the large-scale biochemistry of our ocean is surprisingly incomplete – considerably more effort has been put into finding life on other planets than into understanding how life is sustained on our own small, blue planet. A lot of evidence suggests that the Gulf Stream is beginning to weaken as a result of warming, something researchers are following with concern. But as things stand today, one thing is clear, and that is the extensive impact acidification has on the ocean – and will have for tens of thousand years to come, because carbon dioxide that's already dissolved in the ocean will stay there for geological eras.

Every ocean researcher I've met has been visibly worried when I've asked about ocean acidification. Some of the most distinguished in the world have delivered messages that are not far from the desperation of the researchers in Adam McKay's film *Don't Look Up*, when they try in vain to make the world understand that we're going to be hit by an oncoming comet. The only difference is that ocean acidification has already hit us, and the ocean will continue to swallow excess carbon dioxide from the atmosphere long after humans have (hopefully) stopped burning coal and oil. Sam Dupont has called this "the silent storm." The realization of what this will mean for the coral reefs within this century was so devastating for American coral reef expert Joanie Kleypas that in the middle of a climate conference in

1998, when she first put the pieces together, she had to go to the restroom and throw up.

I have to admit, I myself get a pain in my stomach while writing this, compiling all the frightening trends and predictions of what is happening to our ocean. What shall we do with these facts? Sam Dupont, with his aquariums and experiments with mussels and shrimp, is absolutely right. The scientists have done their jobs. The results are there, staring us in the face, now we need to act on them.

But it seems that they – and the public – have made one big miscalculation. They thought that facts would lead to change. And that warnings of this existential proportions would be listened to and treated with the utmost seriousness. But they are not. Instead, the logic of political theater has kidnapped too many political parties. And the media.

CHAPTER 2

Political Communication

THE TV STUDIO is like a sea of darkness around a small arena in purple-and-yellow, bathed in light. Here we stand, eight Swedish political party leaders, each at our own slender, white-lacquered lectern. Around us are cameras on rails, cameras on swing arms mounted on the high, black ceiling, cameras on harnesses worn by black-clad cameramen who circle around us on foot, floodlights in a heavy, square formation above our heads, and, far off in the black depths, a single green emergency exit light.

Most of us have brought a page or two with some key words or notes, which we place on the lectern next to our water glass before the two-hour live broadcast. Although party leaders today show more restraint on this point, after a photographer a few years ago zoomed in on my colleague Gustav Fridolin's three words note-to-self ("confidence, control and ambition"), turning this "revelation" into an ridiculing article in a tabloid.

This is my third debate on the live news show *Agenda* since I was elected spokesperson for the Green Party, and the first two weren't successes. They might not have been successes for any of the other party leaders either, but at least they seemed to feel more at home on the debate stage than I did. Right now I feel very much thrown into a ring where the gladiator games are about to start; it's just that I'm not a gladiator.

In my notes – and I have a whole bunch – I've written all sorts of facts, numbers and key words in huge letters so I can see the text without my glasses, stealthy photographers be damned. Though it's many years since I turned fifty and even more since presbyopia set in, I still haven't quite embraced my bespectacled self. And this is TV; I need my appearance and attitude to "jump out of the screen," and I have no margin for error. I'm a new party spokesperson, I have the lowest approval rating of all the party leaders, and I'll be competing for the female spotlight with two professional politicians, Annie Lööf and Ebba Busch Thor, who are also much younger than I.

Now, I wrote that, the thing about age; I might as well get it out of the way. Life in the political spotlight is merciless. The more power a politician has, or the lower their approval numbers are, the more unflattering are the pictures selected by photo editors to accompany articles about him or her. Since my entry into the government I appear to have aged at least fifteen years in all the news photographs, and I always look angry, or as if I've just been notified of a terrible tragedy.

That is why, as I stand here in the *Agenda* arena, my and my staff's collective efforts to make me look happy and pleasant have nearly gone overboard. As usual before an important appearance, I've hurled myself out the door the day before, watched by the Swedish Security Service and the curious eyes of shop employees and customers, to find something appropriate to wear. My staff has delicately suggested I pick something colorful instead of my usual beige palette. So the result is a bit surprising both to them and to me: a light pink blazer and a sparkly pink sweater, probably yanked from their hangers in the hope they'll throw some positive sparks around my fifty-five-year-old self.

My staff has also come up with the creative idea that I wear a particular necklace for the debate. The words on the necklace might have become a tabloid headline if I'd written them on one of my cheat sheets, but I haven't. Instead, keen-eyed TV viewers can read the words for themselves in shiny, silver cursive: "Belief in the Future."

I am not in my comfort zone. But what's at stake is so much bigger than me that I'm prepared to do this. I'm prepared to do almost anything, really, to turn the tide of opinion for my little green party, the only political platform in Sweden with sustainability issues at the very top, the party I'm convinced is crucial to finding a solution, that can make the difference needed to reverse a global development marked by anything but belief in the future. A development the world is so late in reacting to that we now have zero time to lose if we want to avoid large-scale planetary ecosystem changes that could make parts of the world uninhabitable, force hundreds of millions of people to migrate, eradicate species, start pandemics, and put peace and democracy at risk for all future generations.

Issues so huge that few political parties in the world take ownership of them, even though change can be achieved only through national governments pursuing these issues, taking the lead and prioritizing them. Since the Green Party entered the Swedish government, Sweden – albeit far from doing enough to combat the climate crisis – has climbed to the top of international environmental organizations' rankings as the country with the best climate policy in the world. After four years in government, after negotiating the budget three times a year with the Social Democrats and the Left Party and establishing what the different parties really prioritize in critical situations, I know what a difference the Green Party makes and has made, both at a national level and as a model for the rest of the world. I just need to get the voters to understand that too.

The party leader debate takes place less than six months

before the 2018 Swedish parliamentary election. I know the election is a defining moment for climate action, not only for Sweden but also for the direction of Europe and the world. With a strong Green mandate behind it, a small country like Sweden can play an important role when the new European Commission is appointed the following year. I also know that the focus and priorities put forward by the new Commission will affect the entire European Union – the world's largest market – as well as the ambitions of global climate negotiations. And I know all too well that the EU, with pressure from climate-ambitious member states like Sweden (assuming Sweden is still a climate-ambitious state after the 2018 election), is desperately needed for global climate leadership in a world where the United States under the Trump administration has abdicated all responsibility for the climate crisis. No, more than abdicated: actually started an active campaign *against* the phaseout of fossil fuels; which has breathed new life into oil-rich nations like Russia and Saudi Arabia.

So, to me, the issue is much, much bigger than the frightening fact that for several years my party has been teetering on the edge of Swedish parliament and is now at risk of being shut out. The question of the party's survival isn't just about the thousands of Green Party members who, usually unpaid, dedicate large portions of their lives to gradually pulling Sweden in a more sustainable direction in municipalities, regions, and at the national level. And it's not just about the fact that the party's existence or nonexistence will be a deciding factor in the formation of Sweden's future government; if it turns dark-blue conservative with virtually nonexistent climate ambitions or stays red-green with the climate transition as its stated highest priority. It's about Sweden's ability to tip the scales in determining the direction of the new European Commission. The "green wave" that swept across Europe with major successes for green parties in Finland, Germany, the Netherlands, Denmark, Austria, Ireland and Belgium can't afford to lose traditionally green member states like Sweden and Luxembourg to the climate-conservative side – the side that believes it's protecting the EU's competitiveness by lowering climate ambitions and relaxing demands on the automobile industry.

I'd been elected party spokesperson two years earlier, midway through the parliamentary term, because my predecessor had stumbled too many times in word and deed and her approval numbers were bordering on zero. So the party had suddenly set its sights on me. My success in the European Parliament was emphasized, particularly the Swedish Green Party's record result in the 2014 European Parliament election with me as the top candidate, when we received 15.4 percent of the Swedish vote, to become the second-largest Swedish party in European Parliament. Searching for a new spokesperson outside the sitting government would create too much uncertainty for the government's future, and I was already Minister for International Development Cooperation. The male spokesperson, Gustav Fridolin, would stay, which didn't portend major reform in the party leadership. But someone had to fill the female spokesperson's shoes. Both my predecessor and the party's selection committee encouraged me to step up. I received phone call after phone call from party heavyweights telling me the moment of truth had arrived. Heavy sighs on both ends of the call. And then, my bungee jump.

My logic for taking on the role was as follows: The climate can't wait; the IPCC is crystal clear on this point. We only have a few years to make the transition, and when push comes to shove, none of the other parties will prioritize the climate. The Green Party must do the job – now, not later. If other people are saying I can do it, I'll have to trust them. If people say they're tired of career politicians, maybe they'll appreciate someone like me, someone with a more deliberate style, a journalist and writer with a long professional career behind me. Maybe, just maybe, a different tone, a different image could do the trick; after all, it worked well in the European Parliament election. But I honestly didn't know, and I was more skeptical than many others were. But you can't keep hoping someone else will do the things you want done. All arrows pointed to me.

A new party leader can't expect a honeymoon period; quite the opposite. And it didn't take long for the outside world to remove every imaginable kid glove. Female commentators were especially merciless. They savaged my style, my hairstyle, my waistline, my makeup skills and insufficient use of mineral powder. They also proclaimed that I was utterly lacking in rhetorical finesse and altogether boring.

But apparently I wasn't even so spectacularly boring as to be funny. A commentator in one of the major tabloids graciously summed up my first big speech at the political Almedalen Week as follows: "At least she didn't make a fool of herself. She was just bad." Of course, her tone was that much harsher given that I represented power, as my party was in government. Opposition party representatives always have an easier time of it. Such is the dramaturgy; I hadn't expected any different. Still, perhaps I hadn't expected that the media, amid a raging climate crisis, would opine after every political debate that I was irrelevant, weird or uninteresting because I didn't talk about what all the other party leaders talked about.

But media logic is rock solid. If no one else picks up the gantlet to debate the climate transition, the media loses interest. So after the party-leader debates in parliament, column inches galore were written about what the other parties decided was most important to talk about, namely immigration, shootings and crime in the suburbs. Head-line-friendly, scripted one-liners doled out in the party leaders' speeches were rewarded faithfully by editors, while my remarks about how acute the climate crisis is, and how the other parties wanted to cut the climate budget and make it cheaper to emit carbon, scarcely got a single mention. Off the table. Uninteresting. Humanity's greatest crisis, which can only be resolved with policy, and which *can* actually be resolved with policies and reforms that involve nearly all of society, was constantly dismissed as something tech-nical, fringe, something for scientists and voluntary industry initiatives – not for politics.

With each debate I felt a stronger sense of unreality. Do other party leaders really not see the imminent risk of ecosystem collapse facing our planet, or do they not care? And seasoned political commentators who've graded the parties' policies and ploys for decades, how can they not see that the climate crisis is a political issue, the *defining* political issue for the future of our society?

It was like a bad dream, where no one hears what you're saying as you try to speak more and more clearly and gestic-ulate and explain that a speeding train is coming towards us, but everyone just looks on blankly and signs to you that they don't understand a word.

So, okay. I've changed my strategy. Sparkly sweater. Mineral powder. And one-liners.

My staff has prepared meticulously for the *Agenda* debate. In addition to the clothing issue, they've gone through every imaginable debate topic. Binders have been assembled for the most likely topics: immigration, the job market, health care and criminal justice. We've role-played under the chandelier in my office at the Ministry of Foreign Affairs, with high cafe tables dragged in from the staff kitchen. My collabora-tors have brought heaps of candy and are amazing at playing the characters of the Sweden Democrats' Jimmie Åkesson, the Christian Democrats' Ebba Busch Thor and the Moderates' Ulf Kristersson – so good, my pulse quickens as if these political opponents were actually in the room.

I recognize all too well the arguments from the other party leaders. That Sweden is responsible for just microscopic parts of global emissions and that China and India are the ones that really need to make changes (Sweden Democrats), that "ordinary people who lives in the countryside" can't afford to buy electric cars or pay an airline passenger tax (Christian Democrats), that Swedish industry is already the best in the world and shouldn't be punished further with new regulations, which would make companies move abroad (Moderates).

The role-play is done in a playful way, but it makes me genuinely upset. I hammer away with my best arguments: "Jimmie Åkesson, if everyone in the world lived the way we Swedes do, we would need four planets! Anyone can make the excuse that they're small, but together with all the other small countries our emissions are actually greater than China's and India's combined!" "Ebba Busch Thor, why do you want 'ordinary people to pay for gas from Russia and Saudi Arabia, and why should the aviation sector be exempt from all environmental taxes?" "Ulf Kristersson, the Moderates aren't credible when you say you want to move all climate legislation to the EU level. You then oppose every ambitious proposal by the EU!"

It drains me emotionally to hear these dismissive arguments again and again, especially knowing I'll soon be in a TV studio on a live broadcast and won't have nearly as much time to strike back, and also knowing my arguments will carry as little or even less weight than those of the other party leaders because their approval ratings are considerably higher than mine. And knowing the TV audience will perceive everything as nonsense or ambiguity and that the truth is probably somewhere in between, even as out-and-out absurdities or lies are presented by the other side.

The whole thing raises my blood pressure. I can literally feel the whooshing in my blood vessels, my head seemingly expanding and my pulse pounding at my throat. If only I could see this as a play. A game. But I can't. Plus, lately I've been struck by a terrible thought, a thought worse than anything else I can imagine. What if it's my fault? What if it's ultimately my fault people don't care about climate change? Because I'm the wrong person, because I can't ignite the masses, can't bring the doubters around, can't convince the ones who've got it wrong.

Because I'm not a good enough *communicator*.

With less than four months until the election, this thought is not helpful. I can't quit now to make room for someone else who might be a better party spokesperson. But the thought is there. Smoldering like a bed of hot coals, which now I have to dance on, quicker, better, giving everything I've got. Because no one else can do it for me.

The practice continues now with "Ulf Kristersson" attacking the Green Party's "ineffective climate policy," and I've completely lost my flow. The comments and critiques that had circulated freely in the room when we analyzed the earlier duels have now come crashing down like stop signs on my every line of thought. If I say x someone thinks y; if I say y someone else thinks x. Not too positive, not too negative, not too boastful, not too aggressive, don't say anything that sounds evasive. I've started to see myself from the outside and I've abandoned my earlier theory, that I should just be myself. That's not cutting it anymore. I open my mouth to say something, change my mind, then realize self-critically that I'd hesitated and that it wouldn't look good on live TV. Suddenly everything just stops. It's too much; my pulse is pounding wildly, the blood seems to push through my veins and tighten around my throat. I can't get any air. Alarmed, my chief of staff interrupts. "You'd better get some rest," he says, as I struggle to utter a single sensible word to reassure my colleagues. Their faith in me is crucial if I'm going to complete my mission, our mission. I don't want my exhaustion to burden my staff. I'm supposed to be showing them where we're going; they shouldn't be taking care of me. After all, we have a planet to save.

It had been four turbulent years in government for the Green Party. Rookie mistakes had been made, such as going public with issues during the campaign that the party knew were technically impossible to pass with less than a Green majority in Swedish parliament or in the Stockholm Regional Council – instead of sticking with the message that our policies were system-changing in the long term. After all, the main campaign promise in the Green Party platform was that Sweden would implement a new climate law and a new climate framework that in the long term would systematically transform the whole country, including the transportation and energy sectors. But we'd spoken out adamantly on other issues. And so, like a tired refrain, journalists repeatedly declared these issues major failures: closing the Bromma Stockholm Airport to make way for housing, blocking construction of the Stockholm Bypass Highway, and selling German coal mines operated by Swedish state-owned energy company Vattenfall. What these issues had in common was that they all constituted a physical reality, something tangible; and, to be honest, that was why my predecessors in Green Party leadership had chosen them to illustrate the climate issue, so they could *communicate* about it clearly. Of course, the party also had ambitions to achieve these goals, and we battled to the bitter end using all possible means – short of leaving government – before we were forced to give up the fight against indifferent Social Democrats, with no support from a Left Party that preferred to attack us rather than condition its budgetary cooperation with the government to make sure the Vattenfall coal mines were closed.

But by pushing for these issues, we'd made a rod for our own back. The issues were beyond our control in many ways, particularly because we had just a scant 7 percent of voter support since the 2014 election, and now for the whole parliamentary term they'd obscured the real work the party had done to move society in the right direction: how we'd finally pushed through what was then the most ambitious climate law in the world, established billions of kronor to support climate adaptation for heavy industry, created a platform – Fossil-Free Sweden – for climate transition in all business sectors, which has resulted in ambitious action plans for everything from aviation to the concrete industry, representing about 70 percent of Sweden's emissions. How we'd adapted Sweden's extensive foreign aid to help developing countries invest in sustainability, how we'd pushed the World Bank to start to divest from fossil energy, and in particular how we'd successfully negotiated at the EU level to tighten the EU Emissions Trading System, increasing the price of emissions by 500 percent as a result of a proposal that I as a minister, thanks to my Green collaborators, brought to the EU Council of Ministers.

But how could I communicate all that? I honestly didn't know, because apparently it didn't ring true when I said it. The journalists looked skeptical; no one outside the Green Party was telling this story, and as soon as I tried to explain how Green Party initiatives had made green steel production possible in northern Sweden, or how coal power in the EU was being shut down because of the high emissions costs we'd successfully negotiated, out came the impatient counterquestion, predictable as the skip in an old record: Yes, yes, but you agreed to sell Vattenfall's coal mines?

And the Left Party, which was not in government, played the same card as often as they could. I knew that their leader, Jonas Sjöstedt, would play it in the *Agenda* debate, and it was a simple, effective one-liner that took two seconds to say but required a minor political science lecture to respond to:

"You sold Vattenfall's German coal mines to a shady Czech company!"

"Yes, but Vattenfall is a profit-driven, state-owned company. We would've needed a majority in parliament to revise the ownership directive so the company could keep the mines and shut them down, which would've resulted in an even greater loss than the sale. That majority didn't exist. Also, German coal power emissions must decrease anyway. Germany is responsible for implementing the Paris Agreement, just like Sweden is."

It wasn't exactly as catchy as the bit about shady Czech companies. We'd scored an own goal on this issue, and I wish the symbolic piece of coal I'd used in the final debate against the Moderates' Gunnar Hökmark before the 2014 EU elections, to illustrate the importance of tightening up EU emissions trading, wouldn't later have become a symbol of the Vattenfall coal mine issue. An extremely complicated issue that ultimately boiled down to whether the Swedish government could impel a state-owned company not to sell a loss-making operation, and then shutting down substantial energy production in another country. An issue that didn't actually appear in the Green Party's platform but was highlighted during the campaign because it sparked emotion, unlike the climate law.

So it was partly a communication error. But it was also a sign of understandable desperation by a small party struggling to "come out" to the public with issues that are concrete and clear. Things that can be visualized and create debate and not be dismissed with "well, everyone wants to stop climate change." Which we knew all too well, after years of negotiations with other parties, that nowhere near "everyone" wants when it comes to the practical measures required, such as taxing emitters, investing in railways and ending fossil fuel subsidies.

So how could we, a small party engaged in issues essentially no one else was discussing, reach out to people? Opinions within the party varied widely, but there were a few main themes.

One was to "speak so that ordinary people understand." Describe how the climate transition will affect people's everyday lives. How buses will run on biogas, bicycle routes will be expanded, solar cells will be mounted on roofs and organic food will be cheaper. This theme has long been the dominant one, but it has also resulted in a strong backlash. Many now think the Green Party's only solution to environmental problems is for every citizen to take personal responsibility and ride the bus even if they live in the country and the bus only makes two trips a day, buy organic food even though it's more expensive, and so on. This has led to allegations that the Green Party is a party only for middle-class people living in big cities, and that we're blind to the massive emissions produced by industry and other countries. Self-righteous and oblivious to reality, we sip our fair-trade, oat-milk lattes and ride our electric cargo bikes as we look down on all of the – ah, yes – "ordinary" people.

Another theme was that we would stick to facts and science, and thus credibly explain exactly how we will remedy each problem, down to the minutest detail, before we go out and "fight like hell for technological solutions to problems no one knew existed," as one self-deprecating Green Party member described it.

Green Party supporters often have academic backgrounds, are solution-oriented and may take a somewhat excessive interest in science and technical details. That's a good thing, because our policy is usually well grounded in technological reality, but in terms of communication it often poses a challenge: we don't just talk about things no one else talks about, we describe exactly how they should work, so people lose the thread before they've even understood what the problem is that needs solving.

Interestingly enough, this problem in particular is what distinguishes the Green Party completely from the rest of the environmental movement. A political party can't simply point out the seriousness of a problem, it also needs to provide concrete solutions; that's why it is a party and not a movement. But it's much harder to inspire engagement in carbon dioxide limit values for cars in a bonus-malus reform than in climate change as a whole. And despite the considerable progress we've made on untrodden ground, Green Party members constantly risk coming across as technical, hard to understand and irrelevant, especially since few other parties even dignify these issues with a discussion – at least not unless a strict legislative proposal poses a threat to emitting activities and is brought to their attention by lobbyists.

A third communicative approach was about green values. We need to broaden our appeal; people need to get to know the Green Party, know what our values are and what we think about all issues, not just environmental ones. If people know what we think about education, health care, taxes and law and order, they'll also have confidence enough to vote for us. I've supported this approach, as has everyone on the party board, who decides on the party's strategies. It's a fundamentally wise but also fairly flexible approach, which I've found most people in the party interpret in their own particular way. Everyone agrees that we have green values, but is it a green value to refuse to budge an inch from what we believe is right and proper and to sooner leave the government than compromise, or to gradually, compromise by compromise, guide the world in the right direction? That is also a question of values, and a critical one for a party in government.

And how do we weigh different green values against each other? Does the climate issue trump the refugee issue, or vice versa? Here the opinions diverged, but in recent years the balance had become clear: We should take responsibility for both planet and people and, step by step, nudge society in a sustainable direction, but not at just any price.

And finally, the approach I myself had advocated: that we are the party that should demonstrate a greater vision, the only party that actually rises to the major global societal challenges: the climate crisis, species extinction, the threat to democracy and peace. I called us "visionary realists" in my first speech as party spokesperson, and I said that those who don't see or hear what's happening to our planet and who have no plan for how to change society – they're the ones who aren't realists.

But what will a sustainable society look like? If we want to bring people on board, we need to be able to paint a picture of our vision and describe a possible way to get there. Explain that it doesn't require all people to live "alternatively," that we want everyone to be able to shape their lives as good citizens without having to burn themselves and the planet out in the process. That we must have a system that serves us, instead of us serving the system. That we must rid ourselves of a fossil-based market system that seems to have become an end in itself, not a means for living a good life. That we ourselves can create the story of what's important and what kind of society we want.

This vision, this freedom of action and inclusion for

everyone, was what I wanted to convey as spokesperson, but I found myself pretty much alone among party leadership in preferring "Lift Your Gaze" as our proposed slogan for the upcoming campaign. "Too preachy" and "too evangelistic," "too holier-than-thou," the majority thought, and considering the party's low confidence numbers, I had to concede: it would probably just fire up the country's jeering commentators. We risked becoming the self-righteous party with its head in the clouds while others dealt with "reality". Instead, our message for the 2018 election was short and sweet: "Now." With the subheading, which actually worked really well: "The climate can't wait."

*

There's been a barrage of opinions about what I should emphasize during the *Agenda* debate. Should I point to facts that can't be disputed? Or appeal to people's emotions? If so, which emotions? Fear? Or hope? Attack my opponents, or stand above the "bickering"? Ideally I should be passionate but not overly aggressive. Use body language. Don't get stuck on numbers, and no long explanations.

To "lift my gaze" and talk about the fact that a different society is possible, about the green vision, will be very difficult. Time is limited, and the debate is so scripted with leading questions from the moderators that I'll probably seem as weird as usual if I even try.

My political subject-matter experts certainly have a very important job, and they carefully pilot me to where they see a landing zone for me. But I can't hide that after two years fighting in vain against poor opinion numbers, I'm sensitive, and even if certain things are only intimated discreetly, I immediately get the message loud and clear. I'm given an extremely thin binder containing hardly any facts, so I can't read too much and get too intricate and fact-heavy in my arguments. They time my answers to show me I'm too long-winded, that I need to get to the point. They don't think I should show my reasoning self but instead use the seconds I have to attack, don't go on the defensive but unload on my main opponent, which we agree is the Moderates.

Basically, they want me to jump in with both feet. And I agree. This isn't about me anymore. It's about the team, the future of the whole party, the fact that it's fallen on my shoulders to reach out to an electorate that sees itself more and more as customers, picking and choosing from the offerings in every parliamentary election, that isn't persuaded by any ideology, isn't presumed to have time to listen to arguments longer than thirty seconds, and no longer sees or hears the difference between the parties. Except, of course, the one party that stands out from the rest. The party the *Agenda* editors decided should stand in the middle between the two blocs in the yellow and purple arena and be the very last party asked for their opinion. The party whose leader, Jimmie Åkesson, eyebrows raised and arms thrown wide, will proclaim like clockwork that "all of these parties are just bickering, but ordinary people understand that they're not doing their jobs, otherwise we wouldn't be seeing all the problems we're seeing." And that the only real alternative to the other parties, with common sense and a different vision of belonging and concern for citizens, is what the Sweden Democrats stand for – a party with its roots in Neo-nazism.

After long discussions our team has agreed it's impossible to skip describing how dire the climate crisis is before I can start talking about solutions. We are looking for a clear picture that people understand, and my staff has brainstormed and come up with some suggestions. In the end we agree on this carefully double-checked fact: that for each minute we party leaders stand there in the live broadcast *Agenda* studio, the Arctic sea ice will shrink by 200,000 square meters.

It isn't perfect, because it doesn't show "how the climate crisis affects ordinary people's daily lives here and now," but at least it's easier to visualize than the fact that carbon dioxide levels in the atmosphere are the highest they've been in 800,000 years, or that humans' remaining carbon dioxide budget to stay within 1.5 degrees warming will be gone in eight years if we continue with business as usual.

What's most important now is to try to say something unexpected that will at least get people to sit up and pay attention, so they might then listen to how climate change will affect so many other policy areas: how it will drive millions of people from their homes (migration), transform ecosystems (forestry and agriculture) and create conditions for new viruses and pandemics (health care). But there's also the positive side, that is, how the climate transition provides a goal and a purpose, how it will create thousands of new jobs in green steel, wind power, the largest battery factory in Northern Europe (job market) and competitive advantages for Swedish industry (economy) – which will also give so many young people who feel hopeless today a reason to believe in the future. We're going to build the world's first fossil-free welfare state, and we need everyone involved! That's another message that needs to be emphasized.

So, how does the debate go, then? I only remember one thing clearly, which is when I'm given the floor during the first topic: "welfare and jobs." After just having listened to the Liberals' Jan Björklund expound on his favorite subject, education, although the subject was jobs, I begin by talking about all the new jobs being created through the climate transition, especially in northern Sweden, which has led to huge investments in fossil-free steel, mining, wind power and battery factories – but I'm quickly silenced by the moderator, who says I should stay on topic. "We'll get to the climate later!" she snubs me and gives the floor to someone else. "But there are no jobs on a dead planet!" I manage to get in, not quite hitting the right tone, but what does that matter? It's a quote-friendly one-liner that makes it on the news, and after the first hour of the debate it's the biggest impact I've made.

Toward the end of the debate it's finally allowed to talk about the climate. I start my reply by announcing how many square meters of ice have disappeared since the debate started, and then the discussion is largely about the possibility of shifting the climate issue to international negotiations. The Liberals' Jan Björklund – in addition to the same old position that Sweden should build more nuclear power plants – pitches the idea that we negotiate a global carbon tax. I'm not against this in principle, but I'm also convinced it would be used as a pretext for inaction, while the world enters into global negotiations that experience has shown would go on for decades and would from the outset be absolutely impossible to get a large number of countries to join, not least the United States.

After the debate I was pleasantly surprised when SVT's viewer poll actually declared me the winner of the segment on climate, with most judging me to be "knowledgeable." Jimmie Åkesson won both "criminal justice" and "migration," while the Moderates' Ulf Kristersson won "welfare and jobs." So I'd defended the government side, which was seen as a great success.

My colleagues were happy, and I breathed a sigh of relief. But it wasn't over.

A few days later I saw a headline circulating in several media outlets and shared gleefully by all manner of internet trolls and malicious op-ed writers: "'Mostly false' by climate minister." It was a collaboration between Sweden's leading media companies, which, in a segment called "Faktiskt"

("Factually") had performed a thorough fact check and concluded that I'd made factual errors in the debate.

At first I went cold, considered the possibility I'd had a brain cramp and mistakenly said something very wrong. But as I started reading the article, my jaw dropped. It was the data about the Arctic sea ice that had earned me the red light. Those who ventured into the complicated text could read that, yes, the polar ice caps had been shrinking at record speed in recent years, but on May 8, the day the *Agenda* debate took place, the ice cover hadn't shrunk anywhere close to as much per minute as I had claimed, because it was so early in the year. On the other hand, between then and autumn it shrank much more. On average over a whole year, yes, the data seemed correct, but not specifically between 8:00 and 10:00 PM on May 8. So, you see, the minister was untruthful.

That's a wrap.

Where does this get us? What do these debates lead to? Does anyone get any wiser? Most people I know outside politics can barely stand to watch this choreographed battle with clumsy attacks cheered on by the moderators because it makes "good TV." But it doesn't make good TV. Time just goes by. And the Arctic ice keeps melting, for real.

CHAPTER 3

The Glacier

HOW QUICKLY DOES a glacier actually melt?

We're standing on the floor of the glacial stream itself. It appears to be covered in a sort of giant gravel, but the gravel is actually big, round rocks, and to make our way we have to leap from round rock to round rock. Black, mottled, pink, cracked, spotted, striped, gray, white. Around us, towering sheer rock walls flecked with green. A raven flies way up there against the blue ceiling. I can hear its wingbeats – the air is still, it's as quiet as an empty concert hall, except for the distant hum of a waterfall etching a bright, thin streak behind us. Otherwise, no sound, no people, not so much as a light breeze. The glacier in the background is still; a slow river of meltwater flows under its gravelly nose. When we get closer I see the water is the color of grape tonic. Cloudy, filled with white sand that's been ground from the earth's crust and is now set free, after perhaps a hundred thousand years.

The sun is shining, and feisty, soundless gnats gravitate around our sweaty faces. My guide in Greenland, Ole Guldager, hands me a jar of Tiger Balm. The cool menthol aroma scares off the flies and brings an unexpected element of civilization to the untouched scenery. In the stillness it

– 51 –

occurs to me that Ole's back and his faint sweaty scent are needed to give the place their human proportions. The glacial valley is like a cathedral times ten thousand. Or a hundred thousand. I can't even imagine how many St. Peter's Basilicas could fit here. The breathtaking vastness and the silence goes on and on inside me; it's as if life is flashing before my eyes, over and over again. But not my life. The planet's.

We stride ahead on thick hiking soles in the Arctic high-summer heat, and Ole shows me stream after stream where trout flutter along in the pristine water. Look there, between a pair of rocks; look there, under a creeping shrub. Unafraid fish without a single experience of fishing, maybe even without a single enemy on earth. We could have an endless number of fishing tourists here, Ole says. This is just one fjord, and look how many streams there are here. And there are thousands of fjords in Greenland!

He says there's no land ownership on the island. You can lay claim to a piece of land, but not buy it. If you want to build a house, graze some sheep or establish a farm – well, then you simply ask the others for permission. If the community thinks it's good for everyone, you get your approval. That's why there's farmland over there in Blomsterdalen, Ole says; it's because there's a need for hay to give the sheep in winter, not because the farmer owns the land. No one owns the land, because no one has ever owned the land here.

Greenland is the world's largest island, five times the size of Sweden, but it has only 56,000 residents. Here, well into the 21st century, when globalization, waves of refugees and environmental problems have reached nearly every corner of the planet, is a type of land use that must have been obvious to the very first humans. That no person can claim to own nature. That all are welcome to work and contribute what they can to the common good. Raise sheep? Sure, go ahead. Build an inn? Sounds great. Let's build a hospital here, and an airport there. My few days in the town of Narsarsuaq, population 135, on the site of a former air base in south-western Greenland, have turned my European perspective around and brought me close to what feels like civilization's infancy. Everyone here has two or three jobs. One person has to be an electrician, teacher and auto mechanic. Another a dental technician, mason and baker. My guide, Ole, is a museum director, handicraft worker and writer. And guide. That's how they get through the winter when communications are down. Everyone helps everyone. And who would deny someone permission to build their house here? Who would sell the land? No one owns it.

We've been walking for an hour or so through the valley, which doesn't actually have a name but lies between Kiat-tuutdalen and Mellemlandet on the map. Incidentally, Ole drew parts of the map, too, since no one else was doing it. When we arrive at the edge of the glacial river, he asks if I want a cup of coffee. He gets our provisions from his back-pack, offers me store-bought jam cookies and, after a while, breaks the silence:

"It must be five years since I was here last. I've had so much other stuff going on. So I wasn't prepared for this at all. I thought we'd be able to see the glacier properly from here. It actually used to extend all the way to where we're sitting now."

He looks over at the valley landscape, the dirty tongue of ice just visible in the distance. I look around at the rounded boulders arranged like a ridge on a kilometer-wide field around us, all the way from the glacier to the sea, and I suddenly understand what I'm seeing, why they look so new and clean. The rocks have recently emerged from under a thousand-year-old layer of ice.

"You're kidding," I say.

"No," Ole says. "Well, shit. We'll have to redraw the map

again. This one obviously isn't right anymore."

I'm struck by what he says. Global warming isn't something abstract; it's here, and it can be touched, just as we – maybe as the first humans ever – can touch these round rocks. I ask Ole, who's Danish but has lived in Greenland since childhood, how he feels when he sees this rapid transformation. I'm surprised by his considered answer. Well, he's mainly worried about Greenland. The immense natural resources, everything that's untouched, could provide a positive development for Greenlanders but could just as well cause their downfall. The world's largest island, with its scarcely 60,000 residents, thousands of fjords, unexploited mineral fields and vast marine resources in the soon-to-be-accessible Arctic, has hardly gone unnoticed by the outside world. Donald Trump hasn't yet offered on behalf of the United States to buy the self-governing island from the Danes, but Chinese companies have already been here for years, wooing the local government with promises to build entire cities in exchange for concessions to build mines for rare earth metals and diamonds. So far, the Greenlanders have said no, but it's so fragile, Ole says. Sooner or later opinions will change, and what will happen then?

"They want to build a whole city for 3,000 Chinese guest workers. Sure, okay, if they'd stay there and keep to themselves and pay their own way, but of course on the weekends they'll want to relax. They'll go to Nuuk and meet Greenlandic women. And then there'll be lots of children. What will happen to Greenlandic culture then? How long can we hold on to our autonomy, prevent companies with economies a thousand times bigger than Greenland's from taking over?"

I take a sip of lukewarm coffee and again take in all that's still untouched – and yet not. Greenhouse gases and soot particles caused by humans far, far away have made the glacier we have before us, Kiattuut Sermiat, retreat several hundred meters in just five years. The conference I'm here in Greenland to attend on behalf of the European Parliament is about the existing conflicts between the EU, Iceland and the Faeroe Islands over fishing in the North Atlantic, conflicts that have arisen because large stocks of mackerel and herring have moved north as the ocean has warmed due to climate change. This place on earth, which feels unreal in its sublime seclusion: how long will it remain untouched?

"That's the question. The ice cover on Greenland has been here for more than a hundred thousand years, so it'll probably stay a little longer," Ole says, adding in a light tone, "although the glacier is probably only ten thousand years old."

"*Only!?*"

He laughs and munches on the last bit of hard cookie. The raven cawing high above us in the blue sky is the only other living creature in sight. It gives us its measure, like the coin that provides proportion in a photo. Everything around us is endlessly big.

As I leave Greenland on a propeller plane to Reykjavik the sky is clear and the view of Greenland's whipped ice cover spectacular. I open my notebook and try to capture what I see. The glaciers have a sort of plastered-looking surface; the stripes are ancient waves of paste, now covered with small, swimming pool-colored lakes. Out in the sea, countless large icebergs. In Narsarsuaq we saw them every day in the fjord, but from here you can see how inconsequentially small they are compared to the enormous Greenlandic ice cover. I can see only a fraction from the airplane window, but suddenly I can make sense of the fact that if Greenland's ice were to melt, sea levels around the world would rise by seven meters.

How deep is this ice, anyway? How old? The ice crinkles atop its hidden interior, like the skin of an elderly person. The outer layer of powder cracks, reveals that the glacier isn't standing still. What look like ruptures in the snow are the tracks of ice rivers running down toward the turquoise fjords in the sea, like tractor tracks in snow. Or dirty, stiff whipped cream. I have to stop now. Why am I searching so desperately for the perfect analogy for what I see? Because it's all so untouched? So untraveled?

I'm seated next to an Icelandic fisheries biologist, and he's also gazing down at the armada of variously sized peaked icebergs floating along the coast. But he doesn't offer any poetic reflections. Instead, he starts talking about the productivity of the ocean.

"Fish production is low now," he says. "It's just shrimp. But as the climate changes, that will change. There'll be real hot spots here. It'll be worth millions of dollars annually, and they know it, the Greenlanders."

The man also spoke at the West Nordic Council's fisheries conference, and his remarks on probable future changes elicited much interest from the attendees. There were many questions, and many declarations meant to scare the EU and other world powers out of claiming northward-moving fish stocks for themselves; Icelanders and Faeroe Islanders aren't known for their diplomatic parlance. This is ours. Don't come here.

Meanwhile, no one expressed any concern over the fact that the Jakobshavns Isbræ glacier in western Greenland had set a new world record for ice loss that summer at 46 meters per day, or that all the pool-blue water we saw atop the ice cover was reducing the albedo effect – the reflection of solar radiation away from the earth's surface – and accelerating the rate of ice melt. On the contrary, they talked about the possibilities. Fishing! Opening the Northeast Passage! Extraction of oil and gas! Rippling glacial streams might be disappearing into the sea, but maybe the cod will come back! The same tone I'd heard at myriad Arctic and ocean conferences in the EU. New opportunities associated with climate change will be exploited "sustainably"! Amen.

I left Greenland feeling deeply worried, a worry that would give way to deep dejection six months later. On May 12, 2014, in the midst of the campaign for European Parliament, NASA and the University of Washington simultaneously published studies on the ongoing collapse of two glaciers on the other side of the planet, in western Antarctica. The studies had both, independently of each other, arrived at the same conclusion: the collapse is now irreversible. The sea based parts of the glaciers had been undermined by warm ocean currents and had passed a threshold to where nothing will be able to stop them from calving, causing a gradual global sea-level rise of 3–4 meters.

Once the sea level has risen that much – it's uncertain how rapidly this will happen – island chains such as the Maldives, Kiribati and the Marshall Islands will be completely under water. The same goes for large parts of Bangladesh, and highly populated coastal cities like Miami, New York, Calcutta, Guangzhou, Lagos, Alexandria, Hô Chi Minh City, Bangkok, Yangon, Tokyo and Amsterdam will all face existential threat.

In Sweden, almost all of the daily newspapers published this news based on the same telegram from a news agency. Some of them buried it several pages back. Not one newsroom took the story any further, and neither did a single editorial writer. It would have created more buzz if two economists had simultaneously predicted an increase in the federal funds rate.

About a month later, I heard the glaciologist behind one of the studies speak at a seminar in Bonn, at one of the UN's countless preparatory meetings leading up to the big climate conference that would take place in Paris in 2015. He explained that it's impossible to say exactly when the glacier in western Antarctica will calve and cause this sea-level rise, but he can say with certainty that it will happen.

"The same certainty with which I can say a piece of ice in a room at a temperature above freezing will melt. It can be slowed down or sped up. It could take a hundred years, a thousand years or even two thousand years, if we make the right decisions today and keep the temperature increase as low as possible."

Another researcher at the conference described the findings as lit fuses that couldn't be extinguished. But he stressed that that doesn't mean it's too late or pointless to do anything now. Quite the opposite, he said. We who are alive today have a very special responsibility. And then he said, and I wrote it down since it was an unusually strongly worded statement coming from a scientist:

"Our children, grandchildren, and all generations, as long as they can remember us, will say it was us, our generation, who did it. We had the ability to change the living conditions on this planet. Never before has the planet's fate been so unmistakably in the hands of one single generation."

Seven years later, in 2021, 23 international cryosphere researchers signed an appeal to the world's leaders before the climate conference in Glasgow. The message, from scientists from Australia to Alaska, reflects a similar gravity and desperation. The cryosphere, the 10 percent of earth's surface that is covered in ice and glaciers and is very far away from where most of us live, is heading toward thresholds beyond which self-reinforcing processes won't stop within human time horizons; that is, they'll continue for thousands of years. In particular, the researchers warn that the changes won't be limited to the poles or the cold mountain ranges but will affect the entire world. Like the irreversible sea-level rise caused by calving glaciers. Like the fact that hundreds of millions of dollars worth of the world's largest fish are threatened when the ocean's acidity and temperature change. And, not least, the fact that fully 70 percent of all fresh water on earth exists in frozen form, and that the melting of the glaciers has accelerated tenfold in the last forty years in the Andes, Hindu Kush, Himalayas and Alps, which is very serious since they are freshwater reservoirs that provide several billion people with drinking water and water for energy production. If people don't have drinking water, they'll be forced to migrate. What happens in the cryosphere does not stay in the cryosphere.

The outcome document of the 2021 Glasgow conference includes limited increases to certain ambitions, but the international community still is far from meeting the challenges scientists have articulated so clearly for decades. At our current level of commitment we're still headed for at least two degrees of warming, which means at least double or triple that amount in the polar regions, where the difference between minus one degree and plus one degree is perhaps the most definitive threshold effect, or so called tipping point, we can see in nature. "We cannot negotiate with the melting point of ice," as it says in the *State of the Cryosphere Report 2021*.

We live in the Anthropocene, the geological era named after humans (the Greek word for human is *anthropos*), because we are the ones who affect living conditions everywhere on earth. In the Mariana Trench, earth's deepest point, and on Mount Everest, its highest, plastic bags and trash have been found. We've transformed the biochemistry of the atmosphere and the ocean, we've eradicated species and assumed a totally dominant position among living creatures. Of the bird populations on earth today, 70 percent are hens and other domestic birds. Of the total biomass of mammals today, humans make up a staggering 36 percent, our livestock 60 percent, and wild animals – everything from mice to whales – less than 4 percent.

This is almost inconceivable, as is the fact that, as the legendary nature filmmaker David Attenborough says in the film *A Life on Our Planet*, in his 90-plus-year lifetime alone, the space occupied by wild nature has shrunk from 66 percent of the planet when he was a boy to 35 percent today. The result of all of this, aside from weakened ecosystems throughout the planet, among many other things, is that humanity is pushing closer and closer to wild populations of animals that can transmit diseases and viruses to humans, including Ebola and COVID-19.

None of this can come as much of a surprise. Researchers have been speaking in plain language for over fifty years to anyone who'll listen; the scale of the problem became clear to the world in 1972, when the first United Nations environmental conference was held in Stockholm. The facts existed then and they exist now, and each new generation that discovers them is equally horrified that nothing has been done, that humanity hasn't been able to unite behind the science, or, in the words of Greta Thunberg, to act as if our house were on fire. But maybe we're making a big mistake by continually turning to scientists for more knowledge and trusting in rational action, when something else is staring us in the face.

Gus Speth, who has worked for many years on environmental issues, including as founder of the important think tank the World Resources Institute, as a White House advisor to Bill Clinton and others, and as administrator of the United Nations Development Programme (UNDP), has said in a famous quote:

I used to think the top global environmental problems were biodiversity loss, ecosystem collapse and climate change. I thought that with 30 years of good science we could address these problems. I was wrong. The top environmental problems are selfishness, greed and apathy, and to deal with these we need a spiritual and cultural transformation, and we scientists don't know how to do that.

CHAPTER 4

Reaching Agreement

HOW DO WE solve global problems? If research and data won't get us there, politics has to pick up the baton. And if national politics isn't enough, can international policy do it?

The first United Nations conference I attended was Rio+20, the big conference on sustainable development in 2012. I felt a great solemnity in being part of something I saw as the highest possible forum for international cooperation. Reverentially I sat, along with hundreds of parliamentarians from almost every country in the world, in the former Brazilian senate building in Rio de Janeiro, at a pre-meeting before the actual UN meeting begun. The discussions were about how we as elected officials could support the process going forward, cooperate with each other, and exchange experiences. The meeting was organized by the Global Legislators Organization (GLOBE). I listened attentively to what was said and took in every detail of the scenery: the senate's high cupola ceiling with the beautiful round, leaded window edged by frescoes of angels and clouds. The mahogany-paneled walls and floor-mounted furniture in dark wood and leather. The text "Câmara dos Deputados" engraved in the brass ashtrays at each parliamentary seat. The grand words and gravitas of the speakers up on the high dais: "There is no plan B, because there is no planet B!" "This may be the most important meeting of our lives!" One of the speakers said what I had long been thinking: "We need a new world order!"

I looked around me. Small, blue tabletop flags with yellow stars stood in front of me and my European Parliament colleagues. In another corner of the chamber, a Swedish parliament member sat with a Swedish flag. In between, rows of red Chinese flags, American, Norwegian, Japanese, and all the flags I didn't recognize. Micronesia. Malawi. Mongolia. South Sudan – the world's youngest country. I'd flown half a day to get here, as had most of the others. Now we were here, and the world didn't feel so big anymore. Everything and everyone seemed within reach. Here we were. Part of the world order.

But of course, this was just a pre-meeting; the real meeting would be held at an enormous conference facility outside Rio. The 2012 Conference on Sustainable Development was the fourth conference of its kind; the very first one, as mentioned earlier, took place in Stockholm in 1972. Twenty years later came the Rio de Janeiro Earth Summit, where the world adopted Agenda 21. Then it was Johannesburg in 2002, and ten years later, Rio+20. And ten years after that, Sweden would host another conference, Stockholm+50, which I took the initiative on when I was Sweden's minister for the environment. Not being able to see the initiative to its completion in the summer of 2022 was probably the hardest part of my decision to step down as party spokesperson and minister.

But of course, I had no inkling of this latter fact as I, European Parliament member, tried to get a handle on what this huge sustainability conference was about and, in particular, where it might lead. Agenda 21 had made a big impact at the municipal level in Sweden; I remembered this quite well. This time, several questions were on the table: first, the civil society organizations were pushing for the world to start negotiating a new global agenda to replace the Millennium Development Goals, which expired in 2015; goals aimed at decreasing global child and maternal mortality. The civil society wanted this new agenda to be something much bigger, a new way of looking at sustainability, where the three dimensions of sustainability – social, economic, and environmental – cooperated with and strengthened each other, and where we stopped treating environmental sustainability and eradication of poverty as two completely separate goals. They also wanted the new global agenda to include all countries, not just the poor ones. It would thus lay the groundwork for a reexamination of every global policy area, and a decision text on this new framework (which would later be named "Agenda 2030") would need to be included in the resolution in Rio.

Another key window that was open during the conference was the negotiation of a new global agreement on oceans. Two-thirds of the world's oceans are considered international waters; that is, they don't belong to any country, or, more correctly, they belong to all of us. Gaping holes existed in the current international agreements on who has the right to use the ocean and how it should be protected, and many in Rio, myself included, hoped we could agree to start negotiating such a new agreement. As the European Parliament's rapporteur for the European Union's international fisheries agreements, I'd been invited to speak at a side event, and of course I hoped to contribute in some way to making this long-awaited and, for the oceans, urgent decision.

In addition to these two extremely important issues for the earth's future, host country Brazil had wanted to highlight the concept of the "green economy," and the large group of developing countries, the so-called G77 countries, had endorsed this. But the draft text wasn't particularly progressive; for example, it mentioned nothing about fossil fuel subsidies or carbon pricing, but focused mainly on the serious concerns that developing countries had about a green transition. In paragraph after paragraph, they'd written not what a green economy is, but what a green economy must *not* be. A green economy must not hinder the development of developing countries. A green economy must not constitute a justification for trade barriers against developing countries. A green economy must not prevent developing countries from extracting their natural resources.

The text illustrated the world's dilemma in a nutshell. Rich countries have become rich by exploiting the global south and the planet for centuries. Poor countries have a right to development. But should the poor countries take the same route the rich countries have? And what right do the rich countries have to tell the poor countries what they can and can't do? The balancing act in how the world expresses itself on these issues is constantly in focus and equally sensitive in all international negotiations. And from a sustainability perspective, it's a constant struggle to find a path forward that assures developing countries of their right to grow in a sustainable way but doesn't give *carte blanche* to those who use developing countries' right to development as an excuse to continue on as before, giving subsidies to fossil fuels, chopping down rain forests, or fishing the oceans to death.

The difficulty in finding the right words was reflected in the draft text on the table. Green economy had gone from an "absolute necessity" to lengthy circumlocutions about how it could be "[one of the important tools available for achieving] sustainable development" that could "provide options for policymakers [but should not be a rigid set of rules]."

The square brackets mean that the countries disagree on that part of the text. Because the only method of decision-making in these meetings is the consensus method – that is, all countries are in agreement – there would be many more square brackets and circumlocutions before the meeting was over. A humorist on Twitter had already articulated the likely result of Rio+20:

"We [agree] [noted] the [need] [opportunity] [possibility] to [discuss further whether to] take action [long after] Rio+20 [or not]."

The proposed text about the oceans was good, however. Without any square brackets, it stated that the world should agree, as soon as possible, within the framework of the UN General Assembly, to begin to negotiate a new agreement on the conservation and sustainable use of biological resources outside national jurisdiction.

This issue had been ongoing for many years. Two-thirds of the world's oceans lie at least 200 nautical miles from any coast and are thus so-called international waters or "high seas", or "Mare Liberum" – a term coined by Dutchman Hugo Grotius in the early 1600s. Because the ocean covers such a large amount of our planet – over 70 percent – this means that half the surface of our planet is not yet controlled by any laws. There are conventions for certain activities: the International Maritime Organization (IMO) regulates shipping, regional fisheries management organizations (RFMOs) regulate fishing of certain species, and the International Seabed Authority (ISA) has the mandate to authorize commercial activities on the seafloor in "the Area," as this common heritage of humankind is called.

However, in a shrinking world, where microplastics can be found in every liter of water in the ocean, where the interests in mining, aquaculture, wave power, and exploitation of the ocean's genetic resources are perhaps only in their infancy, the existing regulations were not enough. The ones that deal with protecting biological diversity had no instruments for implementing this protection outside of the countries' economic zones. For example, the agreements in the Convention on Biological Diversity (CBD) about protecting areas in the oceans (at first the Nagoya-target of 10 percent of the ocean, and since 2022 the Montreal target of 30 percent by 2030) were essentially impossible to implement, because no international authority had a mandate to establish a marine protected area in international waters. The different organizations within the international system (shipping, fishing, mining) were working in silos and shared inadequate information with each other, and much more developed environmental impact assessments and clear enforcement mechanisms were needed.

The international community also had to resolve the question of who should be able to make money from what is out there in these Areas Beyond National Jurisdiction (ABNJs as they're usually referred to in the UN context). Should fees be charged, and how should the revenue from those fees be distributed between countries? How will the ocean be monitored, and how will disputes be resolved? All of this and more needed to be clarified in an amendment to the world's prevailing international law, which, after many decades of negotiations, was finally passed in Montego Bay, Jamaica, in 1982: the United Nations Convention on the Law of the Sea (UNCLOS). A law that has already helped the world avoid so many border disputes and lawsuits that Hans Corell, former legal Counsel for the UN, has called it one of the most important agreements for strengthening peace and security in the world.

*

At the massive exhibition complex where the Rio+20 conference was held, there was a huge food court where I could sit and observe a sampling of the thousands of accredited participants. I saw Tibetan monks taking pictures of each other with their phones, indigenous South Americans in traditional dress looking for a table, nuns in white, Western climate activists in t-shirts emblazoned with messages, women and men of all ages having conversations, introducing themselves, eating and checking their email. Brazil had announced that there would be several large consultations with civil society, including one on the matter of a new global agenda, and in the middle of all these people I again felt that giddy feeling of taking part in a sort of global democracy in full swing. Just like everyone else, I was here because I was engaged in and passionate about these issues, because I'd gone into politics and people had voted for me. It felt huge and consequential.

Monitors hung from the ceiling announcing the meeting rooms for various important discussions and events, and suddenly the word "oceans" scrolled into view. I noted the room number and the word "restricted," which meant access to the meeting was limited. I didn't know if I'd be allowed into the room with my "observer" status, but I didn't hesitate. Feverishly I scanned the signs hanging from the ceiling and found that I was already in the right exhibition hall, not far from the right corridor. The room was just a few meters away, and, to my surprise, the guard who checked my plastic badge let me in without a second thought.

I saw right away that I'd come to the right place. There were many familiar faces from my international work on fisheries issues in the room, like Matt Gianni from the Deep Sea Conservation Coalition with his narrow, brown chin beard; grizzled professor Alex Rogers from the British Royal Society; blond, almost-always-smiling Kristina Gjerde from the International Union for Conservation of Nature (IUCN); and white-haired Tuiloma Neroni Slade from PIF, the Pacific Islands Forum, with his characteristic bow tie and white blazer. The room was quiet and the people who recognized me nodded discreetly in greeting; what discussions were had were had in whispers. Matt Gianni and Alex Rogers briefed me: Pretty much everyone was in agreement to start negotiating the new treaty to regulate international waters – everyone except the United States, Canada, Japan, and Russia. The EU was livid. Nauru had submitted a new proposal, which was now being considered.

Breathless, I set my bag on a chair along the wall and looked around the nondescript room. Light grayish-purple walls and ceiling, fluorescent lighting, light-gray tables arranged in a rectangle with empty floor in the middle, laptops and black tabletop microphones with no nameplates or flags for the participants. And here they were: the US, EU, Brazil, Japan, the Pacific Island countries, Australia, Norway, Iceland, China, Venezuela, and all the other countries with an interest in the world's oceans. The people in here – some stood in small groups and talked, some pored over documents on each other's computers, others sat alone, yawned and stretched – may have looked like ordinary people, women and men of different ages and with different ethnic backgrounds, but they were not. They *were* their countries. They were here to put forward positions that had been hammered out in different ways through political discussions and lobbying in their respective nations. Many of us – politicians, special interest groups, businesses, researchers, activists – had worked extremely hard for many years to get to this moment: to bring an end to the lawlessness on half the planet and finally be able to establish rules for the preservation of biological diversity in international waters, something that was, incredibly enough, still absent thirty years after the UN Convention on the Law of the Sea was signed in Jamaica. Many others had strong interests against this. The Russians and the Canadians didn't want new regulations that might prevent new oil and gas exploration, and the mining and fisheries industries in certain countries would

– 69 –

rather that the free sea continued to be controlled by no one – and exploited by them.

I noticed that a large group had gravitated to where the delegate from Nauru sat at her laptop with the American negotiator standing behind her. Some in the group were engaged in discussion, and others peered surreptitiously at the proposed new text. The original text presented by the Brazilian chair was as good as it could be, stating that "we", (the world): "agree to initiate as soon as possible, the negotiation in the framework of the United Nations General Assembly, of an implementing agreement to the UN Law of the Sea, that would address the conservation and sustainable use of marine diversity in Areas Beyond National Jurisdiction."

All of the NGOs had celebrated this text, and the EU and G77 had already endorsed it, but apart from the US, Russia, and Canada, which had expressed reservations, none of the other countries had actually taken a position.

Kristina Gjerde, an expert in marine international environmental law at IUCN who, like me, was an observer without the right to speak at the meeting, appeared at my side and whispered the identities of the people around the laptop, one by one: "USA, Norway, Japan, Venezuela, Russia, and look – now New Zealand, South Africa, Singapore and Australia have joined them. Whoa. A scary bunch," she said, looking genuinely concerned.

The American negotiator, a woman in a white shirt with long gray hair in a low ponytail, glasses, and a blue wool sweater over her shoulders – no doubt to endure the ice-cold air conditioning – stood behind the woman from Nauru, pointing at the screen and suggesting changes. The people behind them followed what was going on with the text, mumbled a word or two, furrowed their brows, nodded, pondered. What was at stake was almost immeasurable and would affect the whole world, but the stumbling block for the original text seemed to be... domestic politics. The United States had a presidential election coming up in a few months; President Obama was battling strong headwinds and facing a real chance of not being reelected. A guy from Greenpeace in a Hawaiian shirt, also an observer, hissed to me: "Last week the Tea Party movement took out a full-page ad accusing Obama of secretly selling off American oceans and sovereignty to the UN. If he wants to win the election, he can't afford to sign. The conservatives will use any means necessary to paint him as weak. In the Fox News world, the UN is some kind of global communism that has to be fought."

I was reminded that the US hadn't even ratified the Convention on the Law of the Sea, because strong conservative forces had vehemently opposed it from the beginning. The opposition is rooted more in a hostile attitude toward the UN than in issues with the convention itself, which the US, like all other countries, nevertheless abides by and respects. One of the principles they dislike is that part of the profit from resources extracted from the seabed outside national jurisdiction will be allocated to the international community. They also strongly dislike that the United States would have to pay more than other countries due to its size, but it would only get one vote, like all the others. Some defense hawks have also warned that the convention would lull the Americans into a false sense of security, which could cause a decline in military expenditure and readiness.

Based on these arguments, the United Nations Convention on the Law of the Sea, abbreviated as UNCLOS but typically referred to as LOST (Law of the Sea Treaty) in the US, has never been ratified by the US Senate, despite having the backing of three presidents – George W. Bush, Bill Clinton, and Barack Obama – as well as the Army, Navy,

Coast Guard, and the American oil industry. Not even when then-Secretary of State Hillary Clinton, along with a highly unusual coalition including the American military, the oil industry, and various environmental organizations, argued in favor of the convention in the Senate did a majority of senators dare oppose the Tea Party's stance. This was perhaps first and foremost because it would be a win for Obama – which, obviously, no conservative wanted right before the election. The global communism argument was also a natural fit for those who wanted to portray Obama as a "non-American" (remember the dispute over his birth certificate!) who just wanted to sell off American interests and hand over power to UN bureaucrats.

The scene before me – the groups of people in the row of seats in front of the glowing laptop screen with its handful of words being tweaked and re-tweaked, the way they whispered among themselves, the way someone leaned forward and pointed to some word that could be crucial to life on half our planet – suddenly reminded me of da Vinci's famous painting "The Last Supper." The whole room vibrated with the magnitude of this historic occasion. Would the United States successfully persuade the nations around the computer to bury the new treaty and instead relegate the discussion to a so-called "ad hoc informal open-ended working group" for the areas outside national jurisdiction? Would Russia and Canada go against all the other countries just to protect their own fossil fuel industries, which wanted to be able to plan new Arctic exploration without UN interference? Or would the world reach agreement on what everyone knew was best for the planet and humanity as a whole?

The discussions dragged on. I stayed in the room until a proposed text from the US so upset the EU that the EU's negotiator accused the US of insulting the participants' intelligence, and the Brazilian chair adjourned the meeting.

The negotiations weren't completed until several days later, when I was already back in Europe. The environmental organizations were extremely critical of the final result, but given the distance I'd witnessed between the countries' positions, I was relieved.

The outcome document from Rio+20, "The Future We Want," contained the long-awaited statement that the world would now begin to negotiate a new global framework (what would become Agenda 2030) to succeed the Millennium Development Goals. In addition, there was actually a section about a new global oceans agreement. It would be negotiated "on an urgent basis," although no more urgent than to give the General Assembly three whole years to make a decision to even start negotiating – a somewhat unorthodox definition of "urgent." Also, it was no longer a "treaty" but an "instrument." It bore all the hallmarks of a watered-down text, but even so, it would lead to slow steps toward the negotiations that were concluded more than ten years later, in March 2023, after the first edition of this book was published.

The United Nations Convention on the Law of the Sea took thirty years to negotiate, and it left half the planet unprotected. What now goes by the name "International legally binding instrument under UNCLOS on the conservation and sustainable use of marine biodiversity in areas beyond national jurisdiction," most often abbreviated as BBNJ, is about finishing the job. Back in 2012, of course, I didn't know the issue would be on the table two years later when I entered the Swedish government, and that it still wouldn't be resolved seven years after that, when I resigned as minister. Or that Obama would be replaced by Donald Trump, that the EU's long-standing political focus on the climate and the world's oceans would be redirected toward Brexit negotiations, or that a virus would shut down the whole world and halt the final negotiations of a new BBNJ agreement, or that Russia would invade Ukraine which would make this huge coastal state uninterested in any international agreements. All I knew was that I had witnessed one of countless historic baby steps in the art of reaching international agreement, and that the reasons the steps were so small were not pretty.

CHAPTER 5

Political Will

THE 2014 EUROPEAN Parliament election was over, and the Green Party's amazing result had made it the second largest party in Sweden. But the Greens in Europe had lost ground overall, and the xenophobic and Eurosceptic forces had advanced their positions considerably. As a result, the Green group was now the second smallest group in European Parliament with just 50 members, and we had to pack our things and move to another part of the parliament buildings in Brussels. I had been a member since 2009, and now I had to bid farewell to my view of the park and Parliament's round, glass tower, and resign myself to a new office with a view of a dreary courtyard. The losers' lot.

I took the opportunity to go through the piles of papers that had collected in a filing cabinet in my office over the past five years, and the memories came alive. Much of it I'd saved because it had once sparked such wild joy in me, or because I'd had a feeling it was a historical document that needed closer analysis before it could be thrown away. There was the agenda from the session on September 30, 2009 that showed up at the bottom of a dusty stack of wrinkled papers, and the voting list from the vote on a Fisheries Partnership Agreement with the Republic of Guinea, with my Spanish colleague Carmen Fraga as rapporteur. I'd scribbled the vote totals in big numbers at the bottom of the list: 13-11. And then a big exclamation mark.

Wow! This was the first time in the history of the European Parliament that the Committee on Fisheries had voted no to a fisheries partnership agreement with a developing country. And I knew that I, a newly elected, first-time parliament member, had been key to persuading the members of the other political groups to change their positions. I'd personally visited the poor, West African country of Guinea and written a report on EU fisheries agreements for the Swedish Society for Nature Conservation. The EU typically justified the fisheries agreements by pointing out that part of the payment would go toward strengthening the local fisheries sector in the developing country, but I hadn't seen any of this EU support in Guinea.

I'd spent days at a conference with small-scale fishing organizations in the capital, Conakry, and I'd seen for myself the small wooden boats the fishermen, who often didn't know how to swim, took farther and farther out to sea to find fish in the overfished waters. I'd met widows whose husbands had drowned, and who now sold their bodies for fish. I'd seen troops of children hanging out on the stinking, litter-strewn beach instead of going to school, and I'd told my new colleagues in the Fisheries Committee all about it. Another not-insignificant factor had also come into play. Since I'd visited the country, it had been taken over in a bloody military coup at Christmas 2008 – a development that, outrageously enough, hadn't deterred the European Commission from continuing to negotiate for European fishing in Guinean waters.

Not even on September 28, 2009, two days before the Fisheries Committee was to vote on the agreement, when the military carried out a massacre of civilians at Conakry's football stadium with mass rapes, 157 dead and 1,200 injured, did the European Commission withdraw its proposal. They thought the EU should still enter into the agreement, using the sketchy argument that fishing was one thing and human rights another – which was handled in a whole different part of the EU system. And then the EU officials at the Directorate-General for Maritime Affairs and Fisheries insisted that if the money wasn't paid out, the local fisheries sector would suffer.

That's when I'd had enough. My staff and I decided to go at the Fisheries Committee with everything we had. We distributed news articles about the massacre of civilians in Spanish, French and English to all members of the committee. We wrote a preliminary press release stating that the European Parliament had approved payments of nearly two million euros to coup leader Captain Moussa Dadis Camara in exchange for continued access for European vessels to the poor country's waters, and we showed it to the political groups' political advisors – and told them we'd send it to the media if the committee voted in favour. When the matter then came to a vote in the parliament committee room, I took the floor right away and requested that the vote be held by Roll Call Vote instead of the usual anonymous button-pushing, so that each member openly needed to declare how they voted. To my surprise, I got the support of enough members so that the chairperson, Carmen Fraga, couldn't dismiss my request. And look at that! It worked. The committee rejected the proposal. The Spanish and French boats had to return home empty-handed, and Captain Moussa Dadis Camara, with his signature red beret, would go without the cash injection he'd been expecting from the EU.

This was my first big political win, and I remember how incredibly momentous it felt. How I almost had to pinch myself to know it wasn't a dream. How, when I was back home in Sweden, I sat in my garden in the autumn evening chill and looked up at a brilliant starry sky that I knew I shared with the fishermen in Guinea thousands of kilometers away, and I remember thinking how relieved they must be that the gigantic EU trawlers had left; maybe the catches in their small, colorful wooden boats, so called pirouges, would be better now. And most of all, I thought: politics work. Democracy works. To my astonishment. And a shiver went through my body at the thought of what I'd done, and at the thought of what would have happened if I hadn't taken action. The outcome of the whole situation had hinged on me. It was my responsibility. There was no question that I'd made a difference, that my actions mattered. Just as my non-action would have mattered.

At my old office at the European Parliament, I had to part with what was easily a few hundred pounds of papers. The cabinet I was emptying contained documentation from five years of intensive work to reform EU fisheries policy. Heaps of position papers from NGOs, reams of internal communications between me and my colleagues. Agendas from workshops, green strategy papers, scientific reports and basic documents. The Commission's proposal for a new fisheries policy. Parliament's first position. The Council's first position. A whole folder on "the points battle", perhaps the most critical battle in my parliamentary term: a technical fight, totally incomprehensible to an outsider, over the interpretation of the so-called d'Hondt system, which determines how different groups in the European Parliament can "buy" the important rapporteurship for various legislative proposals with an internal point system. The conservative EPP group cajoled shamelessly to get new points and thereby seize the rapporteurship for the important basic regulation of the new fisheries policy, even though the Socialist group had priority according to the d'Hondt system. This developed into a rule-interpretation thriller of the highest order; we fought tooth and nail, bringing in the parliament's legal services, group leaders and the Bureau of the European Parliament itself to prevent the EPP from finagling its way to the rapporteurship.

This battle alone is worthy of its own chapter, as is the long battle over the fisheries agreement with Morocco, where in 2011 we narrowly succeeded in stopping EU fishing in the Morocco-occupied Western Sahara waters. And the battle over shark finning, where we imposed an EU ban (which sadly hasn't worked as well as we'd hoped), and all the dossiers on fish discarding, and the mountain of scientific studies on the topic of maximum sustainable yield (MSY) that would form the basis for future quotas, and all the material on individual transferable quotas (ITQs). Classified documents leaked from the Council of Ministers, top-secret communication between me and the Socialist group, the kinds of things we exchanged only on paper and not via email, so they wouldn't fall into the wrong hands.

I flipped through hundred-page work documents and saw that I'd written notes all over them, highlighted words in yellow and pink and put exclamation marks in the important spots. We'd sat in negotiations and preparatory meetings for weeks, months and years. And the result had been an entirely new basic regulation with binding rules for all European fishing inside and outside of Europe, a legal text in which we'd stated for the first time that fishing shall take place in a sustainable way. Not just *should* take place in a sustainable way, but *shall* – that little word that means so much in the context of legislation. It was a paradigm shift. Overfishing had been made illegal in Europe, exactly what we'd wanted five years ago when we brainstormed our slogan, "Make Overfishing Illegal," and had it printed on t-shirts, postcards and tote bags.

How did it happen? Where do I begin? Fisheries reform could be its own book, but I don't want to write it just now. Instead, I want to write about political will, about how change really is possible – as long as the will is there. Just a few weeks into the new parliamentary term I'd seen it was possible: that a single member of parliament could change important processes, as was the case with the Guinea fisheries agreement. It strengthened my conviction about what to do next. I had to advocate for a whole new fisheries policy, both inside and outside parliament. To get there, I'd use every resource available to a member of European Parliament. Hire staff with this specific issue in mind, use my ample information budget, create a special website and invite environmental organizations and journalists to follow each step of the reform with full transparency (this site would be named CFP-Reformwatch.eu) and build coalitions across party lines. There was no time to lose; I hadn't gone into politics to avoid doing something useful with my life – on the contrary. The goal was clear. We simply had to get to work.

And we did. We created an unconventional majority coalition between the Greens, Liberals, Socialists, the Left, and certain Conservatives from primarily Nordic countries, and we succeeded in breaking up the traditional coalition between the two major party groups, the Socialists and the conservative EPP group, which had steered fisheries policy for so long. The fishing lobbyists were blindsided. The EU got a brand new fisheries policy, which, at least on paper, mandated what was obvious but had never been written into the legal text before: that all fishing shall be sustainable, that discarding of fish shall be forbidden, and that the EU, with regard to fisheries agreements with countries outside the union, shall be permitted to catch only surplus stocks that the country itself lacks the resources to fish.

As I flipped through all the news articles from the spring

of 2013 about the vote and the agreement on the new policy, the jubilation bubbled up again. Change is possible. Democracy works!

Politics make a difference. Not everyone believes that. I honestly didn't particularly believe it myself before I saw politics from the inside. As a Swede, you sort of expect the vast majority of things to be automatically looked after by "society" for the common good, without reflecting more critically on what society actually is or how steady a foundation it stands on. But then, to my surprise, I saw cracks in that foundation. Fisheries policy was a clear example of society not looking after "the common good" but instead looking away and allowing the appalling overexploitation of a commonly owned natural resource by an industry that takes more in taxpayer subsidies than it brings in – without creating any socioeconomic benefit and without taking into account the research on the irreversible losses of vital ecosystem services.

Climate change is another obvious example; in this case, the entire global climate system, and all associated ecosystems on land and in the ocean, are jeopardized for the continued profit maximization of a small number of companies – clearly against "the common good."

So, why didn't we as a society put a stop to this long ago? How can we be sawing off the branch we're sitting on? Why can't we as a global community simply come together for the common good?

These are questions I've been asked so often by voters, journalists, children and college students, anyone trying to understand why the acute threats against our planet aren't simply being dealt with by those in power. Why don't they just do it? And in fact, these were the same questions that finally made me take the step into politics. Because my conclusion was that from a community perspective, there's no rational reason we can't come to agreement. There are, of course, psychological, political and other reasons based on the dirty profits of a few. But it really boils down to one thing: a lack of political will. Because if we want to, we can.

But why don't "we" want to?

One possible explanation for why so little is happening when we know that what we're doing to the planet and therefore to ourselves, may be life-threatening, is that we lack technological solutions. We're stuck in our fossil fuel dependency and the ocean is too big for us to monitor, and every conceivable alternative to our current situation is so incredibly complicated and expensive that unless we want to send development back to the stone age, we'll just have to accept that we're watching the earth's ecosystems slowly collapse.

This does sound like the most reasonable explanation, and many politicians persist with it despite experience and data speaking loud and clear. Technological solutions do exist, or can be invented very quickly, if the political will is there. History shows countless examples of companies adapting and doing what's needed to develop Freon-free refrigerators, chlorine-free paper, phosphate-free detergent, energy-efficient light bulbs, lead-free batteries, recycling systems for end-of-life goods and packaging – everything that seemed so gosh-darned impossible when the problems were being debated – when politicians show they're willing to ban the thing that's wrong or dangerous.

In hindsight, when I look at how rapidly new technologies and new systems can be developed when industry's back is to the wall, politicians seem at best cautious and at worst flat-out counterproductive; it's not uncommon that a lack of political will has actually worked against voluntary technological developments that could have solved problems.

Some technological solutions have been snuffed out

directly by politics. The clearest example is electric cars. Most people today might think electric cars are a recent invention, and that the internal combustion engine and the astronomical consumption of oil our civilization has engaged in for over a hundred years has been unavoidable, because there was no acceptable technological alternative. But the truth is that the electric motor has existed as a perfectly good alternative all along.

The very first electric vehicles were designed in the mid 1800s, and for a long time they were actually more common than cars with internal combustion engines in both Europe and the United States. In the late 1800s a whole fleet of electric taxicabs popularly called "Hummingbirds" (for their quiet humming sound) were tooling around London. The electric car was seen as a true "lady's car" because it was cleaner, quieter, simpler to drive without a gearbox, and considerably easier to maneuver than the heavier automobiles with their noisy, smelly combustion engines. The main limitation of the electric car in its infancy was that electricity was available only in cities. But the conditions changed when electrical power lines started to expand outside cities, and in 1914 the auto magnate Henry Ford announced plans to start mass-producing electrically powered Model T's in cooperation with Thomas Edison, who'd developed batteries for the cars. Edison waxed lyrical about the electric car: "Electricity is the thing. There are no whirring and grinding gears with their numerous levers to confuse. There is not that almost terrifying uncertain throb and whirr of the powerful combustion engine. There is no water-circulation system to get out of order – no dangerous and evil-smelling gasoline and no noise."

But a disastrous fire in Edison's workshops and the outbreak of World War I put the electric Ford on the shelf. Had this not happened, the global automobile industry would probably look totally different today. Because once the war was over, oil companies started pumping a seemingly infinite black sea of oil from the earth's crust, and they needed a market for their product. Thus the fate of the electric car was sealed. Close ties were established between the automobile industry, the oil industry and political representatives. Some politicians in the US were so enthusiastic about motoring and so eager to benefit their financial backers that they opposed both public transit and expanded sidewalk construction. And – lest we forget – started wars and supported dictators in various countries in order to secure oil assets.

It wasn't until the 1990s that a new window of opportunity emerged for electric cars. That's when politicians in smog-choked California threatened new legislation that would get rid of internal combustion engines by requiring car manufacturers to produce a certain proportion of totally emission-free vehicles (the so-called Zero Emissions Vehicle Mandate). This sent car manufacturers into a flurry of activity. Within a short time, Ford, GM, Nissan, Honda, Toyota and Chrysler came out with various models of electric cars. Not small-scale experimental cars but fully functioning cars, which, in the first phase, were leased or loaned to test drivers, some of them celebrities. In the highly informative 2006 documentary *Who Killed the Electric Car?* Hollywood actors including Tom Hanks, Mel Gibson and Danny DeVito talk about how they instantly fell in love with the speedy, cool, emission-free cars, and everyone else who leased them felt the same way.

But then the oil lobby's machinery started firing on all cylinders. The electric cars were way too good; their window of opportunity had to be sealed shut before it was too late. Suddenly, new "grassroots initiatives" emerged in opposition to plans to build public charging stations in California, which they said were a waste of taxpayers' money. Think tanks produced so-called life cycle analyses questioning whether electric cars were better for the environment than fossil-driven cars, and cost-effectiveness analyses showing that an electric car mandate was an inefficient way to reduce emissions – and that it would probably even increase emissions, since people couldn't afford to buy new electric cars and would therefore keep their old fossil-driven cars. According to the lobbyists, the state's and citizens' money would be much better spent in a thousand other ways, which they illustrated in various calculations. Newspapers were flooded with letters to the editor from people who were angry that these new electric cars promoted inequity because only the rich could afford them, and politicians in both California and Washington, DC, started to think twice. The proposed legislation was watered down and ultimately became the nonbinding agreement that auto companies must provide zero-emission cars "in accordance with demand."

But then the oil lobbyists, not satisfied even with this loose wording, set to work ensuring there would be no market demand. The auto industry stuffed the test drivers' rave reviews into the bottom of a drawer and never published them. Then they produced advertisements sure to quash ordinary people's desire to try an electric car. In *Who Killed the Electric Car?* we see a so-called commercial for GM's EV1 – in black and white, with long black shadows and an ominous voice-over that's more evocative of the Ingmar Bergman film *The Seventh Seal* than a typical seductive car commercial. It was such an obvious attack on the cars that a group of e-car enthusiasts financed more enticing e-car ads from their own pockets and took the initiative to compile waiting lists of many hundreds of customers who wanted to buy the new cars. But the auto companies had crunched the numbers and probably found that the soon-to-be-developed SUV concept promised significantly higher profit margins than electric cars. People on waiting lists to buy electric cars, to their immense surprise, got phone calls from car sellers who described every imaginable downside of electric cars and not a single upside.

In 2001 the auto manufacturers had finally succeeded in proving no demand existed, and they began resolutely taking back all the e-cars from their lessees. In *Who Killed the Electric Car?* test drivers complain loudly that they weren't even given the option to buy their beloved cars, and enough of them had become so attached to their e-cars that they organized a surveillance mission to try to figure out where the cars had been taken. Ultimately, a video shot from a helicopter documented the discovery of long rows of EV1s crushed into rectangular packets and stacked in the Arizona desert. A journalist found brand-new Honda EV Plus cars at an auto scrapyard, and the confused employee said he'd been told to grind the cars into metal confetti, for reasons unknown to him.

The car manufacturers, however, seemed quite satisfied and shifted their sales efforts to the burgeoning new segment of fossil fuel-driven SUVs, with that bellowing monster the Hummer as the ultimate symbol of America's freedom to pollute. By coincidence, in 2003 the Bush administration introduced a $100,000 tax credit for small businesses that bought vehicles heavier than 6,000 pounds, which directly supported Hummer buyers. Meanwhile, people who chose a hybrid received just a $2,000 tax deduction. This *political* – not technological – course of events was what paved the way for the fossil-based SUV's triumphant march around the globe, and in the most recent decade (2010–2020) these heavy vehicles made up the second-highest emitting sector in the world. In other words, the SUV has emitted more than, for example, heavy industry, and is surpassed only by electricity production from fossil fuels.

The Swedish (now Chinese) auto company Volvo – despite its branding campaign to be seen as safe and environmentally responsible, with images of untouched Swedish nature – has been quite late in transitioning its auto production to plug-in hybrids or fully electric cars. Instead, they've banked on heavier and heavier luxury SUVs, even into the 2020s. Why?

The truth is, they haven't actually been that late at all. On closer inspection, it turns out Volvo may actually have been too early. Back in 2011, four years before the Paris Agreement was agreed, a fully clean-running electric Volvo was ready to launch in Sweden. A C30 with an attractive design, a quiet electric motor and a 150-kilometer range per charge. Advertisements depicted a new, emission-free, noise-free vision: by 2020, between 5 and 10 percent of all cars in Sweden would be e-cars, and a few years later the whole EU would be electrified. "0 to 70 km/h in 6.0 seconds" and "Full driving pleasure, virtually free of carbon dioxide emissions," read an enthusiastic Volvo press release.

But this e-car, too, was discontinued, after just 250 cars had been manufactured and leased. I don't know exactly why. What I do know is that the then-conservative Swedish government didn't respond to this technological shift by investing in the necessary charging infrastructure, and that it created uncertainty in the green car market first by removing the green car subsidy in 2009, then in 2013 by expanding the term "eco friendly car" to suddenly include heavier diesel cars. They did this by adopting a scandalous formula that factored a car's weight into whether it counted as a green car; the heavier a car was, the more it was allowed to emit and still be "green"! It was a fat bundle of cash directly into the pockets of heavy cars that, under the guise of "clean diesel," could suddenly be approved as green cars by companies with environmental policies – which, of course, kneecapped

Volvo's more expensive e-car with its shorter range. So in this case, politics actively hindered an attempt by the market to make a needed technological shift.

It's also interesting to look at the Norwegian example. In that oil-rich country, politicians – in a government with an understandable weight on its conscience – did the exact opposite. At around the same time, through tax breaks, free parking for electric cars and many other supportive reforms, Norway became the world's most e-car-dense country and the springboard to the European market for e-car company Tesla. Speaking of Tesla, that company would barely have survived its first year if not for politics and the variant of the Zero Emissions Vehicle Mandate that belatedly became reality in California, which forced manufacturers of emitting cars to purchase a sort of zero-emissions quota from e-car manufacturers.

Without supportive policy, the market very rarely makes great leaps in environmental technology. Every business leader I've met will attest to this. "Just tell us how much we're allowed to emit, and we'll get it done!" is something I've heard for as long as I've been involved in environmental issues. "But", the industry always emphasizes, "the rules of the game have to be the same for everyone, so competition isn't skewed. We need a level playing field. As long as that's clear, we have no problem at all reducing emissions."

On the other hand, political disunity, and the risk of environmental regulations being scrapped after a shift in government, are a company's worst nightmare. They want a long-term outlook for their investments. In 2020, when the oil refinery Preemraff in Lysekil, Sweden, dropped its plans for expanded operations that would have made the company Sweden's largest emitter, an important factor in this decision was the Swedish Climate Act, which establishes a clear framework for how Swedish emissions must decrease to net zero by 2045 – a framework with no room for additional emissions by Preem. The fact that the government itself had chosen to be the final arbiter in Preemraff's approval process – something the Green Party had to push through against a reluctant Social Democratic government partner because we believed the issue was so fundamentally important from the perspective of both the Swedish Environmental Code and the Climate Act – clearly played a role. As did all the negative publicity the company got from environmentalist protests. But according to Preem, the pivotal factor in their decision not to go forward with their application for higher emissions was that the government had introduced clear economic support to encourage the transition to renewable and new technology with green hydrogen. This is what made the company change its plans for an expanded fuel oil refinery and instead invest in producing biofuels and making the technological leap to green refineries. The combination of legislation and economic support was what changed their game plan.

Another example where political will, not technological development in itself, has changed the game is the expansion of wind power. The recent explosion of wind power in Sweden isn't a coincidence or the result of a self-sustaining technological development; it's the result of an interparty political agreement in 2016 to have a one hundred percent renewable electrical system by 2040. The market reacted immediately and extremely positively to this clear, cross-party political message, and in just a few years Sweden doubled its wind power production and has become the Nordic leader in land-based wind power, and has also attracted Europe's largest wind farm, Markbygden in northern Sweden. (This positive development came to a halt in 2022 when the new conservative Swedish government decided to leave the cross-party agreement to focus all its efforts in the energy field on nuclear power.)

Another example of technological solutions just waiting for the right political conditions is how the Swedish steel company SSAB after the Swedish cross-party supported Climate Act was agreed, has become the world leader in a brand-new technology for manufacturing fossil-free steel using green hydrogen. And how now the Swedish mining company LKAB is investing hundreds of millions of dollars in fossil-free mining, and brand-new company, H2 Green Steel, is establishing itself in Boden and a huge battery factory, Northvolt, in Skellefteå, both towns in the sparsely populated northern Sweden; it's not because the technical feasibility didn't exist before – it's because the political conditions didn't.

As long as the political parties' focus has been to ensure that Sweden gets as large an allocation of free emission allowances as possible and that Sweden's industry won't be "punished" in comparison to other global or European industry, the status quo has prevailed. But when Sweden reached an interparty agreement on a climate law stipulating that all industries in the country must reach net-zero emissions by 2045, when at long last there's a political majority in the EU for increasing the price of emissions, when the European Commission has passed its Green Deal and when Sweden has linked climate goals to comprehensive climate investment programs – well, then it's possible. It's possible!

It's not the lone engineer in the lab who solves the climate crisis. It's policy, which must make demands on and provide conditions for both the engineer and the corporations. Without this political guidance and leadership, the electric car wouldn't have made it to the market on its own merits, even though the technology has been there all along. Those who still believe market forces alone will solve the climate crisis might consider the fact that the automobile industry – while making gargantuan sums of money on a polluting internal combustion engine that's put the world in a climate crisis – still, to this day, dedicates most of its extensive research and development budget and its creativity to things like electronic rear-view mirrors, cup holders and designed, "expensive sounding" door-closing sounds, not to lowering emissions. Meanwhile, global road-traffic emissions have increased from 2.2 to 3.2 billion tons per year since the year 2000. And that when car sales ramped up again after shutting down during the 2020 COVID-19 pandemic, it was SUV sales, not e-car sales, that increased the most – five times more, to be exact. It's simple: As long as the industry can make money out of the combustion engine, they will.

Another common hypothesis for why humanity fails to act despite its better judgment is that it's so incredibly expensive to make the transition to an ecologically sustainable society, and that the cost impacts not only big corporations but also ordinary people, who are hit disproportionately hard. Closely linked to this theory is the narrative that sustainability is an elitist virtue that privileged people on their high horses can engage in, but not "ordinary people."

This narrative tends to focus on rural car owners, coal miners, professional fishermen and the tremendously expensive investments needed for a climate transition, and politicians from left to right tie themselves in knots trying to assuage groups they're afraid will otherwise show up in yellow vests or dump tons of rotten fish on the streets of Brussels.

But is it true that these particular groups are impacted unfairly? Would people rather work in coal mines and on oil platforms than with biofuels and wind power? Would fishermen rather vacuum up the ocean for a few short years than have a sustainable income for the rest of their lives? And even if they would – is that a legitimate reason to keep supporting unsustainable activities?

When I visited the steel company SSAB in Luleå – a town close to the Arctic circle with 79,000 inhabitants – in 2018 as Minister of the Environment to break ground on the world's first fossil-free steel mill, the union representatives were as happy as I was. They were beaming with pride, and with belief in the future. From being stuck with a blast furnace technology from the Middle Ages that relied on a massive supply of coal to make steel – SSAB alone represents 10 percent of Sweden's emissions – to seeing major new investments in northern Sweden, foreign interest, an order book filled with orders for green steel that hadn't even started being produced yet – now they felt like part of the solution to the climate crisis, not part of the problem. Rarely has a pat on the back given me such sincere happiness as the one I got from the president of the of the IF Metall trade union.

Today the green success story is almost unreal in northern Sweden, where highly educated people and youth previously hadn't seen a future and had chosen to move away. Now, hundred million dollar investments in battery factories, wind power, green hydrogen, green steel and green mining are pouring in – the kind of investments the northern part of the country hasn't seen in a hundred years.

So, the claim that a climate transition will cost people their jobs might be true of certain sectors that can't adapt and become fossil-free, but other fields are seeing new opportunities and chances to create jobs, probably many more than are being lost.

But yellow-vest arguments aren't just about jobs; they're also about everyday life. "Organic food, who can afford it?" "Electric cars, they're just for millionaires in big cities, not for ordinary folks."

But is that really true? First, I'm convinced that everyone would prefer sustainable production of everything we consume. No one wants animals to suffer in factory farms that create antibiotic-resistant bacteria or viruses to fuel potential pandemics. None of us wants the earth's climate to collapse, or wants California and Australia to go up in flames or the conifer forests in Scandinavia to light up like fire-crackers in arctic heat waves that turn the forest into tinder.

So what the protests are about, presumably, is the prospect of high price tags, not the environmentally friendly principles. And it's easy to understand how someone with tight financial margins, who has to choose between buying sneakers for the kids and organic food, might resent being lectured by all these know-it-alls who can afford to buy both. I understand completely. But what I don't understand are the politicians who exploit these emotions and pretend to be on the side of "ordinary folk" while actively working against reforms that would create market conditions for the green transition and defending an income tax system that favors the very rich. Politicians who, in the middle of a climate crisis, vote to lower gasoline taxes so that "ordinary people can afford to drive to work," but whose only answer to the climate crisis is extremely expensive nuclear power and/or carbon capture and storage (CCS) technology to potentially pump emissions back into the ground – neither of which can be financed by the market but will instead draw from the taxes or electric bills of ordinary people – those ordinary people they pretend to protect. Politicians who feed the myth that electric cars are for the elite, even as prices of new electric cars have plummeted in a short time and people in rural areas have the most to gain from the green transition, since people who live in single-family homes can charge their cars at home with solar power from their own roof instead of paying dearly for fossil fuels from the Middle East or Russia.

Of course, individuals can be affected in different ways when changes happen, but why do both the political right and the left point specifically to the green transition as a source of injustice, when major structural changes are happening all the time? Just look at how work has changed as a result of computerization and digitalization, how our lives have been transformed by globalization, how women's rights and access to the employment market have altered the conditions for men. Look at the incredible changes in travel, social and work life worldwide as a result of COVID-19. Look at how the outbreak of a war can change the landscape of the whole planet. The world is constantly transforming, and not always for the better for each individual person, and in every such transformation policy must take responsibility and help those who get left behind. But societies will continue to change in one way or another no matter what we decide, or don't decide. The climate transition does represent a small added cost compared to business as usual for the corporations and countries of the world – but in the long run it's a fraction of what we'll pay for the disasters of climate change if we fail to stem rising temperatures.

According to a 2015 calculation by the World Bank and the IMF, the world will need to invest $89 trillion in energy and other infrastructure by 2030, whether we make climate adaptations or not. If we do make them, the investment is a few percent higher. The European Commission has done similar calculations. The added cost is within the margin of error for all infrastructure projects and is in fact negligible, and it's quite modest compared to the added costs of combating COVID-19 or the damages to the world economy resulting from Russia's invasion of Ukraine.

So, is it true that it's too expensive to make the change? No. What is true, however, is that the costs we'll pass on to future generations increase with each day we don't act, and that new fossil fuel infrastructure projects cynically base their calculations on the assumption that someone else will pay for the externalities, that is, the damages their activities cause to the environment and the climate.

And even if we could use some sort of economic argument to claim that it's rational to destroy the only planet the human race has to live on, but that it would be rational to start investing in and planning for exploration and colonization of the red deserts of Mars, as some "techno-optimists" seriously believe: well, then we'd have to change the rules of the game as to what can be considered economically rational. After all, money and the economic system are human inventions, not laws of nature, and if money is eating up the very ground we stand on, then it's time to take control over our own mental construct; saving the planet ought to be worth the marginal cost.

A third hypothesis for why nothing is happening is about corruption and self-interest. Everything is controlled by large corporations and a few countries, and politicians' campaign coffers are filled by industries that don't want any regulations.

After twelve years in politics, I can confirm this hypothesis, but – with a big "but." Namely that it would apply to *all* politicians, corporations and countries. However, it's remarkable how rarely this factor is actually highlighted. The debate wants to revolve around the effects of climate change on "ordinary folks," or the uncertainties of new and presumably expensive technology, while the larger political battle, between the countries and political forces that are directly steered by these economic interests and the ones whose actions are unaffected by them, is much less often addressed in media analyses. The fact is that every time I've raised these issues for discussion as Minister for the Environment or as Green Party spokesperson, the reactions have been as dumbstruck as if I'd asked a fish to imagine an alternative to water.

In other words, it seems we're so accustomed to the current state of things that the connection between climate, oil, war in the Middle East and authoritarian regimes goes unnoticed by most people. The close ties between the United States and Saudi Arabia, or the fact that the Russian economy is totally dependent on oil and gas exports, are issues that, at least before Russia invaded Ukraine, were very rarely even mentioned in the climate debate – and neither was the fact that the unholy alliances between these interests use the megaphones of nationalism and populism, both in Europe and elsewhere in the world, to feed into the image of climate policy as a project of the elite that harms ordinary people.

I've seen Saudi Arabia's seasoned chief negotiator manipulate climate negotiations too many times. The tricks in his book are innumerable. Delay tactics. Agenda items. Challenging the Intergovernmental Panel on Climate Change. New agenda items. Technical details. And the skillful use of development perspectives. Before you know it, some impoverished developing country is on the same team, protesting against agenda items while countries with vast fossil resources like Russia and Australia rub their hands together.

This obviously explains we can't just "resolve it" the way most people would like. But since the media spotlight is focused less on the multibillion dollar interests at stake and much more on how readers' and listeners' wallets are affected by climate policy, few people make the connection. If they did, perhaps more people would be outraged about fossil fuel dependency and turn their anger on the oil companies and countries that want to keep making money from a growing climate crisis – not the environmental movement and parties that want to ban fossil fuels.

In Swedish national politics as well, I've seen baffling positions taken by parties with loose or direct links to strong lobbying groups. Among the most skilled are the Forest

Owners and the Federation of Swedish Farmers, who more or less dictate what a majority of members of the Swedish parliamentary Committee on Environment and Agriculture think about forestry issues and issues around bioenergy – which, among other things, has led to Sweden repeatedly disgracing itself on the EU stage, for example by refusing to provide correct calculations of carbon dioxide removal in woodlands, the so-called Land Use, Land-Use Change and Forestry (LULUCF) sector; or by doggedly opposing the entirely reasonable Taxonomy Regulation: the proposed EU regulation for classifying environmentally sustainable investments. In none of these cases has the focus been what's best for the climate, only what's best for the industries.

Nor was it Norway's proudest moment when, in closed-room meetings in Washington, DC, they opposed the idea that the Nordic-Baltic constituency of the World Bank Group should push to stop financing new oil exploration in poor countries. Oil-rich Norway could envisage an end to coal, but not an end to oil.

A final hypothesis for why nothing is happening is perhaps the saddest one of all. And that is that politicians aren't even corrupt, just cowardly and populist, with their fingers in the air to see which way the wind is blowing. Maybe they don't care at all about the climate crisis but simply exploit every opportunity to say what they think "ordinary people" think: We must be able to drive fossil fuel cars. We must be able to fly. We must be able to eat meat. China should lower its emissions, not us. These politicians avoid challenging voters' everyday lives at all costs. They pretend to be on the side of the people when in reality they're on the side of the OPEC countries and the fossil fuel industry.

Unfortunately I must also confirm this theory. I see far too many politicians who appear to care very little about what the issues are about, and more about "getting it right" with respect to the voters.

An example of this was when the leader of the Swedish Christian Democrats, Ebba Busch Thor, in a live televised party leader debate before the election in the fall of 2018, came out with a whole new position on nuclear power with no forewarning and no decision from the party conference. In an instant, the antinuclear stance the Christian Democrats had held since the 1970s changed, and the long-term, inter-party agreement on one hundred percent renewable elec-trical systems by 2040, which the party had entered into two years earlier with the Social Democrats, Green Party, Center Party and Moderates, was broken. The reversal was so out of sync with the party itself that the party's own spokesperson for energy policy, Pernilla Gunther, expressed her utter bewilderment in the media after the debate. The whole thing definitely suggested that in preparing for the debate Ebba Busch Thor had struggled to answer the question of where the party stood on climate change. In the summer of 2018 Sweden had been hit by a frighteningly long heat wave and drought, which gave rise to the worst forest fires in modern history and even led to the emergency slaughter of Swedish animals due to a lack of feed. Climate change had there-fore emerged as one of the most important issues to voters, and the Christian Democrats didn't have a single climate proposal in their election platform, whereas they clearly opposed important climate actions such as introducing a flight tax and increasing the gasoline tax. I don't know how she could change positions on an issue as important as nuclear power without including the whole party in the decision, but apparently the temptation to do so was irresist-ible. After all, the new position seemed to give a satisfactory answer to the climate question in a single, punchy one-liner: "The climate transition requires more electricity, and it isn't windy every day; therefore, we need more nuclear power!" Plus, this position didn't require any changes to the voters' everyday lives. Perfect.

It didn't seem to trouble Busch Thor that all the plans for nuclear power in Europe in the past fifteen years had been hit with significant delays and cost increases, that in many cases the plans had been put on hold, that nuclear power is not considered competitive with new wind energy anywhere, or that the final nuclear waste issue still is not resolved. And the voters thought it sounded good and rewarded the party with several percentage points as the Christian Democrats hit the afterburners in the final sprint, quite probably based on this issue, which seemed to appeal to people's common sense.

Obviously, the reason populist politicians gain power in many countries is that voters actually vote them into office. So the mirror should also be pointed back at the people who give them their vote, or at the media that give them a disproportionate amount of coverage. What's the reasoning? How can a majority of Australians vote for parties that want to expand coal power when Australia is one of the world's most climate-vulnerable countries? How can a climate denier like Australian member of parliament Craig Kelly be given VIP access to Sky News and the tabloid press with false claims such as that the Arctic ice isn't melting and that socialists and arsonists, not climate change, are behind the 2020 Australian bush fires, in which more than two thousand families lost their homes and three billion animals died?

Is it about entertainment value? Viewer numbers? Clicks? Advertisers? Absolutely. But to get a deeper answer to the question, I believe a psychological, sociological and moral-philosophical analysis is needed, of how we're drawn to fake news and alternative facts that enable us to keep behaving the only way we've ever felt comfortable behaving.

How we've been carefully trained by advertising to think of ourselves first, how we've accepted that the most important thing in life, what gives us an identity and worth, is to be consumers, and that this is absolutely nothing to be ashamed of. And how we instinctively point fingers: why should we, when they're not?

It's striking to see the same thing everywhere on earth in this context. In Sweden, the message from parties on the right is that since Sweden produces less than 1 percent of global emissions, it doesn't matter what we do. And the EU doesn't play much of a role, either, as it produces less than 10 percent of emissions. No, it's China we should be focusing on! Similar arguments are heard from Australia, Japan, South Africa and Venezuela. Russia and Brazil point to their large forested areas, which can absorb carbon dioxide, and say their countries are carbon sinks, not emitters. China and India point out that they have low emissions per capita and historically low emissions overall. So do all the developing countries in Africa, Asia and Latin America that want to exploit untapped gas and oil reserves.

But the truth is that there are 193 countries on earth, and almost every one of them represents less than 1 or 2 percent of the earth's emissions. If all the countries in the world that emit less than 2 percent of the total were combined into a single country, that country would be the world's largest emitter, larger than China and India put together. And if we count cumulative emissions – the total emissions a country has produced historically – or consumption-based emissions – the emissions created through importing goods – the numbers would look completely different, and the finger would point unequivocally at the inhabitants of countries like the United States and Great Britain, but also at Sweden and the whole European Union.

But none of that actually matters too much. In this childish rationalization contest, there are no winners. Because if we fail to limit global warming, we're all losers. If we succeed, we're all winners. We must go from "I'll make sure I'm safe" to thinking "only together are we safe."

Humanity's collective inability to envision anything other than what is here and now is also a major reason why so little is happening. I remember the debates in European Parliament as recently as 2010, and the endless seminars on biofuel, solar energy and carbon capture and storage (CCS), which many believed in when the EU was setting its first target for reducing emissions by 2030. It was mainly environmental organizations and small green tech companies that were interested, while industry, business and most political parties seemed to think what we were talking about wasn't serious. Not fully "realistic" or "balanced," to use two of the most misused words in the EU debates. They seemed to think it was some kind of naive charity that the EU was even setting these targets – even though it would soon turn out that, in principle, the targets could be met simply by slightly tweaking the directives for car and heavy vehicle emissions and by changing the light bulbs in the whole EU.

But they didn't see a transition ahead of them then. That we really were headed for a technological shift away from dependence on oil, coal and gas. Now, however, the realization is starting to sink in. But not completely. And not for everyone.

In 2021, the EU agreed on a new climate law in which the target is net zero emissions by 2050 and before that the Union must reduce its emissions by at least 55 percent by 2030. The European Parliament wanted to see a reduction of 60 percent by 2030. Sweden, Finland and Denmark wanted to go even further; Sweden was prepared to set the target at 65 percent, not counting carbon sinks.

So why did it end up at 55 percent reduction by 2030?

Because it's technically impossible to reach 65 percent? Because it would be too expensive? After the multi billion dollar deluge of aid to communities in response to the COVID-19 pandemic, can anyone seriously claim that money is a scarce resource? We also know that technology evolves, more rapidly than anyone can foresee, when policy sets up the framework and creates the conditions. And we know that those on the leading edge of the climate transition will have an enormous competitive advantage when the whole world is making the shift.

So, what is standing in the way of a more ambitious climate law? Political will. Or, more correctly, the lack of it. If brave politicians in more countries had communicated a vision of the benefits the climate transition will bring, and particularly if more voters had dared to believe in that vision and voted for politicians who were already prepared to implement climate reforms in the industrial, transportation and agricultural sectors, the climate transition could have happened much faster.

No other external reality is stopping us. Only this. The voters can't expect change without giving their politicians a mandate to make change.

*

When I leave my office at European Parliament, the last thing I do is take down what I'd hung on the walls. A few posters about threatened fish species, a cod-shaped postcard and postcards with the text "Make Overfishing Illegal" (and again I think: we actually did it!). I take down the worn paper with the words of pastor Dietrich Bonhoeffer that I'd hung at eye level at my desk. Bonhoeffer, a member of the German Resistance, and one of the people involved in a serious attempt to kill Adolf Hitler, wrote this in his prison cell in the midst of a nightmarish reality that was becoming the water everyone swam in.

> *The essence of optimism*
>
> *is that it takes no account of the present,*
>
> *but it is a source of inspiration, of vitality and hope*
>
> *where others have resigned;*
>
> *it enables a man to hold his head high,*
>
> *to claim the future for himself*
>
> *and not to abandon it to his enemy.*

CHAPTER 6

Leaving No One Behind

AS WE SPEED through the streets of Mogadishu I try to absorb as much as I can about life outside the car window. No one takes any particular notice of the convoy, despite the huge UN Jeep and the trucks carrying heavily armed local security officers who plow death-defyingly into every turn, slamming on the brakes and blocking every street corner so no one can attack the convoy from the side. Women flutter by like colorful exclamation marks against the gray, bullet-riddled facades. Children standing at the side of the road are so used to the sight of men in truck beds with machine guns that they don't even turn their necks; it's just another day for the residents of Mogadishu.

Somalia's capital was once called "the white pearl of the Indian Ocean" for its many white Italian palaces along the long, white beach. Then came the war. I remember the images on the news in 1991. *Black Hawk Down.* The American soldiers dragged behind Jeeps through the city. Now, almost thirty years later, I see the rubble, the piles of debris, the bullet-peppered walls up and down each street. The devastation is unbelievable, yet life goes on. Here and there I see a blue or red tarp and some scraps of wood at the edge of the sidewalk, makeshift walls that might belong to someone, might be someone's night shelter, someone's home.

The shops have images of their products painted in bright

colors directly on the outer building walls. In these images I see everything from brooms and mobile phones to syringes, sick people on stretchers, and blood. The latter might be a sign for a pharmacy or clinic. Garbage everywhere. On a street corner I catch a glimpse of a lone little girl admiring a special pile of treasures she's pulled from a mountain of junk. She's in her own world; she doesn't see our armed, white Jeeps and military escort as we fly by, just her glittering pile of glass fragments and beautifully colored chips of concrete. This is her everyday. Not sitting at a school desk.

Three million children in Somalia don't go to school, according to UNICEF. Literacy is low, which must be why the shops paint their goods on the walls instead of using words. I think about the mind-boggling fact that half of Somalia's population of fifteen million are under 17 years old. That means a majority weren't even born when the country collapsed in 1991 and have never experienced any other reality than this one. A reality I'd never truly had to confront before I became Sweden's Minister for International Development Cooperation.

I entered the Swedish government in 2014. My decision to leave the European Parliament wasn't an easy one; I enjoyed my job and felt I'd accomplished a lot. But to be part of Sweden's first ever Green government, and as aid minister at that, was a key opportunity to work further to resolve issues around the resources and capabilities of developing countries, which I'd come to realize was critical if we wanted to save the oceans and the climate. It would be four extremely exciting years, with trips to many countries I never thought I'd be able to visit. Countries that don't belong to the minority of countries in the world with welfare systems and high GDPs; the so-called developing countries, many designated as fragile states, post-conflict countries or countries in conflict, including Somalia, South Sudan, Afghanistan,

Iraq, Mali, Lebanon, Liberia, Sierra Leone and Myanmar. And poor, climate-sensitive countries like Bolivia, Bangladesh, Kiribati, Tonga, Mozambique, Kenya and Ethiopia. And European countries hard-hit by war, like Bosnia and Ukraine.

I went into politics because I cared about the environment, particularly the ocean. But it wasn't long before my concern for cod in the Baltic Sea brought me to West Africa and into debates in European Parliament about the EU fisheries agreements in the Pacific and Indian oceans. Fisheries aren't just an environmental issue; they're also a global justice issue. For us in Europe, the hunt for fish doesn't end when we've exhausted our own seas with our overly efficient boats; we can also fish the waters of poor countries. Seventy percent of the fish eaten in Europe are imported or caught by EU fishermen outside European seas. The world is interconnected this way on issue after issue. It's rarely possible to introduce sustainability at a strictly local level. Cross-border regulations are often needed and can just as often run aground, since operations can always be moved to another jurisdiction. Vessels swap their flags for those of countries that sell so-called flags of convenience; companies move to where taxes are lowest, or nonexistent. The arguments against stricter regulations in the EU or in Sweden always sound the same: If we don't fish in West African waters, the Russians and Chinese will just do it instead. If we toughen emissions regulations or raise taxes, companies will just move somewhere else where the taxes are low and the environmental laws are weak.

My environmental engagement, which in the beginning was focused mainly on a single issue, broadened quickly as I realized that the issue couldn't be isolated from other issues, and that to save the ocean, or the climate, we must cooperate internationally. I also realized that we'll never fully succeed as long as there are poor countries with weak laws and zero capacity for monitoring and enforcement. Somalia is one of many examples where the collapse of the state gave fishing vessels from all corners of the world free rein to empty the war-torn country's waters of fish. This in turn made the situation in the country even worse, as some local fishermen who saw their waters being plundered armed themselves and joined up with pirates, who controlled the coast for many years. And this in turn fortified and financed the terrorist group al-Shabab, which in turn has created fear and violence that's made it impossible for Somalis in Sweden and other Western countries, or in refugee camps in Kenya, to go back and build up their homeland.

"Poverty is the greatest polluter," Indira Gandhi said at the opening of the first UN environmental conference in Stockholm in 1972. Fifty years later, the link between poverty and environmental and climate issues is just as relevant. Today, 750 million people worldwide live without access to electricity. Women are oppressed, wars and conflicts hold many countries in a bloody stranglehold, people are losing their homes, their lives, 84 million people are refugees (2021), and a million babies have been born as refugees since 2018 alone. To then ask that all countries put climate first on their agenda is to ask the impossible, although more and more people are starting to see the connection between wars and conflicts and climate change. This is the case on the Horn of Africa, where many years of extreme drought have led to crop failures, which has made it easier for al-Shabab to recruit. In Somalia I learn that very few join al-Shabab for religious reasons. Instead, it's about money, pure survival. When it's impossible to find a normal job, or when the crops fail, the terrorist group can recruit far more easily among uneducated boys with no future prospects and desperate men needing to support their families.

It's impossible to describe the global dimensions of climate change without talking about the development aspect. Or the justice aspect. Rich countries have put the planet in this situation, there's no question about it. In 2014 one of the first things I did as a Green aid minister was to announce that Sweden would contribute four billion kronor (at the time roughly 600 million dollars) to the UN Green Climate Fund. This was a first step toward fulfilling Sweden's part of the promise rich countries had made to poor countries at the Copenhagen Climate Change Conference in 2009, namely that we would create a financing mechanism to help poor countries reduce emissions and adapt to the damage caused by climate change. Sweden's financial contribution was one of the first and largest, and it prompted other countries to follow suit. It was seen as crucial to the success of the Paris Agreement that the fund be fully stocked and able to do its job.

During the Green Party's time in government Sweden became the world's largest per capita donor of climate assistance, and we were included in many renewable energy and climate adaptation initiatives via our bilateral aid, the UN and the EU, and the development financier Swedfund. I feel it is important to write this, because money is often a focal point in international climate discussions, whether it be the one hundred billion dollars a year promised by rich countries to poor countries at the climate meeting in Copenhagen, funding for a just transition for people working in the fossil fuel industry, or compensation for the loss and damage poor countries experience due to climate change.

I'm well aware of these financing discussions, and equally aware after my years as Minister of International Development Cooperation that the money we're potentially talking about is just a drop in the ocean compared to what's needed to build up the world's broken countries. These countries certainly benefit from access to renewable energy, but what they may need most are social welfare systems to provide security for people who are ill or unemployed. They need democracy, rule of law, efficient institutions, free education systems, health care, and peace. I'm not saying the hundred billion is insignificant in any way, but I fear it obscures our view of what the Western world most urgently needs to do in its partnership with the Global South, something that could change the whole playing field. That is, eliminate tax havens where corrupt leaders and global corporations can stash the money they've stolen or made from developing countries' resources; put tight reins on multinational companies so they'll pay taxes instead of bribes in countries where they extract natural resources; support countries in combating terrorism, in particular by helping to design social welfare systems that make it unnecessary for a person who's lost their job or suffered a crop failure to join one of the terrorist groups that have attacked developing countries with more virulence than any plague, such as al-Shabab, al-Qaeda, IS or the Taliban. Realize that all countries are interconnected, that we're dependent on each other, and that wars, conflicts and poverty threaten the security of all of us, which keeps us from focusing on the overarching threat, which is the destruction of our planet. Fair and just trade isn't a sacrifice for Western consumers; it's critical for global security. Climate aid isn't charity; it's life insurance for ourselves.

In his book *Moneyland*, investigative journalist Oliver Bullough describes the holes in international law that allow the world's kleptocrats, oligarchs and dictators to empty their countries – not uncommonly oil-rich countries – of money and, under cover of anonymity, open bank accounts and buy penthouses in New York, dream villas in the Caribbean or swanky houses in the UK and Switzerland. "Moneyland," as Bullough defines it, is the borderless international space that some of the world's most cunning tax attorneys and lawyers have found, or sometimes created in conjunction with micro-states, where the immeasurably rich can establish an address and proceed to move around unhindered as their homeland's tax collectors and prosecutors stand powerless at the border and stamp their feet. Every year at the UN climate summit the world devotes two weeks to discussing a hundred billion dollars in climate financing for poor countries – which isn't wrong, of course. But the world's failure to come together in a similar way to stop at least the same amount (according to Oxfam) or ten times as much (according to Global Financial Integrity) from being stolen or swindled away annually by tax evaders and corrupt leaders and their families and hidden in tax havens, is a stain on the world order – as is the fact that many of the world's tax havens are in the EU, whose hypoc-risy in this matter defies all understanding.

Because if the money from so-called poor countries' rich natural resources stayed in those countries with full trans-parency and was taxed there, I'm convinced that the spiral of poverty could be reversed and that the important social contracts that must exist between a people and its govern-ment could be established.

That said, I still think the rich world must show solidarity by contributing money, expertise and capacity-building support, as well as support for human rights defenders and women in developing countries. But that can't replace the political legitimacy and accountability that result from a government itself levying taxes and distributing social welfare in a country.

In Somalia, great strides have been made toward creating a new, peaceful federation of states in a previously completely divided land, and Sweden has invested a great deal of polit-ical and economic energy and power to help build new insti-tutions and facilitate dialogue between different parts of the country. I'm incredibly proud of the Swedish diplomats and development cooperation officials who've fostered trust in this work, and of the unusually well-functioning cooperation with other donors and representatives of the new Somali state, which has resulted in a shared development plan and several steps toward parliamentarianism and democracy. To show Sweden's support, I visited the country twice during my time as minister of international development cooperation, despite it being perhaps the most dangerous country in the world to visit.

My experiences from those visits are forever imprinted on my memory. The machine guns my bodyguards carried at all times, the stiletto behind the headrest in the car in case we were attacked, the machine-gun bursts we heard nearby. The bombproof bunker where I had to spend the night. The brave women I met, many of them exiled Somalis who'd returned to build up their country. A young aid worker whose sister was shot and killed just a while after I'd left the country. None of these stories fit into the climate story, or the ocean story – or do they? Most developing countries aren't war-ravaged, after all. But Somalia is an example of how long it can take to heal a country once it's fallen apart, how the artificial borders and exploitation of colonialism have left their mark, and how the ripples of those periods in history still affect countries to this day – as far away as Sweden's lower income suburbs, where young, rootless people who aren't absorbed into mainstream society, search for an identity and sometimes find it in criminality. And where many media companies and politicians prioritize the issue of immigration-associated criminality stratospherically higher than the issue of climate change, with no solutions except to call for harsher penalties and no more refugees.

If we're going to get through the climate crisis, the perspectives of developing countries must be accounted for, but without simplifications. A hundred billion dollars a year won't solve their problems when at least as much is being pumped out of these countries to tax havens, and Western oil companies are propping up dictators and corrupt governments by paying bribes. And climate funds can't be an isolated section of the world's wallet – *all* money must be spent sustainably and must support a transition that saves our planet and ourselves; the Paris Agreement even stipulates as much. And if the world is to live up to our promise in the UN Agenda 2030 to "leave no one behind," we must see the whole picture, and we must look in the mirror. We can't hand issues of justice over to aid ministers when they belong in the hands of prime ministers, finance ministers and business leaders. Of all the countries I've visited as aid minister, I've never been invited to the most important one: Moneyland.

CHAPTER 7

Political Unwillingness

Katowice, Poland, December 10–14, 2018. COP24

IT DOES NOT begin well. Just before the meeting, Brazil announced that they no longer plan to host the next climate summit in 2019, which has caused many to fear that their new president, Jair Bolsonaro, like Donald Trump, will withdraw from the Paris Agreement. Then, the United States and Australia organized a big flagship event to promote "clean coal," which makes the environmental organizations scream bloody murder.

After that, the news travelled around the world about a loud conflict in one of the negotiation rooms. It's about how the meeting should word its response to the scientific report just released by the Intergovernmental Panel on Climate Change about how the world will be affected by a temperature rise of 1.5 degrees. The conflict is over one single word. All countries want to "welcome" the report. All except Saudi Arabia, the US, Russia and Kuwait, which merely want to "take note of" it. Considering that the panel of researchers behind the report had worked for three years and delivered their comprehensive findings as commissioned by the countries within the United Nations Framework Convention on Climate Change (UNFCCC), it would be nothing short of a sheer provocation if the international community now would simply "take note of" the report.

On top of this, Turkey has hijacked several days of negotiations, refusing to approve the agenda unless a new agenda item was added making it possible for Turkey to be deemed a developing country in the context of climate change, since they've taken in so many refugees of the war in Syria. This would entitle them to many benefits, including access to the massive climate funds contributed by rich countries to help poor countries. Naturally, Turkey's antics have inspired many other countries to point out why their own diverse hardships should give them the same right. Enormous efforts have therefore been required of the Polish Presidency to stem this flood of arguments so they could even have the agenda approved and start the meeting.

So when I arrive in Katowice, the mood is at rock bottom. Fossil fuels are clearly present, not just politically but physically: outside, as a strong odor of burning coal; inside, as a stubborn smell of stale smoke that never goes away. From my hotel room on the tenth floor I see one of the causes of this stink: Katowice's coal-fired power plant with its tall, red-and-white striped chimney that sprawls on the horizon like the silhouette of a belching dragon. After just a few hours in the country I desperately crave fresh air, but there's nowhere to get it. I gaze down at the landscape with its dirty patches of snow and wonder what it must be like to live day in and day out, all year long, with nowhere to go to take a clean breath. A claustrophobic thought.

Coal power represents more than 70 percent of the energy production in Poland, the highest percentage of any country in the European Union. Poland also has the most respiratory health problems in the EU. The campaign "See What You Breathe," in which the organization Polish Smog Alert placed models of lungs in several cities and within fourteen days the soft material in the "lungs" went from bright white to pitch black, was an eye-opener for many Poles. According to the European Environment Agency (EEA), around 46,000 people die prematurely each year because of air pollution. Still, statistics show that this air isn't even close to what hundreds of millions of people in other parts of the world live with. On the list of the fifty most air-polluted cities in the world, none are in the EU; the vast majority are in India, China or Pakistan.

Why Poland now wants to host its second climate summit (the first was COP19 in Warsaw in 2013) is a question many have asked themselves. The Poles have insisted that among the EU countries they are best placed to overcome the divisions between rich and poor countries by showing that they have similar problems to other coal-dependent economies and the same interest in an orderly climate transition that safeguards both jobs and energy security. In thirty years, the number of people employed in the Polish coal sector has decreased from almost 400,000 to 80,000 without the economy taking a beating; quite the opposite.

Poland has also been more resistant to climate action than any other country in the EU. They held off ratifying the Paris Agreement until the last minute, and only the same month the meeting in Katowice was to take place they submitted their ratification of the Doha Amendment to the Kyoto Protocol, long after all the other EU countries, and after an exceptional procedure in which the EU finally tired of waiting for the COP24 host country and decided to ratify before Poland had done so.

Actually, this meeting should have been a fairly uninteresting one. The Paris Agreement has already been signed and ratified in record time, the principle of a bottom-up system in which countries voluntarily submit their commitments is already in place and everyone has already agreed that the Agreement will be followed up with a rule book where countries will report how much they emit in a more or less transparent way, as well as how much their emissions are decreasing, so everyone can keep track of how the world is doing and how much more needs to be done.

That's all that has to be finalized now. A rule book for what we've already agreed on. It should be a cakewalk.

But without political will, nothing is easy. And right now, the political focus is elsewhere. The euphoria of the Paris Agreement has evaporated, the opposing forces have mobilized, and what should be in the common interest of the whole global community now seems to be anything but. Few people want to talk about the climate transition, or about raising our ambitions; instead, technical matters have turned political and the devil lurks in a thousand details.

In short, suspicions between south and north from before the Paris Agreement have flared up again. Of course, the poor countries have every right to feel betrayed. Before the ink had dried on the United States' ratification of the Paris Agreement, the American people elected a new, climate-skeptical president in Donald Trump – who let climate skeptics like Myron Ebell and Scott Pruitt handle environmental policy and appointed ExxonMobil CEO Rex Tillerson as his Secretary of State. The US also announced that it wasn't going to fulfill its commitment to contribute two million dollars to the Green Climate Fund. This was a flagrant breach of the promise that the countries primarily responsible for causing the climate crisis – which have built their wealth by emitting greenhouse gases – would compensate the poorer countries and help them adapt to climate change.

But the rumblings in Katowice come not only from the poor countries but also from the oil countries, who see a threat to their income if the Paris Agreement becomes a reality. Oddly enough, these two groups often align with each other. For example, when the interest in having more flexible accounting rules for developing countries overlaps with the fossil fuel industry's interest in having the vaguest rules possible that allow for all manner of loopholes. The EU is fighting tooth and nail in Katowice to keep the Paris Agreement rule book from having two different sets of rules, one for the rich and one for the poor (it's unclear who would be included in the poor group, as major emitting countries like China, India and Brazil are still part of the G77 group). Capacity-building support for developing countries, yes, but the same rules must apply to everyone.

At the same time, countries like South Africa, India and Brazil have started mobilizing to include the concept of "equity" in the global stocktake, something the rich countries don't like; they want to look forward, not backward. Partly because an "equitable" compensation for loss and damage could amount to uncountable sums of money, and partly because it would shift the world's focus from a common transition to pained demands for accountability. Equity is important in many respects, of course, but it's also a perfect conflict-generating wedge to drive into the work on the rule book. Many people remember the last time the word was discussed, late one night at COP17 in Durban in 2001, when the chief negotiator for the US, Todd Stern, quite undiplomatically blurted out: "*If equity's in, we're out!*"

The exhibition halls in Katowice are like exhibition halls everywhere on earth. In one part of the facility the countries each have a white modular office with four walls; Sweden's is among the smaller ones and is filled with coats and hats, printers, a couple of meeting tables and a Swedish coffee machine. Someone has spruced up the atmosphere with Christmas decorations in the form of a poinsettia and red tinsel; it's getting close to St. Lucia Day, anyway.

We have a delegation of more than twenty people, and

there's always someone in the module working. It's cramped, the lighting is bad, but at least it's a safe place to kick off our shoes after long, arduous negotiation sessions that often run late into the night. Occasionally other Swedes show up at the little room. A couple of Swedish parliament members, some Swedish journalist wanting an answer to some question, a European Parliament member. Sometimes there's someone catching up on sleep in a corner. It's an informal atmosphere, which I as minister appreciate. It also makes it easier for all of us representing Sweden to work as a team. Civil servants from the various ministries, experts from our agencies and chief negotiators are all in one place and can be quickly consulted if needed, and everyone at all levels can pull in the same direction.

As an EU country, Sweden also acts in conjunction with the other 27 member countries (the UK is still in the EU at this COP). The EU has submitted a common Nationally Determined Contribution (NDC), the EU's collective commitments to emission reductions; the EU's positions have been negotiated jointly, and the EU community is represented in the negotiations by the European Commission. The member countries are also present, of course, and in constant coordination.

But there's still plenty of room for an individual EU country to act and exert influence at the climate summits. This can happen through organizing or participating in the numerous seminars and initiatives at the meeting, where Sweden has high visibility on issues including oceans and climate, the climate transition in business and industry, and climate financing. It can also happen when a minister from the country is given a special role as facilitator to try to untangle difficult knots in the negotiations. The host country, together with the UNFCCC, can make such requests of individual ministers, the idea being that a tough question that has stumped professional negotiators for months or years might be solvable at the political level.

I both hope I will and hope I won't be assigned this role. On the one hand, it would give me a unique insight into how the countries reason; on the other hand, something in the air tells me success is far from guaranteed. Despite the assurances I give in every interview, that the world will keep working as usual with the Paris Agreement, that the climate transition will happen with or without the United States, I don't feel so sure, myself. Of all the countries in the world, only a few groups are working to raise ambitions and ensure the agreement is implemented. These are the EU, the small island developing states (so called SIDS), and then a few countries here and there, like Canada, New Zealand and Costa Rica. The rest of the world seems to sit quite comfortably in the shadow that emerged when all the light turned toward Donald Trump.

Every morning there's a coordination meeting for the delegations of EU countries, and I meet the other like-minded ministers with the customary cheek-kissing. These include the Green climate minister Carole Dieschbourg from Luxembourg, the German climate minister Svenja Schulze, Teresa Ribera from Spain, João Matos Fernandes from Portugal, and Kimmo Tiilikainen from Finland. We don't all belong to the same party groups, but along with the ministers from a few other countries we make up an important inner group that coordinates us and pushes the EU for higher ambitions. How important we are becomes clear when we've sat down at the long, horseshoe-shaped conference table and donned the obligatory headphones, and the Executive Secretary of the UNFCCC, Patricia Espinosa, takes the floor.

"It is you in the EU who have the most important leadership role now," she says. "This is the most important conference since Paris. The UN Secretary General has said that we have no other choice than to succeed here! We will not take the path of division, the one certain countries are now on."

Espinosa, with her short, dark hair and lively brown eyes set in a round, sympathetic face, looks genuinely concerned. She represents all of the UN member states and is trying not to be overtly critical of any individual country.

"Obviously, everyone wants a good outcome from this meeting. No one is saying otherwise," she stresses. "And the 1.5-degrees report has had a good effect. With all the media attention, no one wants two degrees anymore."

But she's concerned about the fight over which words should be used about the 1.5-degrees report, "welcome" or "take note of."

"We absolutely don't want to open this meeting up for a political debate about science. The independence of the research must be protected. We must distinguish between opinions and facts. People can have different opinions on what should be done, but they can't have opinions on facts."

We all know what she's referring to. Since the 2016 US presidential election, the bizarre concept of "alternative facts" has gained ground in populist circles, and just the thought of opening the floor to a political discussion of the IPCC's integrity is frightening. The large EU coordination room in Katowice, with tourist posters on the walls from Austria, which holds the EU presidency, the continental breakfast with coffee and croissants and the proper, unsmiling top officials from the European Commission at the head of the table feel in this situation like a safe but also shrinking haven in an uncertain sea that's suddenly changed character. I look at our British colleague, climate negotiator Archie Young, who since the Brexit vote has worn the same expression of apologetic guilt and dejection as almost every Brit I meet, and try to process the fact that he and the

UK will soon leave this room and will no longer participate in this extremely important setting together with the EU. Sweden will lose a key ally on so many issues, including climate change. It's as if a Bond villain has hatched a scheme to influence the elections in various countries in order to weaken the Paris Agreement. Stone after stone is being snatched from the foundation of the climate transition: the US, Brazil, a weakened EU preoccupied with Brexit. And then there are the unrelenting attacks against another cornerstone: the science and the IPCC.

So the assignment Patricia Espinosa then gives me couldn't be more critical. A mediator is needed to help resolve the wording issue in response to the 1.5-degrees report. Would I be willing to do this, together with another minister?

The fact that, out of everyone here, I'm being asked to do this clearly reflects Sweden's high credibility on climate issues, in that we are major donors of climate aid and are ranked highest in terms of our own climate policy. I've also made a lot of contacts in developing countries during my four years as Minister for International Development Cooperation, and also with the leaders of the small island states, whom I know well since Sweden together with Fiji co-hosted the 2017 United Nations Ocean Conference in New York.

So naturally I say yes, albeit with some trepidation. Of course, it's also a red line for me and Sweden that we "welcome" the report from the UN climate panel, so it won't be easy to find a middle ground between "welcome" and "take note of." But I know that when it comes to the UN, consensus is the only way. Failure to find a solution is not an option. It's all about the art of the possible.

Soon I'm sitting in a meeting with my Costa Rican climate minister collegue, Carlos Manuel Rodríguez, a bearded man with an attentive gaze who's been appointed as the other facilitator for this very difficult and symbolically important question. We agree on a strategy that starts with taking the pulse of the US civil servant negotiator; we're both well aware that the US isn't present in Katowice on a political level. If the US relents, we reason, the other countries probably will too. And why would the US oppose anything anyway, when they're just going to leave the Paris Agreement? It would be, as someone remarked, "like being invited to dinner and complaining about the food even though you are not going to eat it."

But of course, it's not that simple. We meet the American climate negotiator, Trigg Talley, an affable man with a thick shock of gray hair and dressed in a white shirt and a tie, who has worked under many presidents before Trump. He listens intently to our arguments that the US shouldn't create conflicts over climate science and spoil things for the rest of the world, but he quickly interrupts. We're mistaken, he explains, if we think anyone in Washington thinks criticizing climate science is a bad thing. It's more the opposite. The president's base likes that sort of thing.

"My advice is to not elevate this to the political level," he says. "It would be best if we could find a solution that's within my mandate. Otherwise you run the risk of escalating things and getting an even firmer position in response."

Talley shrugs sympathetically as we digest what he's said. Reluctantly, I realize he's right. The Americans have already blocked several joint statements, including in the Arctic Council, where they refused to include wording about the climate or even Agenda 2030 once the document had been sent to Washington.

But Talley doesn't want to make the first proposal of wording that could loosen the knot. As long as we find language that's accurate, and that doesn't imply that the US welcomes the 1.5-degrees report, it should be fine, he says.

Grudgingly I realize I'll have to swallow my instinct to fight for the word "welcome" at all costs, and that now my task is to try to soothe everyone's outrage and find another, sensible way forward.

My colleague and I spend the greater part of the following day in back-to-back meetings with pretty much every country in the world. To make consultations easier and to give their positions more weight, the countries have formed various groups. We meet with the EU, the Alliance of Small Island States (AOSIS), the Least Developed Countries (LCDs), the African group, the Arab group, the Association of Latin America and the Caribbean (AILAC), China and Brazil, and, finally, the Umbrella Group – a motley collection of countries that may at one time have been like-minded, namely Australia, Belarus, Canada, Iceland, Israel, Japan, New Zealand, Ukraine, Russia, Norway, Kazakhstan and the United States.

Most of the people we talk with are very disappointed and upset that the four countries – the US, Russia, Saudi Arabia and Kuwait – object to welcoming the IPCC report. The small island states are among those least willing to compromise. Many have historically had very close ties to the US and feel deeply betrayed. They're also in shock over the report's harsh message, including the almost unfathomable conclusion that 90 percent of coral reefs will die even at 1.5 degrees of warming. A minister from the Caribbean exclaims: "We can't simply make note of it, we must own this report, it can't just be allowed to die at this conference!"

No one understands which "knowledge gaps" Saudi Arabia and others are talking about, either. A minister from the Least Developed Countries says: "We can't compromise on science! Why should we question it? The Presidency must put its foot down now. It must be brave!"

At our meeting with the Arab group, Saudi Arabia is represented by the highly experienced negotiator Ayman Shasly. This is a recurring problem at the climate summits, that while the high-level week is intended for ministers to resolve conflicts with each other, certain countries still choose to send their regular, technically minded negotiators to the meetings with other countries' ministers. The stout man with the elegant suit and tidy, combed-back gray hair starts to describe insistently and in detail all the knowledge gaps and inaccuracies that he believes apply to the 1.5-degrees report, information that's impossible for me or my Costa Rican colleague to be familiar with or address. We can only say that Shasly's opinions aren't consistent with what's been approved and adopted by the IPCC, in which Shasly himself is Saudi Arabia's representative. The knowledge gap he refers to seems mainly to be about his lack of cost estimates for what restricting the global temperature increase to 1.5 degrees would cost the world. The IPCC's estimates are far too "rosy," Shasly says; they only talk about the benefits a climate transition would have for health and the environment, not about the financial costs!

The discussion gets us nowhere, and later I note that the Saudi negotiator is also on the board of the Green Climate Fund. There, he has, among other things, asked that the fund approve aid for a project in Bahrain where the oil industry wants to purify and recycle water used in oil extraction. The project didn't pass, however, because Sweden and several other countries flatly opposed this absurd interpretation of what climate aid should be used for. Everyone I talk to confirms that Saudi Arabia, which has the role of coordinator for the entire Asian group in the fund, is the single most important reason the board has been dysfunctional from day one, with constant conflicts similar to those that plague the climate negotiations. An experienced diplomat tells me that in his many decades in international organizations, he's never witnessed such dirty play as in the Green Climate Fund.

Our next meeting is with China. But if my colleague Carlos Manuel Rodríguez and I had any hope that China would want to use its weight to pressure the intractable countries or take on the mantle of climate leader formerly worn by the US, that hope is very quickly extinguished. China's veteran climate negotiator, Xie Zhenhua, just smiles dismissively and announces that the country has no position whatsoever on the matter. "We'll join the consensus. We won't block anything," he says in a neutral tone.

But then he suddenly adds that China, too, sees "knowledge gaps" in the 1.5-degrees report. Which is extremely concerning. After the meeting, Carlos and I can only conclude that China is very far from wanting to take a leadership role on climate, not even when Donald Trump has served them the opportunity on a silver platter.

In perhaps the strangest meeting of all, with the wildly sprawling Umbrella Group, several of the countries are on a direct collision course with each other. The ministers from New Zealand, Canada and Norway insist that the report absolutely *must* be welcomed, while the anonymous representative from Russia says in a neutral tone that he absolutely can't do that, he only has a mandate to "take note of" the report – which doesn't surprise me in the least. On many occasions I've heard high-level Russian representatives openly say they think global warming has many "positive" effects, such as opening the Northeast Passage and providing access to frozen areas and fossil resources in the Arctic. I've even heard some of them express skepticism over whether climate change is caused by humans. I put on a brave face and listen to the tenuously cohesive group, and in the end I'm thankful that at least the oil countries Norway and Canada, though they continue to permit new oil and gas extraction, are honest enough not dispute what consequences it will lead to.

When the final consultations are done for the evening, my colleagues and I have barely had a bite to eat all day, which is what usually happens at meetings like this one. But despite my waning energy, I don't want to go back to the hotel just yet. Greta Thunberg is in Katowice, and she's scheduled to speak at the plenary session. I don't want to miss it.

This was before she'd made her famous sailing voyage to New York and scolded the entire international community at the UN, but she'd already led a number of major climate marches in Europe, and she'd made a very strong impression internationally. Almost all of my colleagues had asked me about her and her improbable but true story. The lone fifteen-year-old girl with her braids, serious expression and hand-painted climate strike sign in front of Swedish parliament, who it then turned out had a photographic memory and had read most of the IPCC reports herself. And who also had a preternatural ability to express herself clearly and with a scathing logic: "What is the point of learning facts... when the most important facts given by the finest science... clearly mean nothing to our politicians and our society? Why should I study for a future that soon will be no more?"

There was something about her unpretentious aura and total incapability of being flattered or embarrassed by the attention that shone through in the interviews she gave, and it wasn't just the media and world leaders who took notice. Above all, it was the children. Children all over the world had participated in Greta's climate strike, and it was incredibly moving to see the power in that. For example, in the video clips from climate marches in different capital cities, where groups of children act as her bodyguards to protect her from intrusive photographers and fans, or that amazing scene where a public address system isn't picking up Greta's voice and the children and young people standing around her solve the problem by shouting her speech, sentence by sentence, to the thousands of spectators farther away.

At five minutes to eleven that night, it's time.

"Miss Thunberg, you have the floor."

A male functionary dressed in a suit runs up and places a step stool behind the podium. Greta climbs the stage from the side, dressed in a dark plaid shirt and purple skinny trousers, walks purposefully to the podium and steps up onto the stool.

Her voice is high-pitched like a child's, but her English is perfect, with a slight British accent. She looks calmly out at the room with a furrowed brow and speaks in short, punchy sentences. Every passage in the short speech could be cut out into a quote. Her criticism of the adult world is merciless:

"You are not mature enough to tell it like it is," she begins. "Even that burden you leave to us children."

The speech is about how the rich part of the world tries to pretend we can fix the climate through more economic growth that we call "green." She points out that very few people can take part in the abundance created through destroying the biosphere, and that it is "the sufferings of the many which pay for the luxuries of the few."

My colleagues and I are sitting in the front row, and there aren't many others in the plenary hall, certainly no other ministers. But her speech is being recorded and will circulate on social media, and it's an important speech – she represents the children, the youth, the billions who can't yet vote, the untold generations that haven't yet been born. Many more people support her than the representatives of countries I've met today, and Greta knows it.

She closes by saying that in sixty years she'll celebrate her seventy-fifth birthday, and that if she has grandchildren, maybe they'll spend the day with her. She looks out over the deserted conference hall.

"Maybe they will ask me about you. Maybe they will ask why you didn't do anything while there was still time to act. You say you love your children above all else, and yet you are stealing their future in front of their very eyes."

After the speech I find Greta, backpack on and eyes to the floor, waiting with her father to go home. We've never met before, and she says a quiet hello and thanks me when I praise her speech. She's so small and pale and it's so late at night that I can't help saying something about how she shouldn't overdo it, she needs to rest and take care of herself. Greta looks up quickly and says:

"You, too."

She has Asperger's syndrome and selective mutism and, by her own account, speaks only when she must, so not much more is said. But her thoughtful "you, too" fills me with unexpected joy and new energy. If she can do it, then damn it, so can I.

See, it hadn't just been a tough day in Katowice but also a dark day for Sweden as a climate role model. As mentioned before, since entering the government in 2014 the Green Party had taken the country to the number one ranking for best climate policy. We'd passed the world's then most ambitious climate legislation, more than doubled the environmental and climate budget, introduced airline passenger tax, increased the carbon tax, and established the two major climate transition support programs, *Klimatklivet* (The Climate Leap) and *Industriklivet (The Industry Leap)*, which enabled local governments, businesses and heavy industry to begin transitioning.

But the fall 2018 election didn't go well for us, and the overall result was so close between the political blocs that there wasn't a new government yet in Sweden. So, in Katowice I was representing a transitional government, and the fruitless talks between the party leaders and the speaker of parliament had already been going on for months. Now, the Swedish Parliament, despite the fact that we in the transitional government had secured the other parties' support for a neutral transitional budget – a budget that would allow Sweden to keep moving with no policy changes until we could form a new government – had thrown all parliamentary practice out the window and passed a completely different budget, which was negotiated by the conservative Moderates and the Christian Democrats and which the Sweden Democrats predictably couldn't resist voting for.

Thus the government's transitional budget was sunk, and in one fell swoop the climate budget had been cut by over two billion kronor. On top of that, the recently introduced airline passenger tax had been repealed, the tax on gasoline and diesel had been lowered, agriculture had received increased carbon tax exemptions and the support for solar cells, electric vehicles and climate adaptations had decreased sharply. And most of these changes were set to happen overnight at the new year, meaning that in a few weeks our agencies, primarily the Swedish Environmental Protection Agency, would have to lay off employees after a cutback that was larger percentage-wise than the ones Donald Trump made to the US Environmental Protection Agency when he took office.

On the way back to the hotel after Greta's speech I scroll through Swedish news sites and read the triumphant comments from the opposition parties and their scornful condemnations of the "weak" transitional government, and ask myself, as I have so many times before, if the other party leaders don't know how serious the situation is, how little carbon dioxide the world has left to emit if we're going to meet the 1.5-degree goal – or if they simply don't care? Is cutting the transitional government down to size the most important thing to them, more important than trying to solve the climate crisis we all find ourselves in? When I go to bed at night, the only thing I wish for before I fall asleep is that the international media won't pick up the story about the Swedish "budget catastrophe"; it would be yet another destructive blow to the trust between rich and poor countries. After all, Sweden is the country that wants to convince all the other countries at the meeting that a climate transition is a positive thing, that it's an investment and not a sacrifice to put money and resources into the climate. If Sweden won't even stand up for climate action – who will?

Should the world "note with concern"? Or "express gratitude"? Or "appreciate"? Or "welcome the work on the report"? Or "welcome the researchers' answers"? Costa Rica's minister and I, along with our team, weigh the words back and forth and conclude that we should move away from welcoming the report itself, but still find a way to use the symbolically important word "welcome." Then we must thank the researchers for their work and emphasize – most importantly – that the meeting takes the report's conclusion into account.

Our solution is to focus on many paragraphs. One where we thank the IPCC. One where we "welcome that the IPCC's special 1.5-degrees report was finished in a timely manner." And one that urges the parties to use the information in the report in all relevant contexts, and one more that urges the parties to continue supporting the IPCC's work. It's a solid package, and the four opponents of welcoming the report agree to it, and AOSIS and the EU are reasonably satisfied as well, so we can exhale.

Now I also have time for a meeting with the UN Adaptation Fund, where I'm scheduled to speak. On my way there, I get word that my civil servants have been forced to make last-minute changes to my talking points on the amount of money Sweden can pledge, because of the uncertainty of the Swedish budget. But when I give my speech I say nothing about potential Swedish cutbacks, and no one at the meeting seems to have heard the news about the Swedish budget chaos. I can exhale again.

The week is coming to a close, and many other details are nearing resolution. The EU ministers have been facilitators on almost all the tough questions, and throughout the meeting the EU has undeniably been the force holding negotiations together and propelling them forward. During Friday's final EU coordination meeting, EU Commissioner for Climate Action Miguel Arias Cañete says the text is still somewhat unstable, but that the EU will keep working and that all parts of the decision must be taken as a package. We won't give anything before we've got something at the other end.

My blond Finnish colleague, Kimmo Tiilikainen, asks for the floor to make an observation, which he delivers in English with a strong Finnish accent:

"Do you know why we, the EU, are so good at this? Because we have practiced so much in the EU Councils!"

Everyone laughs, because it really is an apt remark. In a transnational world where we need to get along, it's a good thing there's at least one well-oiled negotiating machine like the EU, accustomed to finding compromises in all possible areas, always prepared to solve tough problems between countries.

Our British colleague, Archie Young, also asks for the floor.

"This is probably the last time we'll see each other," he says. "I just want to thank you all for the great teamwork."

He looks emotional, and the applause that erupts in the room seems never-ending. Many of us have tears in our eyes. The UK is leaving the EU in a world where power dynamics are shifting, where many people want the EU's role to be marginalized and where the values we promote in all contexts, like women's rights, democracy, and environmental sustainability, are being swept under the rug. It feels frightening and unreal that the Brexit vote pushed through by Nigel Farage and the Murdoch press has now made us less united. "Take back control" was the Brexiteers' slogan. As if there were strength in being alone in a world of trans-border problems like climate change, terrorism and authoritarian regimes on the march.

But it's done now. The Brits believe they've taken control of their own lives and their cod, and we've lost one of the most important members of the EU.

"We'll meet again. We'll miss you," we assure him, and we truly mean it.

Essentially all the issues with the rule book have found solutions at the meeting. All except perhaps the most important one, which is about how climate action should be accounted for in cases of international cooperation. The Poles have postponed it because Brazil refused to budge from its position, which ran the risk of double counting in the system. The meeting has now run over-time for more than twenty-four hours, and the exhausted delegates gather in the plenary to see the President at last gavel through this year's decision. But the President's seat is empty. Nothing's happening. Time ticks by, and there's no sign of the Polish Presidency. People start to leave their seats on the benches and wander around the place trying to figure out what's going on. What's the problem? What's happening? Many people are checking the time and have trains or flights booked; the irritation is growing.

A rumor starts to circulate. Now it's Turkey again. President Erdoğan refuses to support the climate decision if

Turkey isn't granted "special status" and given access to the climate funds, which he's pushed for throughout the meeting. And now the Poles have asked the UN Secretary General, António Guterres, to call the Turkish leader on the phone.

I sink down onto a chair and sigh. All the drama and the work we've put in this week hasn't exactly been matched by the result we'll soon make official. No accounting rules for efforts in other countries. No raised ambitions. No whole-hearted welcoming of researchers' work, just a text that manages to avoid taking steps backward. The climate negoti-ations have fallen back into being an arena for all the world's injustices and an easily hijacked victim of different political agendas without direct links to the climate.

After an hour, the Polish conference president finally comes to the podium; we aren't told what caused the delay. In any case, Turkey's status will remain unchanged, for now, and the year's decision can be taken by acclamation.

Immediately afterwards, I have to do my best to explain to the journalists what we've accomplished, even though nothing that was decided will solve the climate crisis. Then, along with the other thousands of participants, my team and I hurry to the exits and the waiting cold, coal-scented air. I look around one last time at all the people who work essen-tially full time on the climate negotiations, and I wonder when they, and I, will be able to tell our children it's over? That we did it. That from now on we don't have to think about climate change, because the world has decided to take care of it now, without delay.

This was the world's 24th climate summit. Will it happen at the 25th? The 27th? What will Greta's grandchildren say to her? Did we do it, or not?

CHAPTER 8

The Knowledge

IN 1957, OIL companies took part in a report on the effects burning fossil fuels would have on the earth's climate. The study was financed by ExxonMobil, and its results were taken very seriously. The so-called Brannon Report was followed by several scientific studies commissioned by the oil industry, which led to several practical changes.

For example, the industry started to account for future climate changes when they planned for more oil extraction. In the documentary *Smoke and Fumes* (2017), retired Exxon employees recall how in 1970, when the company was building a new oil pipeline across Alaska, they assumed the permafrost would melt within a few decades and therefore made the pipeline's foundation significantly more stable than they otherwise would have. They also made the oil rigs in the Gulf of Mexico much more stable than was normally required because they expected that the greenhouse effect would soon generate more severe hurricanes in the region. In the North Sea and off the coast of Canada oil companies accounted for both rising sea levels and extreme storms, and in the Arctic they assumed the ice pack would change in nature. In 1969 ExxonMobil sent a specially equipped vessel to Alaska via the Northwest Passage to get familiar with the waters so they'd be prepared to use the shortcut in a future, ice-free Arctic – a scenario they could already see coming.

Climate research wasn't drawing much attention at the time, but the fact that increased carbon dioxide in the atmosphere would lead to a warmer climate was undisputed. The first article on the subject was published already in 1896 by the Swedish chemist Svante Arrhenius (a distant relative of Greta Thunberg, incidentally!), and the first American president to mention climate change in a speech was Lyndon B. Johnson, in a "Special Message to Congress" in 1965 in which he declared that "this generation has altered the composition of the atmosphere on a global scale through...a steady increase in carbon dioxide from the burning of fossil fuels."

President Johnson had been informed by his own scientific committee, which included climate scientist Roger Revelle, of the great risks posed by the continued burning of fossil fuels. In a report to the president, the researchers wrote: "Man is unwittingly conducting a vast geophysical experiment. Within a few generations he is burning the fossil fuels that slowly accumulated in the earth over the past 500 million years." The same sentences had appeared in Revelle's first scientific paper on the topic in 1957.

Twenty years later, even more research had confirmed what lay ahead, and oil companies followed the developments closely. In 1977 and 1978 (as exposed by the Pulitzer Prize-winning organization Inside Climate News) Exxon researcher James F. Black gave multiple briefings to company management on the state of the science, saying the burning of fossil fuels had led to a rapid increase in the concentration of carbon dioxide in the atmosphere, and that a doubling of this concentration would cause the earth's average temperature to rise by two to three degrees Celsius – up to ten degrees at the poles – and bring a great risk of extreme weather with floods, droughts and crop failures worldwide. Black summed up his briefings by saying that tough carbon emission regulations could be expected soon from policymakers and that humans' energy strategies would need to change.

Understandably, this message created a strong response within the company. Exxon expanded its research department to work with climate models and conduct its own empirical studies. Among other things, they would investigate other potential causes of increased carbon dioxide levels in the atmosphere, for example, deforestation. They also wanted to know more about the role of the ocean in the carbon cycle – maybe the deep ocean waters could absorb more emissions than researchers had estimated thus far? To that end, Exxon equipped the *Esso Atlantic* oil tanker with measuring instruments, and in 1979–1982 they took comprehensive oceanic and atmospheric measurements along the route from the Gulf of Mexico to the Persian Gulf.

In internal documents, the new Exxon researchers soon expressed the exact same concerns Black had expressed in 1977. To ward off climate change, combustion of fossil fuels must decrease significantly, or else "potentially catastrophic events" could occur. The researchers also warned about a "wait and see" approach: "Once the effects are measurable, they might not be reversible."

It seems many at the company at that time honestly believed the company would assimilate this knowledge and even lead the way in an energy transition for the public good. The Exxon researchers collaborated with experts at the US Department of Energy and participated in conferences on global warming. According to Inside Climate News documentation, they sounded more or less like the average climate-conscious techno-optimists of today. There was no doubt the world was in an energy transition – away from fossil fuels, toward renewables!

In 1988, the issue came into the public eye for the first time in earnest. NASA's top climate scientist, James Hansen, had been invited to speak before the United States Congress about the greenhouse effect, where he stated in a powerful testimony that climate change had already started, and that it was almost certainly a matter of human impact and not natural variation.

Reactions among politicians were strong. Both Democrats and Republicans started talking about the need for regulations, and during his presidential campaign the same year, George H. W. Bush said: "Those who think we are powerless to do anything about the greenhouse effect forget about the 'White House effect'; as president, I intend to do something about it."

He wasn't the only conservative politician to take the threat of climate change very seriously. The following year, British Prime Minister Margaret Thatcher, herself a trained chemist, gave a 35-minute, supremely eloquent speech before the United Nations General Assembly about the greenhouse effect as the new great threat to humankind. She compared what we're doing to our planet with how the people of Easter Island cut down every last tree, leaving themselves not even enough lumber to make boats so they could leave the island when it was no longer possible to survive there. The only difference is the scale of what we're doing, Thatcher said; now it's not just one island but our whole planet:

"Change to the sea around us, change to the atmosphere above, leading in turn to change in the world's climate, which could alter the way we live in the most fundamental way of all."

Thatcher urged the UN to quickly adopt a new convention to limit greenhouse gas emissions. And what she proposed sounds almost like a radical green utopia by today's standards. The new climate convention would be negotiated in just three years and would quickly be followed up with legally binding protocols and effective monitoring and enforcement mechanisms that would apply to the whole world.

"The evidence is there," Thatcher said. "The damage is being done. (...) The problem of global climate change is one that affects us all, and action will only be effective if it is taken at the international level."

The climate change question clearly had strong political momentum in 1989 when Thatcher stood at the podium in front of the famous dark-green marble wall in the UN General Assembly. The cold war was nearing its end and the Berlin Wall would soon fall – the day after Thatcher's speech, in fact. The threat of nuclear war, and many other dark clouds over global politics, suddenly seemed to shrink. In addition, the world had just recently shown, through the binding Montreal Protocol to the Vienna Convention, that it could come together to deal with global environmental threats, in that case by deciding to phase out the substances that break down the ozone layer, which protects the earth against ultraviolet radiation.

And the UN Environment Programme (UNEP) and the World Meteorological Organization (WMO) had already established a unique scientific panel of researchers from around the world, the IPCC, which in 1990 would release its first assessment report on global warming, thus providing a sound scientific foundation for political decisions.

So as Thatcher stood there with her sparkling brooch, well-sprayed coiffure and stern voice, all the necessary puzzle pieces were in place. Facts were there, international forums were there, experience with similar regulations was there, political momentum and will were there. And there was also a unique window in global politics where former enemies suddenly started to draw closer to each other. It was a time of glasnost or détente, and it wouldn't have been at all implausible if the communist countries in this new, hopeful phase of world history, had joined the capitalist countries to unite in a peace project with a shared higher objective: to save humanity and the planet.

"It won't be easy," Thatcher said. "The challenge for our negotiators is as great as for any disarmament treaty. We must not allow ourselves to be diverted into fruitless and divisive argument. Time is too short for that."

The General Assembly resounded with applause. On YouTube you can see the camera sweep across the large hall, and none of the countries' representatives appears to react negatively. Brazil's ambassador nods, the representatives from the Soviet Union and China applaud just like all the others. The commercial oil interests haven't yet taken hold of the Eastern Bloc, and climate science has finally got its message across in the West. A different world was possible there and then.

But the world didn't take the chance. Instead, thirty years after Thatcher's speech, half of all republican members of congress and six percent of Swedes would be climate deniers. Thirty years later, humans would have emitted more carbon dioxide into the atmosphere than they had in all of history before her speech.

How was that possible?

The climate convention (UNFCCC) was indeed negotiated, as Thatcher had insisted, and adopted in 1992, but the tone from the world's leaders quickly started to change. The binding Kyoto Protocol, which the world agreed to in 1997 after painstaking efforts and which took effect in 2005, applied only to certain countries, and the United States, historically the largest emitter of any country, chose not to ratify it, that is, incorporate it into their national law. Canada ratified it but chose to leave the Protocol in 2012. Margaret Thatcher herself reversed her stance on climate change and soon had very little respect for either the Kyoto Protocol or the climate movement and Al Gore, whom she dismissed as a prophet of doom. So, what had happened?

For those who want detailed, intimate descriptions with extensive references to leaked and public documents, I recommend some of the excellent but disheartening books and documentaries on the topic, for example *Merchants of Doubt* by Naomi Oreskes and Erik M. Conway (2010), *Climate Cover-Up* by James Hoggans and Richard Littlemore (2009), German filmmaker Johan von Mirbach's *Smoke and Fumes: The Climate Change Cover-Up* (2017), Danish filmmaker Mads Ellesöe's *The Campaign against the Climate* (2020) or Maths Nilsson's book *Spelet on Klimatet* (The Climate Game) (2021). To mention a few thoroughly researched sources.

For those who are content with a summary, here it is: The fossil fuel companies started spending billions of dollars to sow uncertainty around climate science. The same year Margaret Thatcher stood at the UN and demanded a new climate convention and the Berlin Wall fell, their work began in earnest. Around sixty American companies and organizations, primarily from the auto and oil industries – including Texaco, Amoco, Phillips Petroleum, BP America, Shell Oil, ExxonMobil, GM, Ford, Daimler Chrysler, the Aluminum Association, the National Coal Association, and the American Petroleum Institute – formed a coalition with the green-sounding name "Global Climate Coalition." Their first goal was to make sure the US wouldn't accept any binding emissions reductions under a potential new climate convention.

Soon, the George C. Marshall Institute, a think tank focused on defense policy, partly changed course. It had long worked together with researchers from the defense industry to lobby for the need of a so-called Star Wars defense system against nuclear missiles, but interest decreased after the Berlin Wall fell, so they started looking for new enemies.

Now they found them in "climate alarmists," including the whole IPCC.

Some older, renowned physicists from the early days of the nuclear weapons program – in particular the then nearly 80-year-old Frederick Seitz, who, after retiring, had also worked for Philip Morris sowing scientific doubt about the harmful effects of smoking, and Fred Singer, who'd worked to sow doubt around the causes of both acid rain and the hole in the ozone layer – now switched to sowing doubt about climate science. Like a carbon copy of the strategy for creating uncertainty around the dangers of tobacco, a policy document, a so-called "white paper," was soon produced, which in 1989 started to circulate among various authorities and opinion leaders. The following year, the contents were published in a small volume titled *Global Warming: What Does the Science Tell Us?*

The report's authors, Frederick Seitz, William Nierenberg and Robert Jastrow, had excellent contacts at the White House and were soon able to go there and present the key points. Among other things, they pointed out, using a diagram from NASA researcher James Hansen's own research as support, that temperature fluctuations since the breakthrough of industrialization weren't at all consistent with how the amounts of carbon dioxide in the atmosphere increased. The changes were most likely a result of the intensity of solar radiation, not carbon dioxide, the authors hypothesized.

This made a deep impression at the White House. Chief of Staff John Sununu, himself an engineer, was particularly captivated. In the book *Merchants of Doubt*, climate researcher and Stanford professor Stephen Schneider recounts how Sununu would always wave the report around when the topic of climate change came up: "like a cross in front of a vampire."

On the other hand, the head of the IPCC, Bert Bolin, was never invited to the White House to give the international climate research community's perspective on the issue, and no one cared that the diagram used in the Marshall report was taken completely out of context. What James Hansen had shown, of course, was that carbon dioxide wasn't the only explanation for the variation of temperature. In several different diagrams he showed that various individual explanations didn't give the complete picture, but that if you combined carbon dioxide, solar radiation and the cooling effect of certain volcanic eruptions – for example, that of Pinatubo, which caused a cloud of particles in the atmosphere – then the climate model was right. The Marshall Institute's trick was childishly easy to see through and grossly misleading, as they only selected the diagram that showed that carbon dioxide alone didn't give the whole picture.

At the same time, another think tank, the Cato Institute – funded in part by oil money from the Charles Koch Foundation, picked up the Marshall Institute's report and published it without caring that the IPCC had, in its assessment report, gone through it and dismissed the solar radiation hypothesis. The Marshall Institute's spin now gained even broader distribution. The institute's founder, Robert Jastrow, proudly wrote to the American Petroleum Institute in 1991 that the magazine *New Scientist* had recently described that Marshall Institute "is still the controlling influence in the White House".

Encouraged by this success, the think tanks then set their sights on a particular scalp: Roger Revelle, the patriarch of US climate scientists, the one who'd once written the report to Lyndon B. Johnson but who'd also been the environmentally knowledgeable senator Al Gore's professor and mentor at Harvard. The 80-year-old Revelle had given a presentation in 1990 at the American Association for the Advancement of

Science meeting in New Orleans called "What Can We Do About Climate Change?" in which he'd considered different factors that could mitigate the climate crisis. One was by lowering emissions, another was by significantly expanding boreal forests, and a third was by stimulating plankton growth to increase carbon dioxide uptake in the oceans. Based on these ideas, Revelle had called for more research and had said the following about how global warming would unfold over the coming hundred years: "There is a good but by no means certain chance that the world's average climate will become significantly warmer during the next century."

These words were gleaned immediately at the conference by Fred Singer, who'd known Revelle for years, and he asked Revelle if they could write an article together for the *Washington Post*. Revelle answered with a tentative yes. It's unclear exactly what the article was to be about, but during his trip home Revelle suffered a severe heart attack and had to undergo triple bypass surgery. So, Singer wrote an article himself and sent it to Revelle's sickbed, without receiving a reply. Finally Singer brought his text to the ailing Revelle, who apparently objected primarily to one sentence stating that warming would only be less than one degree in the next century. He crossed it out and wrote "1–3 degrees" in the margin, as shown in the documentation he left behind.

Singer, however, struck out the whole sentence before submitting the article, with Revelle as co-author, to a nonscientific magazine. Revelle died shortly thereafter, and an interpretation war broke out. Revelle's relatives, students, and colleagues insisted that he would never have supported the article's conclusions, including the sentence: "The scientific base for a greenhouse warming is too uncertain to justify drastic action at this time."

Nevertheless, the sentence was highlighted by several political commentators who launched fierce attacks on Al

Gore. The United States presidential election was coming up, and Democrat Bill Clinton had selected Al Gore as his running mate. Gore, who had just written the environmentalist book *Earth in the Balance*, was naturally a strong supporter of the Kyoto Protocol and regulating carbon dioxide emissions, and his objectivity was now being questioned. Gore was a fraud who withheld the truth, critics argued: after all, his own mentor had changed his mind about climate change before he died!

One of Revelle's students fought for years to defend Revelle's legacy but was eventually sued by Singer and had to give up the fight against his well-funded opponent with his arsenal of lawyers. Under the terms of a settlement, the young teaching assistant had to take back what he'd said and promise not to say anything further on the matter for ten years.

Naomi Oreskes and Erik M. Conway, who had written the book *Merchants of Doubt*, have themselves dug through Revelle's archives and found nothing to indicate that he had changed his opinion that humans are creating global warming by burning fossil fuels. And his colleagues continue to assert the same thing.

Bill Clinton won the election despite the attacks on his vice presidential candidate. But the fact that the White House's accommodating attitude toward the oil lobby had ended didn't mean the fossil fuel interests conceded defeat – on the contrary. They'd already succeeded on the most important point, namely getting the media to report on climate change as if there were two sides within the scientific community and significant uncertainty existed – considering that even someone like Revelle had wavered on the issue.

Before the second major assessment report from the IPCC came out in 1995, in which the researchers for the first time clearly stated that there was a human influence on the climate, the think tanks fired yet another punishing broadside. Singer accused the IPCC, and specifically a young researcher named Ben Santer, of every error imaginable. For example, in the chapter establishing the existence of a human impact on the climate, of which Santer was the lead author, he had allegedly deleted the parts that contained criticism and doubts and engaged in what Singer called "scientific cleansing."

The Global Climate Coalition promptly distributed a document titled "The IPCC: Institutionalized 'Scientific Cleansing'" to politicians and journalists, and Frederick Seitz bellowed in a *Wall Street Journal* op-ed in which he put his whole career behind his words, that in his 60 years in the American scientific community, including as president of the National Academy of Sciences and the American Physical Society, he had "never witnessed a more disturbing corruption of the peer-review process than the events that led to this IPCC report."

The accusations were answered in detail by Santer and his colleagues, but the IPCC researchers, who were used to long, nonconfrontational explanations for their positions and methodological choices, were brutally cut by the newspaper's editors, who also chose to omit the names of the roughly forty IPCC lead authors who cosigned the reply along with Ben Santer. Thus Santer appeared to be alone, weak and toothless, and his critics all the more senior, indignant and compelling.

The battle continued, and soon the entire IPCC united behind Ben Santer, but in the end his vindication would come in journals read only by scientists, while the accusations of fraud and the uncertainty around climate change continued to flourish in media that reached the general public.

Climate change had at this point taken on a clear political hue, where conservatives were starting to think climate scientists were driven by a leftist agenda. In 1995, when US Representative Dana Rohrabacher proposed cutting funding for climate research, he stated what had become an increasingly common view among Republicans: that climate research is "trendy science that is propped up by liberal/left politics rather than good science."

Despite this growing opposition, the Clinton administration supported the binding climate protocol that was negotiated in Kyoto in 1997, and the oil interests started to focus on preventing the US from incorporating the Kyoto Protocol into national law.

So in 1998, the fossil fuel industry's biggest trade organization, the American Petroleum Institute, drew up a strategy together with other stakeholders and think tanks, a document that was leaked on the internet a few years ago. The plan was called a "Global Climate Science Communications Plan," and the eight-page document – which includes a goal; an action plan; strategies and tactics; and even a proposed budget of six million dollars to cover media outreach, a new data center, "grassroots campaigns," recruiting of five "new" climate scientists, and activities to provide information on the uncertainties of climate science to members of Congress, journalists, industry leaders, civil servants, teachers and students – is so unabashed in its cynicism it's almost breathtaking. The plan identifies what should be considered future "victories," which was when average citizens, media and industry senior leadership "understand" (quotation marks are from the plan) the uncertainty in climate science and this uncertainty becomes part of the "conventional wisdom." The ultimate victory would be achieved when "those promoting the Kyoto treaty on the basis of extant science appear to be out of touch with reality."

Sure enough, Bill Clinton and Al Gore failed to get the

Kyoto Protocol through Congress, and by the time their term of office was over climate change had become a clear dividing line between Democrats and Republicans. When George H. W. Bush entered the White House in 2001, few were surprised when he announced that the United States would not ratify the Kyoto Protocol.

All of this is history now, and it might seem I'm going into unnecessary detail about it in this book, but for me as a former climate minister and environmentally engaged citizen it's important to understand how the climate crisis has been able to go on so long, despite the science being there from the very start, questioned by no one, until the fossil fuel companies put their strategies in motion. They played their cards skillfully in such a way that the media, anxious to report in a nonpartisan and objective way, started describing climate science as an area in which there were two camps and a great deal of uncertainty, when the truth is that there had never been two camps among published climate scientists – the ones sowing confusion were dozens of vociferous scientists who were, almost without exception, not climate scientists.

In 2004, American science historian Naomi Oreskes searched out every peer-reviewed scientific article about global climate change published between 1993 and 2003. Of the roughly one thousand articles, she found that three-quarters confirmed that emissions from human activities caused global warming, while one-quarter of the articles didn't comment on the cause at all. None of the articles contradicted or disproved the human impact. At the same time, Oreskes found that IPCC-critical and climate-skeptical voices had been included in half of all American news articles about climate change, to "balance out" the content! In other words, the American Petroleum Institute's communication strategy had triumphed. Doubt had become the "conventional wisdom" reflected by the media, and the ultimate result was that the US didn't ratify the Kyoto Protocol.

But of course, the story doesn't end there. The attacks on climate scientists are still ongoing, billions of dollars continue to pour into so-called Climate Change Counter-Movement Organizations (CCCMs), and climate skepticism has taken hold in every possible context, not just in the US but worldwide, including in Europe and Sweden. Gunnar Hökmark of Sweden's Moderate Party has been involved in founding a think tank, the European Enterprise Institute, which has actively worked against the Kyoto Protocol and has given a platform to climate skeptics. In 2006 Maria Rankka, former CEO of the Swedish free-market think tank Timbro, said in connection with a climate-skeptic seminar she was organizing that more climate research was needed to know exactly what causes climate change, that the science isn't unanimous and that "anyone with a pat political answer has no basis for their position." She later became CEO of the Stockholm Chamber of Commerce.

Jonas Pettersson, who was press secretary to the Center Party leader Annie Lööf when she was Swedish Minister for Enterprise from 2011 to 2014, previously worked at the think tank Captus, where in 2006 he came out as a total climate denier in an op-ed in *Aftonbladet* with the headline "Bluffen om klimatet" (The Climate Hoax).

But the campaigns to delay a transition away from fossil fuels haven't focused solely on questioning the science. They've also employed more subtle strategies that can get under anyone's skin. One of them is something I myself feel complicit in, or rather deceived by. It's about the emphasis on individual responsibility and consumer empowerment.

In 1988, the same year James Hansen delivered his testimony to Congress, my first child was born. A couple of years later, deeply troubled by the throwaway culture and environmental destruction I saw around me, I would take my first step toward trying to contribute to a sustainable world when I walked up to the editor of the Sunday supplement of the daily newspaper *Expressen* and made the case for a recurring column with tips on what the average consumer can do to push companies in a more environmentally friendly direction. The editor bought into to my idea, and in the years that followed I wrote every Sunday under the heading "Green Sunday," cheering on companies that took environmentally friendly initiatives and calling out the ones that made it hard for consumers to make environmentally conscious choices.

I was convinced that empowering the consumer would make a big difference; I'd seen how chlorine-bleached paper quickly disappeared from the market once attention was drawn to the problem and consumers demanded a more environmentally sound alternative, just as most detergents containing over-fertilizing phosphates had quickly been replaced by more environmentally friendly variants once consumers understood the problem. During my time as editor, several examples were added to the list: Freon-free refrigerators, "dolphin-safe" canned tuna and environmentally less-harmful fuel for lawnmowers. The phasing-out of Freons was certainly not the result of consumer empowerment but instead one of the clearest examples of how an international convention can achieve success despite industry's lobbying efforts against the government. Leading refrigerator manufacturer Electrolux had long insisted it would take them many years to find an alternative to CFC, the Freon used in refrigerators, so they'd been granted an unreasonably long transitional period before the ban was to take effect in 1995. But when Greenpeace on its own initiative produced a Freon-free refrigerator in the fall of 1992 and 70,000 shoppers put their names on a waiting list to buy the new "Greenfreeze," suddenly it took just three months for Electrolux to get the first Freon-free refrigerators and freezers onto the European market. What was previously impossible to develop for a multibillion industry was all of a sudden very easy to do, with the threat of competition. However, the refrigerator industry did cynically delay introducing the Freon-free fridges outside of Europe, since the environmental and consumer movements weren't as vocal in those markets.

But what I didn't quite understand then was how much my view of how environmental problems should be solved was influenced by a market-economy idea that think tanks, paid by industry, had been pumping into the public debate for years: the idea of consumer responsibility. The notion that it's not the manufacturers, industries or even legislators that should take responsibility – it's individuals. Consumers. The market laws are "neutral" in this view and if only people start demanding more environmentally sound products the laws of the market will correct errors and all will be well. But if they don't, it isn't industry's fault but our own. We, the lazy, irresponsible, comfortable consumers.

The purpose of framing the issue this way was, of course, to avoid clear and binding legislation; a development researchers at the Centre for Studies of Climate Change Denialism at Chalmers University of Technology in Gothenburg, Sweden, have studied. Unfortunately, the environmental movement itself somewhat unwittingly contributed to the narrative of the consumer's individual responsibility, which reinforced the idea that industry is only providing what the people want. And at the same time, industry succeeded in painting the picture – which continues to flourish and is fed by far-right think tanks – of environmentalists as finger-pointing, elitist hypocrites that demand huge sacrifices and don't understand the conditions for ordinary people, while placing the blame for everything on them.

It wasn't until I got involved with the issue of over-fishing in the early 2000s that I seriously started to realize how absurd it is to ask ordinary people to know the status of hundreds of fish species and stocks by checking various consumer guides every time they go shopping. To even dream that ordinary consumers will know trawled cod from Kattegatt is bad while line-caught cod from the Barents Sea is okay – when most people don't even know where those seas are or what a normal cod looks like – is totally unrealistic. And to be like the Center Party's Eskil Erlandsson, who was fisheries minister at that time, and absolve yourself from responsibility and refer to consumer empowerment at the fish counter, isn't just irresponsible but also completely ineffective. No matter how much awareness-raising is done by environmental organizations and the media, only a few percent of the population will absorb the information (often the same people who try to learn what is environmentally sustainable when it comes to clothes, pension funds, coffee, meat or transportation), while the vast majority don't have the time or energy to study all the details, or the money to pay more for the goods. Meanwhile the information that reaches the vast majority of people is that there *are* things in stores that are bad for the environment. Which instills a vague feeling of guilt in many people because they haven't informed themselves enough, or causes people to construct their own inner defense mechanisms that legitimize their reasons for choosing goods that aren't animal- or environmentally friendly... Thus the blame is placed squarely on the shoulders of the individual, not on politicians or industry.

A brilliant strategy, really.

Personal responsibility does exist, obviously, and consumer empowerment can be a great thing. But eco-labeled goods alone aren't enough. For one thing, not everyone can afford to choose pricier alternatives; for another, those with high incomes who actually can afford it generally consume much more than those with low incomes, which creates more emissions as a whole, even if the goods are eco-labeled.

From the left, this fact typically leads to a crudely simplified analysis. Climate change is simply a problem of income distribution, which can be solved by imposing heavier taxes on the rich. I sympathize with the principle of a society with as little inequality as possible, and I share the opinion that the rich people of the world must reduce their consumption, and generally pay more taxes, but if the aim is to reduce emissions in an acute climate crisis, a single-minded focus on income distribution won't bring the structural changes needed to reach a fundamentally sustainable society. Not as long as essential transportation to jobs and hospitals runs on fossil fuels, steel for buildings and bridges is produced in coal-fired blast furnaces, forests are leveled for grazing land and countries use coal and gas as energy sources for heating and cooling. The COVID-19 crisis has made it abundantly clear that we have a long way to go: despite nearly every airplane in the world being grounded for a whole year, people staying home and shops and restaurants closing worldwide, global emissions decreased by just 6–7 percent – and that's very far from enough. We must decrease emissions to as close to zero as possible and, through various solutions, even by creating negative emissions.

The Swedish research project Mistra Sustainable Consumption has delved deeper into the issue of changed consumer behavior, and found that if the average Swede ceased flying and driving fossil fuel cars altogether, switched to a mainly vegan diet, bought furniture secondhand and repaired their belongings instead of buying new ones, they could only reduce their individual emissions by 40 percent, assuming all other consumption stayed the same. Which shines a light to the fact that to get to zero, *the whole society* must change, which can only happen through policy changes and public investments that make it possible for transportation systems, industry and food production to shift to green technologies, and for materials to be used in circular flows within both private and public consumption. What we need is a systemic change.

But opponents of this kind of systemic change hold a lot of trump cards. The story of individual responsibility has taken hold, a story of individual sacrifices and diminished prosperity that is invariably grounded in resistance to change. The language used in climate negotiations within the UNFCCC assumes there will be a burden on various countries – there's constant talk of "burden sharing" instead of transitioning to a healthier society. And since the Paris Agreement was ratified this issue has also entered right-wing populist and nationalist circles. Environmentalists and climate scientists are now a definitive part of the conspiratorial narrative of fake news, the EU, women's rights, immigration and the global elite that make up the swamp people like Donald Trump and Jair Bolsonaro claim they want to drain, the thing that threatens ordinary people's right to live their lives the way they want.

Still, the recipients of this latter narrative are a limited proportion of the population. So, the think tanks are now putting more and more energy toward another, significantly more palatable line of reasoning that has made its way into editorial pages of daily newspapers and reports by certain economists: a cool, ostensibly rational cost-benefit analysis of the climate transition in monetary terms.

The basis for this reasoning is to stop expending energy denying that climate change is caused by humans, and instead prove that from an economic perspective it's much better to invest in more economic growth than to spend money on reducing emissions, because the growth will enable us to afford to simply adapt to a changed climate. This reasoning is usually supported by various numbers and facts showing how many people are dying or are expected to die because of climate change, compared with how many more people die of other causes, like diseases, especially in developing countries. The conclusion is seemingly crystal clear: we'll get more "bang for the buck" investing in cholera vaccines that save children's lives here and now than in renewable energy that might not save a single life in the future.

This is indeed a quantum leap in the climate denial debate, because the reasoning eliminates not only the denial but also what was the basic premise behind the denial: that if humans actually knew the truth, we'd stop using fossil fuels, because anything else would be totally irresponsible and would doom our children and all subsequent generations to a life of extreme weather, food uncertainty, refugee flows, sinking islands and dead coral reefs – in short, enormous problems. Now, with the cost-benefit logic and the question of most bang for the buck, we can both believe in the science and ignore it. We simply have to accept what a mess we've made and make the best of it, and it will even be better this way.

One of the most tenacious advocates of this viewpoint is the Danish political scientist Bjørn Lomborg. He's been very active in the climate debate for many years and has written books such as *Cool It*, *The Skeptical Environmentalist* and *False Alarm: How Climate Change Panic Costs Us Trillions, Hurts the Poor, and Fails to Fix the Planet*. Lomborg is a regular columnist in Swedish daily *Svenska Dagbladet*, and according to the Copenhagen Consensus Center, a think tank he founded and runs, his columns are published in 40 newspapers in 19 languages and reach 30 million people.

In the fall of 2021, I was invited to debate Lomborg at a very serious seminar with representatives from both the highest levels of politics and multilateral organizations, but I declined, shocked that the organizer would give such a prominent platform to a climate obscurant. The explanation I got was that many in the business sector "silently worship" Lomborg, and therefore he must be heard.

Of course, afterwards I watched the seminar online and was glad I hadn't participated. Lomborg's PowerPoint presentation goes by at lightning speed, and he tosses out numbers and cost estimates he claims are based on research from numerous economic research groups and several Nobel laureates. But when I take a closer look at his most important graph, I'm quite surprised. What his institute has done is to analyze the Sustainable Development Goals in the UN's Agenda 2030 from a cost-benefit perspective to guide decision makers, particularly in poor countries, on what provides the most social, economic and environmental benefit per dollar. By far the best-spent dollar would then go, not to climate action or adaptation, but toward removing all global trade barriers; this would return over two thousand dollars per dollar spent. On the other hand, achieving the "2°C objective" in the Paris Agreement (that is, the least ambitious goal), investing in renewable energy, and protecting valuable natural environments are according to this analysis all losing financial propositions. The real screaming deal would instead be to save lives by providing aspirin to prevent heart disease – which the Power Point tells us will give back 63 dollars for every dollar invested!

I wouldn't be bringing up Lomborg's absurd analyses here, except that the Copenhagen Consensus analytical model purportedly guides policy in countries such as Ghana, Malawi, Bangladesh, Haiti and India, according to the institute's website, and in 2015 the institute was very close to receiving major government funding from Australia, (the world's largest exporter of coal), to establish a location at one of the country's universities (which was halted only after an outcry from Australian academics). Lomborg also has Bill Gates' ear, and Gates has promoted Lomborg a few times, like when the two wrote a column together criticizing the setup of the Sustainable Development Goals, published on Gates own blog Gatenotes in the summer of 2023. In other words, Lomborg is part of the in-crowd, despite the reports against him for misconduct in research and the heavy criticism for having deliberately misinterpreted and distorted others' results (something he was originally convicted of, a judgment the Danish Ministry of Higher Education and Science – to which Lomborg appealed – then overturned because they found that his book *The Skeptical Environmentalist* wasn't a scientific publication and therefore Lomborg couldn't be convicted of misconduct in research). Another sign that the school he represents is listened to very seriously is the fact that one of the economists Lomborg often cites, the Yale professor William Nordhaus, was awarded the 2018 Nobel Prize in Economics.

Nordhaus, who once promoted the idea of a carbon tax, has since the early 1980s contributed to various economic analyses on behalf of the White House that have resulted in the advice to "wait and see" rather than take action on global warming. The basis of his award-winning Dynamic Income Climate-Economy (DICE) model is to make different assumptions about what a transition away from fossil fuels would cost (in his Nobel Prize Lecture he mentions 4 percent of global income), compared with what the damages from climate change would cost. According to the model, adapting to a warming of up to three degrees Celsius emerges as a fairly good and "cost-effective" alternative. But, as Nordhaus also emphasizes in his Prize Lecture, his model only considers the influence on the atmosphere, not ocean acidification, which he briefly mentions is "bad for shellfish."

And he also carefully emphasizes that he doesn't include as many parameters as many other climate cost models, that his model is quite "simple."

Many people were surprised when his name was announced as the recipient of the 2018 economics prize to the memory of Alfred Nobel, the same month that the 1.5-degrees report was submitted by the IPCC. Some were devastated. Among them was an American economist who had developed a totally different economic model that – unlike Nordhaus's model, which assumes a linear and steady increase in emissions and temperature – includes so-called threshold effects, or tipping points. The Harvard professor Martin Weitzman had accounted for the fact that ecosystems usually have a certain level of resilience but can then rapidly change to a new state, which can produce much more dramatic climatic effects that what a linear curve shows. Obviously no one knows exactly which incremental temperature increase will cause an entire ecosystem to change character, and Weitzman argued that this insight and the mere possibility of a major planetary catastrophe must justify action; uncertainty can't be a reason for passivity.

And Weitzman was also skeptical that a carbon tax could solve the basic problem of emissions, because the market can adapt to a tax, allowing emissions to continue in perpetuity. Therefore, we need not only a price on emissions but also a ceiling that phases out emissions at a certain rate. Weitzman's ideas have led to the implementation of the carbon trade system, known in many countries as "cap and trade," such as the EU Emissions Trading System (ETS) – the only effective market mechanism for truly steering toward zero emissions.

Weitzman, who has been described as a giant among environmental economists, took the award of the Nobel Prize to Nordhaus very hard, as his research basically went against everything Weitzman's own research stood for. How hard he took it would become clear almost a year later, when, in August 2019, the 77-year-old died by suicide. According to his obituary in the New York Times, he left a note saying he no longer thought he had anything to contribute to in his field of research.

*

The oil companies knew in 1957. Sixty-five years later, the battle over the narrative of reality rages on. Is the threat of climate change real, is stopping emissions too expensive, whose fault is it, who will suffer, who will profit, who should take action, should we take any action at all?

Against the shallow cost-benefit analyses by Lomborg and his supporters stand the IPCC's estimates of what the loss of ecosystems, crops and water, and the increase in extreme weather events, floods and fires will cost us: at 2 degrees warming, 69 trillion dollars, more that what the fossil fuel companies will be able to pay in damages; and at 3.7 degrees warming, 551 trillion dollars – more than all the money that exists on earth today.

But the thought exercise is actually unnecessary. We need to reverse the narrative. The problem isn't money. Money is nothing but an instrument invented by humans to make various kinds of activities easier. The money shouldn't steer us, we should steer the money. The problem isn't even climate change; that's a *symptom* of the real problem. The real problem, as Gus Speth, founder of the World Resources Institute, pointed out, is egoism, greed, and indifference. That we as humanity have accepted these destructive forces as a part of our self-concept and as the premise for the economic system we have created – while at the same time we know that greed, egoism and indifference are detestable qualities in our daily lives, that no one wants such a friend or neighbor, that it's natural for most of us to cooperate, work together and show consideration for each other for the simple reason that we ourselves need help sometimes and it's so much nicer that way.

I'm reminded of the story of the old man who tells his grandchild that two wolves live inside each of us, fighting each other: one good, wise and compassionate, the other evil, greedy and ruthless. "Who wins?" the child asks. "The one you feed," the old man says. So, can we stop feeding the greedy wolf? Can we reevaluate ourselves as a collective humanity in light of the global catastrophe that lies before us, can we become good neighbors and friends, can we pull together? Can we see ourselves as a small part of something much bigger?

Can we?

CHAPTER 9

Political Craftmanship

IT WAS FEBRUARY 2017, and newly inaugurated president Donald Trump had already made it his trademark move to sign executive orders in his Oval Office, surrounded by solemn-faced men. Someone suggested that I also sign a law, surrounded by some of my closest colleagues who happened to be women.

Like billions of others in early 2017, I was in perpetual shock at the new president's statements and decisions. The ban on Muslims entering the United States (except Saudis), the diatribes against China, the wall against Mexico, and the very first thing Trump did: sign the "Global Gag Rule," an order that halted funding of global organizations that provide information about abortion and contraceptives – here, too, surrounded exclusively by men.

Our Swedish government, like so many others, was now wrestling with how to relate to and be able to cooperate with an America led by Trump. After all, the US was still an extremely important party to international negotiations, a country with which we had extensive trade relations as well as collaborations in a number of areas. The suggestion that I be photographed Trump-style as I signed our Swedish climate law aiming for climate neutrality by 2045 was therefore pretty daring from a diplomatic perspective, and I agreed to take the picture without promising my collaborators I'd give the okay to publish it. I had to think it all through carefully first, and not least see if I thought the picture was good enough to get a clear but subtle message across.

That February I was trying, as climate minister and deputy prime minister, to orient myself in a world that was dark in more ways than one, and which had overnight become so much harder to navigate. We were in a completely new situation in the international community, which, of course, is the foundation for all action on climate change. Previously, the EU and the US, under Barack Obama's leadership, had pulled China and the rest of the world along in tandem and ensured that the Paris Agreement was finalized and then ratified in record time. Now, the EU, and therefore Sweden, was suddenly alone and watching longtime alliances collapse like a house of cards. The US refused point-blank to include simple wording about the climate or Agenda 2030 in negotiated documents, and Russia and China essentially shrugged and left the EU alone to do what the world had agreed on to do together just a year earlier.

For certain countries, the turnaround by the US gave them a new, more comfortable position, where they themselves didn't have to look like the bad guys. For countries like Sweden, the big question was how we could keep moving forward at all on issues like climate and gender equality, when the most powerful country in the world was being led by a man who not only intended to leave the Paris Agreement and sung the praises of coal power, but also did totally unthinkable things like publicly mocking people with disabilities, bragging about groping women, saying he could "stand in the middle of Fifth Avenue and shoot somebody" and not lose any voters, impetuously accuse countries and threaten them with trade restrictions, and not only threaten but actually carry out the construction of walls and the imposition of arbitrary travel bans into the US.

These were all things I had to take into account as I stood behind my press secretary looking at a photograph that was nothing short of perfect. I, my two state secretaries, and the female civil servants all looked innocent and homicidal at the same time. The lightning and the blue-and-yellow Swedish flag in the left-hand corner gave the photo the air of a historic painting. Each of my colleagues had her own interesting but serious facial expression and pose, not least my brilliant civil servant coordinator who was nine months pregnant at the time, standing at the far end, staring at the document I was signing with a lugubrious look. You would have thought we'd worked half the day to get this photo, but the truth is that it happened in less than ten minutes: to rig the lights, commandeer people from their offices and seat an extremely stressed-out minister (i.e., me), who had just come from the dentist and whose face was still drooping on one side from the anesthetic, at the table. Click.

It then took me three seconds to decide: I couldn't deprive the world of this; the picture was just too good.

I carefully composed the matter-of-fact tweet saying I'd just signed the referral of the Swedish climate law binding future Swedish governments to zero emissions by 2045. I also added a few solemn words of hope for a better and more secure future as a result of this law. When I clicked on the Tweet button, I was fully aware that the tweet would have been vetoed immediately if I'd sent it through the internal review processes in the Government Offices.

But Trump had shown by example that normal politics no longer applied, not even in international relations or in how we addressed each other: "Bad Hombres," "Crooked Hillary," "Sleepy Joe," "Little Rocket Man".... My tweet was like a good-natured funhouse mirror by comparison, though at the same time it was real, not a joke.

I put down my phone and waited. When I picked it up

a while later, I saw the shares and likes multiplying by the second. Soon my press secretaries came into my office, more or less jumping up and down: all the major media outlets had called! I gave a very neutral comment to the English-language newspaper *The Local*, which could then be cited by the rest of the media. I emphasized the fact that we are in a climate crisis, the importance of women's rights, and that we are a feminist government. Am I trolling Trump? the reporter asked. No, I'm just busy passing important policy, I insisted truthfully.

In the following days I devoted nearly every free moment to reading comments and following the dissemination of the photo throughout the world. It was overwhelming. The tweet was such a release for so many people. Both as a sort of comic relief after weeks of Trump's bulldoggish countenance as he held up one repressive executive order after the other, but also as a real, concrete, true light in the darkness. We were for real! We weren't a group of political satirists; Sweden really had a feminist government that had just adopted climate legislation that will make Sweden climate-neutral by 2045, for real! Another reality was possible, and people the world over were getting that message. The emails, letters and newspaper clippings poured in from every continent, world superstars like Miley Cyrus had shared the picture and the comments under my tweet made me part-laugh and part-cry. So many people thanking me for giving them new hope, for showing them a different reality, and also so many Americans who were genuinely despairing over their country and humanity and who apologized to the world for the US putting us in this nightmare.

Of course, I also got a reprimand, albeit indirect, from the Minister for Foreign Affairs, who earnestly asked the whole government to resist the temptation to score easy points by denouncing the American president, who was unpopular in Sweden, as it could lead to unforeseen problems for our country. And that might actually be what happened. Two weeks later, on February 18, 2017, President Trump stood at one of his "Make America Great Again" rallies and, apropos of absolutely nothing, proclaimed that something terrible had happened "last night in Sweden."

"Sweden! Who would believe this? Sweden?!" he said, repeatedly. And despite the fact that no one could reasonably have understood what he was talking about, the Trump supporters responded with a full-throated "boo."

The only problem was that nothing had happened in Sweden the previous night. It's more likely the president had watched a Fox News report about Sweden that night. But the effect of Trump's statement was that he and his supporters – including a vast army of internet trolls – seemed to spend the rest of his term in office searching for evidence that he was right after all, that Sweden really was a glaring cautionary example of... it's unclear what.

The phenomenon was so tangible that we in the government soon got reports of a clear increase in the number of negative news articles about Sweden from around the world, most of them about particularly vulnerable suburban areas, shootings and violence – problems that absolutely did exist, but that were nowhere near what was found in the US, for example.

I, on the other hand, got to experience for a short time how it felt to be a rock star on the international stage – at meetings at the UN and the World Bank, and particularly on a trip to California to seek climate cooperation at the state level – posing for selfies with young people, receiving raucous applause and putting people in a good mood just by showing my face. One photo, set up in ten minutes, one decision made in three seconds, gave such an enormous amount of joy to thousands, probably millions of women and men all over the world, at a time when everything seemed so dark.

That's how politics can take shape. The work of a moment, something that can be seen, that arouses emotion, that speaks to people. It's a side of politics that can be amazing – or dangerous, if the message is hateful or misleading.

But then there's the other side of politics. The slow, tedious, circuitous side. The political craftsmanship. My Trump tweet actually exhibited both, because the proposal I was signing was a clear example of the result of a long and arduous democratic process that would make a far greater difference than my tweet, though it wouldn't get quite as many hurrahs.

The climate law I signed was an amazing legacy from my Green Party colleagues. It started as a party proposal in the Swedish parliament in 2012, signed by Åsa Romson and others when the Green Party was still part of the opposition – a proposal that was voted down. But the idea of a climate policy framework and a climate law was so good and so potentially system-changing that the party brought it back as the first point in its platform leading into the 2014 election. When the Green Party then entered government, thanks to the long-term strategy of the party leadership at the time, new climate minister Åsa Romson could task the parliamentary Committee on Environmental Goals (MMB) with exploring the possibilities for the climate law.

It was a wise move. With its cross-bloc parliamentary representation, MMB is an outstanding forum for deepening members' knowledge of environmental issues, thus instilling the need for new measures and laws and creating the necessary acceptance and legitimacy in Swedish parliament. After more than a year's discussions and negotiations under the leadership of MMB's chair, Anders Wijkman – a highly environmentally engaged and knowledgeable former conservative politician who'd been appointed for his ability to speak with both political blocs – all of the parties, except the Sweden Democrats, could finally get behind the key elements of a new climate policy framework. This included a goal for Sweden to be climate-neutral by 2045 and a sector-specific goal for transportation (excluding aviation) to reduce its emissions by 70 percent by 2030. In addition to that regulations for how the government will report its work to parliament every year and submit a climate action plan every parliamentary term; and the establishment of a Climate Policy Council in the form of an independent agency that will review and evaluate the government's climate policy.

The Green Party would have loved to see far more ambitious goals than those the other parties were willing to support. First and foremost, goals for reducing emissions within *all* sectors, particularly agriculture, which primarily the Center Party refused to endorse, and a goal for reducing emissions for consumption, which basically all the parties rejected at that time (however, in the spring of 2022 they managed to agree on such consumption-based goals). Still, the end result was good enough to make Sweden the country with the most ambitious climate goals in the world (up to that time, no country had set a net-zero goal earlier than 2050, although a few years later Finland, Denmark, and Austria set more ambitious goals than Sweden's). My and the Green Party's assessment was that as long as there was a framework in place, with the independent climate policy council we'd insisted on as a monitor to ensure goals were met, the goals could and should necessarily be tightened along the way. To do what the Left Party did – that is: express reservations because everything hadn't been accomplished in one go – was as shortsighted and nonproductive as usual; the Left's nay-saying was deliberate, a way to score points with the environmental movement for being, on paper, more ambitious than the government. But we in the Green Party, with nearly twenty-five years of experience being right but not having enough influence, had chosen a different path – things must happen, not only be said.

As climate minister, I then had the great pleasure of presenting the groundbreaking climate law to parliament in the form of a bill we knew had cross-bloc support. This was extremely important, because otherwise there was a risk the law might be changed with a change of government, which wouldn't give business and industry the security they needed to invest in a climate transition; large parts of industry quite rightly praised the climate law for this reason.

The Council on Legislation, however, issued harsh criticism: In their view, legislation was unnecessary; the goals themselves were enough. But we'd had environmental, so called generational goals in Sweden for thirty years without achieving them, and now parliament had actually realized that we needed more than ambitions: we also needed teeth and claws and binding legislation. And I was thrilled to have the law in place, after all we'd been through.

Who should get credit for the Swedish climate law? Me? Åsa Romson? Anders Wijkman? All the party representatives in MMB? Or should we go even further back in time, to when the whole idea of a climate framework, with a climate law and a climate policy council modeled on the Fiscal Policy Council, was pitched to the Party by climate policy expert Gunnar Lind, one of the Green Party's civil servants in parliament in the early 2010s? Or should we thank his sources of inspiration, those who had come up with the idea and introduced similar legislation in the UK and Denmark?

The truth is that everyone deserves credit. Political will is the driving force, of course; without it, nothing changes. But without political craft – concrete ideas about how to move the ball forward, patience, discussions, congressional decisions, election platforms, commissions of inquiry, proposals, bills, and amendments – Sweden wouldn't have a climate law today. Sure, we might still have taken a cool Twitter photo. We might have been signing some other bill, whatever; with our facial expressions, it probably would've flown pretty well in any case. But if we hadn't had a climate law that would then become reality, and which, at the time of the photo, was the most ambitious climate legislation in the world, the symbolic value would have been so much weaker. This picture wasn't about me. My face just happened to front a democratic craft process that came to fruition at a time when the whole world was yearning for just this sort of democratic progress. Getting to post the tweet was like getting to score the perfect goal that the whole team had played for, after training on muddy fields every weeknight for years. Boom! She shoots, she scores. Back of the net.

Of course, an experience like this gives you a taste for more, and it would have been a lot of fun to keep tweeting anti-Trump parodies and getting more applause. But at the same time, I knew it wouldn't work. Not if I was going to continue representing Sweden, not if I wanted to continue to push through policy for real or move processes forward in climate work where the world needed the US on board.

The Trump tweet was also a snapshot of the politician's dilemma. How do we approach democracy and political craft in a time of quick tweets, "like" algorithms, polarization, populism, and, ultimately, contempt for politicians? In a time when citizens seem to be losing patience with what they perceive as bureaucracy and long, tedious processes, and are fueled by a growing band of politicians who say that "anyone" can see in five seconds what needs to be done, and who heap scorn on the politicians who "aren't doing anything." And the risk is great that politicians who receive the people's love for various tweets, but nothing, or even contempt, for political craft that makes a real difference, will tire of spending time on real reforms and instead devote their days to praising what's popular on social media and denouncing what everyone already thinks is bad.

Democratic processes are definitely not perfect. And they can be criticized from at least two diametrically opposed positions. First, because they're too slow and rigid and can't react quickly enough when crises and urgent problems arise. Second, because they're too shortsighted: terms of office are too short, and few politicians are willing to invest in long-term strategies that might punish them in the public opinion. Or, as former President of the European Commission Jean-Claude Juncker once said: "We all know what to do, but we don't know how to get reelected once we have done it."

Another, even more complicated problem is that very few of the big, almost existential issues that threaten our society are within the power of individual governments, something that is apparent to the voters. The climate crisis, wars and conflicts, terrorism, the global economy, pandemics, the power of global tech giants, the threat to democracy – all of these cut across national borders, just like the air, the sea, and the ecosystems. But the democratic decision-making systems do not.

With one striking exception: the European Union.

The EU certainly isn't perfect; it occasionally gets hijacked by certain interests, the substantial aid it gives to the agricultural sector is bizarre, and micromanagement can for sure be excessive. Still, after five years as a member of the European Parliament and seven years as a minister overseeing areas such as foreign aid, environment and climate, I can only emphasize what a miracle the EU is. Twenty-seven member states, some of them embroiled in horrific wars with each other as recently as the middle of the last century, others – the eastern countries – that had lived under a completely different economic system for many decades, 24 languages, different customs and religions – and yet the countries not only cooperate on a voluntary basis but are forced, or, rather, force themselves, to compromise to reach solutions so that the whole EU has good drinking water, protects migratory birds, imposes environmental and human rights requirements in trade negotiations, stands up for sexual and reproductive health and rights (SRHR), and sets fair roaming fees for a half-billion people within the union.

And they actually legislate in a democratic way for the common good. And have done so successfully for over fifty years.

Most EU citizens have a very vague understanding of what the EU actually does and how it is structured, something that is unscrupulously exploited by national politicians in Europe who happily blame everything bad on the EU and take credit for everything good. The British grievance party the UK Independence Party (UKIP) famously talked for decades about how undemocratic the EU was, with bureaucrats from Brussels ruling over the poor Brits. What never came out in the Brexit debate was that the only platform for medium-sized or small British parties like UKIP – or my party's sister party, the UK Green Party, for that matter – is in fact the European Parliament, because the UK electoral First Past the Post system means these parties very rarely win even a single constituency in the whole United Kingdom, even though they have the support of, say, 5 or 15 percent of the UK electorate. So a vote for UKIP is a wasted vote if you want a member of parliament in Westminster, while in Brussels the same number of votes could get you a whole brigade of Union Jack-waving members in European Parliament, collecting high salaries each month for discrediting the work of the EU and praising a country whose political system excludes themselves from political influence.

I saw UKIP leader Nigel Farage up close quite often myself, because we both had seats on the European Parliament Committee on Fisheries. Of course, in the first four years, he never showed his face there. Not until he was publicly shamed by the leader of the European Parliament liberal group, Guy Verhofstadt, who bellowed in the plenary chamber that Farage was a giant waste of taxpayer money because he never did his committee job. Obviously this was a good thing, but less good was that I thereafter had the dubious pleasure of seeing Farage in the committee from time to time. I don't remember him ever speaking. I do remember however that when we voted he instinctively pressed the "no" button every time he spied a key word such as "environment" or "sustainable" on his voting list.

According to the EU treaties, a nonpolitical Commission, made up of commissioners from the different member countries and aided by nonpolitical staffs and expert directorates, shall submit proposals for legislation that lie within the EU's areas of competence, which for the most part have to do with environment, climate, agriculture, fishing, and trade. When the Commission has submitted its proposal, it is considered by the two legislative bodies, the European Parliament and the Council of Ministers. The parliament comprises 705 elected Members of the European Parliament (MEPs), who can come together in various majorities, which makes it different from national parliament where normally a majority of parties are "government parties" that always vote in favor of the government's proposals. Also, many of the MEPs have quite free and personal mandates, and all are valued equally, both those who belong to parties that are in the government in their home countries, and those who belong to parties in the opposition.

If by democracy we mean that all voices are represented and have the same chance to have an impact and be heard, then the European Parliament is a unique exception in which members are not just "voting cattle" following a government whip but are instead real players with the opportunity to exert influence. If we also want decisions that raise their sights above naked national interest, then it's considerably easier to find a majority at the EU level than in national parliaments. An Austrian MEP is simply more inclined to vote for what's objectively more sensible in terms of, for example, fisheries policy, than the MEP elected in a Spanish constituency where a vocal fishing lobby sets the tone in local and national media.

The second legislative body is the Council of Ministers, which includes the governments of EU member states. The Council has 50 percent of the power, and the Parliament has 50 percent. Of course, the European Commission has a great deal of influence over the whole process, but in the final negotiations – the so-called trialogue meetings – it's the Council and Parliament that come to agreement on policy. Then it might happen that members of parliament from a country's opposition negotiate with ministers from that same country, with different entry points. It's hard to imagine a more thorough and better functioning supranational process with democracy as its basis. And with the limited media attention the EU institutions normally attract, political craft, political craft is at the heart, not spontaneous crowd-pleasing histrionics. Member states, political groups, civil society, and industry representatives work constantly and diligently to influence legislation at each small step: the formulation of the Commission's proposal, the selection of a rapporteur to the European Parliament, consideration by the committee, the work of the Council working groups, the first discussions in the Council of Ministers, the Council conclusions, Parliament's position, and the trialogue negotiation. The whole process takes several years and requires tremendous conscientiousness, perseverance, cunning and strength of the person who knows what he or she wants.

The Swedish Proposal

As a member of the European Parliament, I was fortunate to be on the winning side many times on fisheries policy, and to strike the ball into the net by first winning in European Parliament and then bringing the Council of Ministers around in the final battle through pressure via our green network in different countries.

As minister, there's one momentous process of political handiwork I'm particularly proud of: the reform of the EU Emissions Trading System (ETS) for carbon dioxide.

The system was introduced in 2005 after extensive discussions, and after the countries of the EU had rejected adopting a common carbon tax. Instead, it was decided that the EU's industries – which represent around 40 percent of the Union's total emissions – would economize allocated emissions allowances, which could then be bought and sold and slowly decrease in number. The idea was that the price would eventually increase so much that it would be more profitable to invest in low-emission technology than to pay dearly for the right to emit.

The only problem was that EU member states were so anxious for a generous allocation of emission allowances that the total pot started out far too big, and the "linear reduction factor" that decreased the size of the pot by 1.74 percent annually was far too wimpy. Especially when the financial crisis hit in 2008–2009, the economy slumped throughout the EU and demand for emission allowances decreased. The price to emit a ton of carbon dioxide in the EU sank like a stone from 30 to 3–4 euros, cheaper than a latte.

In 2016, it was finally time to do something about the EU Emissions Trading System. At the time, it cost 6 euros to emit one ton – far from the 30 euros normally seen as the approximate pain threshold at which coal-fired power plants start to become unprofitable.

Many proposals circulated in Brussels, and most focused on the linear reduction factor. It clearly needed more ambition. The problem was that Poland had already raised this issue to the heads of state and government in 2014. Many Swedes remember when Prime Minister Stefan Löfven, in his first month on the job, had to build a consensus on Sweden's position in the Swedish parliamentary European Union Affairs Committee, and the opposition parties made a big show of not understanding what he was talking about, using expressions like "number bingo" and "trainee government." It was messy, to be sure, but the real problem wasn't that Sweden needed flexibility in its mandate to negotiate with other EU countries, but that Poland had ensured that issues as detailed as percentages and a whole range of other technical details ended up on the desks of the heads of government – issues that actually belonged with the climate ministers. The reason for this maneuver was obvious: decisions by the heads of government are made by consensus, while the climate ministers can make decisions through qualified-majority voting and thus overrule recalcitrant countries. Poland wanted to avoid this at all costs.

So now the issue was closed; the heads of state and government had already decided the emission bubble would shrink by 2.2 percent per year. And although everyone could see that this reduction factor wouldn't lead to reduced emissions in line with the 1.5-degree goal in the Paris Agreement (which had been adopted in 2015, a year after the European Council's, decision) there was a clear nervousness around trying to change the decision, which would have elevated it to the heads of government again – where countries like Poland and Hungary would impede an ambitious reform.

I had just succeeded Åsa Romson as climate minister in the spring of 2016, when Sweden was starting to formulate a new position prior to the negotiations in the fall. In my first meetings with the civil servants at the Ministry of Environment, I got the impression that it was already too late to do something. According to their assessment, since the European Council (the heads of state and government) had already established the linear reduction factor, the climate ministers now just had to execute this decision.

For me and the Green Party, this was a message we couldn't accept. My state secretary, Eva Svedling, and in particular my hard-nosed and knowledgeable staff member Fredrik Hannerz, had many discussions with the civil servants that summer, insisting it must be possible to find other mechanisms to drive up the price on emissions. To bring it back up to a reasonable level we'd need to scrap emission allowances *en masse*, or alternatively set a statutory price floor for emissions. In any case, the 2.2 percent annual decrease decided on by the heads of state and government was insufficient and would probably not make any difference at all to emission levels.

Our civil servants presented several different proposals that summer, and we settled on one that would come to be called "The Swedish Proposal": a system in which a certain amount of surplus emission allowances were eliminated from the market each year starting in 2023.

Eventually the European Parliament produced another proposal to regulate the emissions bubble: a one-time elimination of 800 million tons of emissions. Obviously this was good and promising, and the European Commission supported the proposal. But we'd calculated that our method would have a much greater impact on the price. As a conservative estimate, 2–2.5 billion emission allowances would be eliminated, and the annual elimination would be an effective regulator in case a new financial crisis (or a pandemic, for example) hit the EU and the emission allowances overflowed again. Our proposal would also bring an end to the "waterbed effect;" that is, when an industry reduced its emissions it had no effect on the climate because the emissions could simply be transferred somewhere else, making it cheaper there. With our proposal, the reserve would continually be emptied of a surplus, and the shutting down of, for example, a coal-fired power plant wouldn't create room for emissions somewhere else in the system. This would eliminate the most tiresome of all the arguments against energy efficiency and technological leaps: "If we decrease, someone else can just increase."

At the civil servant level, several informal meetings were held with different countries to gauge their interest. At the same time, I tried to enlist a few ambitious member states in an initiative to buy up emission allowances and then scrap them to tighten up the system. This was a rather drastic proposal that sprang from the fact that the Green Party, when we failed to stop the Vattenfall deal, had secured a budget allocation we called *Utsläppsbromsen* (The Emission Brake) that would remove emissions from the European market in a different way than by closing coal mines. Between 2017 and 2040, Sweden would spend 300 million kronor per year to buy and scrap emission allowances from the EU Emissions Trading System (ETS) – which with the low purchase price would actually mean that quite large quantities of emission allowances would vanish from the market.

Our initiative was hailed by ETS experts, but the interest from other countries was tepid. The Germans rejected it, and not even green Luxembourg showed any enthusiasm. Still, the proposal attracted attention, and even though some must have thought we were crazy to be willing to buy emission allowances only to scrap them, most in Brussels soon knew that Sweden was very seriously focused on doing something about the inefficient system. They listened to us.

On October 17, 2016, we climate ministers were to discuss reforming the ETS at an Environment Council meeting in Luxembourg. As usual, the trip there had been tiresome, with a stopover in Amsterdam followed by a propeller plane to the small Grand Duchy that is one of the EU's founding member states. The night before the meeting, I and a few other ministers had a late dinner and talked, and early the next morning we gathered in a windowless room in the big EU Council building on the Kirchberg Plateau for a customary breakfast for the 13 EU countries that together make up the environmentally ambitious "Green Growth Group."

Prior to the meeting, Sweden had shared a document, which I'd be presenting. It contained an argument for the need to increase the price of emission allowances and presented several possible ways of doing it, including by placing surplus emission allowances in a reserve for five years and then each year eliminating everything above a specified ceiling.

The meeting was fast-paced as usual, with many brief statements from the ministers, who sat across from each other at two rectangular tables set with coffee cups with EU flags on them, linen napkins, and plates with croissants, marmalade and cheese. One by one the ministers spoke, and I was surprised that so many of them already wholeheart-edly supported the Swedish proposal. France's environment minister, Ségolène Royal, presented an alternative proposal that included a price floor for emission allowances, but it wasn't received as positively, maybe because it would so clearly result in a discussion of what the price tag would be.

I was also surprised that climate commissioner Miguel Arias Cañete wasn't at all enthusiastic about the Swedish proposal, quite the opposite. The European Commission instead supported the proposal from the European Parliament of a one-time elimination of 800 million tons of emissions, which the Commissioner clearly thought was sufficiently ambitious. It became very clear to me that if we were going to get a majority in the Council, we'd have to work for it; the European Commission wasn't going to help us.

So, to get the idea out to a wider community of NGOs and other interested parties in the various member states who might support the proposal, I gave a couple of interviews to Reuters and Bloomberg and hoped it would get the EU ball rolling. At the same time, I wrestled with another problem: We still hadn't formally gained support in Swedish parliament for our proposal of continual elimination of emission allowances. I had the mandate to push for a strengthened price signal on emissions, and in our civil servants' assessment that was exactly what we were doing. A Swedish parliament member from the conservative Moderate Party, Jesper Skalberg Karlsson, who saw a tweet where I'd linked to the interviews with Reuters and Bloomberg talking about our proposal, got to work immediately to question my mandate to act in a report to the parliamentary Committee on the Constitution. Thankfully, detailed, parliament-approved positions aren't needed to have informal discussions, which the constitution committee confirmed later in the spring, but I'd still need a majority support in parliament on a more detailed proposal before we could formally move forward in Brussels.

As usual, there were long discussions in the parliamentary Environment and Agriculture Committee, and the proposal might have died then and there after lengthy reservations by the Moderates, Christian Democrats, Center Party and Liberals, and by the Left Party who thought the difference between our proposal and the EU's proposal was trivial, using the Swedish expression "like an argument on the Pope's beard." The Left thought instead that an increase of the reduction factor to 2.6 percent was a much better tactic, even though I'd explained that it would mean elevating the issue to the heads of government, where Poland would cast its veto. The Sweden Democrats, who are always against anything climate-related and who don't want Sweden to take the lead, naturally didn't want the EU to lead the rest of the world, either. So, several adjustments were needed before the position was approved in the European Union Affairs Committee, but we managed to retain the substance of the proposal, and in the end only the Left and the Sweden Democrats had dissenting opinions.

The next step was to convince 27 member states and a parliament in Brussels. On February 28, 2017, it was time. In the large oval room in the Council of Ministers building, with interpreter booths along the walls and colorful wall-to-wall carpet on the floor, the mood was anticipatory and spirits were high as all the ministers and civil servants started to arrive. My shoulders always relaxed when I came to Brussels. In some strange way I felt more at home here in this surrealistic building, with its facade of old wooden window frames and its enormous enclosed round structure that seems to hover under the roof, than I did in the dreary corridors of Swedish parliament. The throng of people streaming in all directions and speaking different languages always puts me in a good mood, perhaps because I can be virtually certain that the topic of conversation between them isn't how to attack an opponent but how to go about bringing a certain member country or parliamentary party group onside on a certain issue. To me, this was real politics. No posturing, no communicating at the speed of Twitter, no demonizing each other, but a true negotiation machinery with long processes that would lead to binding regulations – laws! –

for a half-billion people across 28 national borders. Laws that would influence the rest of the world, and policy that couldn't be summarily dismissed with "emissions will move somewhere else" or "companies will move," but policy for the world's largest market that would show the way, that was truly world-leading.

I'd pursued issues and sat in negotiations before in Brussels as a member of the European Parliament, and now I was enjoying the familiar feeling. Everyone gathered in one room, groupings of friends and opponents. The European Commission with all of its civil servants in attendance, documents with talking points and proposals, EU ambassadors from each country.

I greeted Cañete with a certain emphasis and razzed him for the European Commission not backing our proposal. He clicked his tongue dismissively in a characteristically Spanish way and explained in his heavily accented English that it would be very bad to do that to Poland and several other countries in the former Eastern bloc. He wanted to get everyone on board without creating hard feelings, which was roughly the same argument that had been used for the past decade of inadequate ambitions on the part of the EU. There's no more time for that now, I said. It was time for the countries with the highest ambitions to set the bar for once, not those with the lowest, as usual. The climate commissioner, who'd received harsh criticism from my group in parliament due to his earlier ties to the oil industry, looked skeptical.

I and the ministers Ségolène Royal from France, Sharon Dijksma from the Netherlands and Carole Dieschbourg from Luxembourg had arranged beforehand to request the floor as early as possible in the discussion and to support each other in the Swedish proposal, which we were putting forward jointly. We sat down at the long, oval conference table of light-colored wood with microphones at each seat, the agenda was opened by the Maltese President and the floor went first to France, as host country of the Paris Agreement. Then it was my turn. Both I and Ségolène urged that the proposal we'd circulated to all the delegations be incorporated into the revised ETS.

In the Environment Council the President always uses the ministers' first names, so when Carole, Sharon, Ségolène and I took the floor we referred to each other by our first names, and because we had the floor one after another it was a very powerful opening with support for the Swedish proposal expressed by four female ministers. I observed the gallant, quite charming commissioner Cañete with his well-groomed gray beard, who, in a famous blunder before the 2014 EU election, claimed that he'd lost a debate to a female socialist because he felt forced to hold back his "intellectual superiority" lest he come across as a male chauvinist – a *machista*. He did not look amused.

Then the round table was filled with ministers of both sexes who expressed various degrees of support for the proposal. Belgium, Denmark, Finland, Germany, the United Kingdom. As I checked each one off in my notebook, I started to realize that we had a real chance. Our Swedish EU ambassador, Åsa Webber, told me about an app that calculates votes in the EU where we could see how close we were to a qualified majority, which requires at least 15 member states and at least 65 percent of the EU population. It actually looked very good, but we weren't quite there yet. Hungary was opposed; Poland too, quite strongly. Italy also sounded negative, and we were very far apart.

I realized that it was important to make sure that we, the ambitious countries, stuck together and steered the discussions during the adjournment that would follow, so the European Commission or someone else didn't start circulating watered-down compromise proposals that most countries could agree to if need be. According to the app, we only needed one more country for a majority, and there were several countries that hadn't taken a clear position during the discussion, among them the Czech Republic.

The Czech minister was actually seated next to me, so I leaned toward him and asked where he stood. He wasn't negative but he needed more information, he said, and happiness instantly started to spread through me. If the Czech Republic came over to our side, we might actually have a majority!

There were several adjournments, and the discussions lasted more than five hours. The ministers and civil servants huddled around various documents with their proposed changes. As soon as I or one of the other ministers walked across the room to speak with someone, we were surrounded by one of these rings of curious individuals wanting to know which way things were leaning. The original proposal was being modified, and France now took the lead, together with the Czech Republic, in refining some parameters. But at the same time, what I'd feared was happening. In parallel with our discussions, the Maltese Presidency had drawn up a different compromise proposal for which they now thought they had a majority. My Dutch colleague, Sharon, intervened in a powerful speech and demanded to know what this new text actually meant. Was it a proposal for a one-time scrapping of emission allowances, or a continuous elimination in accordance with "The Swedish Proposal"? The confusion spread around the table and the President gave the floor to climate commissioner Cañete, who was visibly irritated.

"Why are you asking me!?" he exclaimed. "The Commission didn't make this proposal, you ministers did. I can't answer that."

Finally it was explained that the new proposal the President was trying to gavel through was for a one-time elimination, and many at the table were extremely upset. It was clear there had been work behind the scenes to get to a majority for a proposal other than the Swedish one.

Meanwhile, the clock was ticking, and several of the ministers, including my French colleague, had already left and given their seat to an alternate, and soon there was a risk that the Council would no longer have a quorum.

But then the Czech Republic took the floor and explained that they were willing to support the modified proposal for continual elimination of emission allowances that surpassed one year's emissions at the EU level and had been in the market stability reserve for five years. I took the floor and said that Sweden supported the proposal. With that, it was done.

Nineteen member states voted for the proposal, nine against. The countries that voted for the proposal made up over 71 percent of the EU population.

The Polish minister was livid. He had fought hard to get a blocking minority and I understood that he saw the outcome as a huge failure, even though the decision also meant large sums of money specifically for the most coal-dependent countries through the so-called Modernization Fund. But although the decision had already been made, he requested the floor several times and insisted that it went against the decision by the European Council. "We feel deceived!" he exclaimed in closing.

He almost seemed to be in shock, and on a personal level I felt for him. But the President explained that the procedure would now proceed to negotiations with the European Parliament, and that the issue would then return to the Council of Ministers, all according to the EU's cumbersome decision-making process. No one had been deceived; these were the rules of the game.

A long round of applause erupted spontaneously in the

room after the Maltese minister's explanation, something quite rare in an EU context. Many of us sensed that we'd taken a big step toward what would be the beginning of the end for coal power in the EU and the starting point for a real transition throughout EU industry.

After lengthy discussions, the proposal also survived the negotiations with the European Parliament, which of course was a prerequisite. When the new regulations went into effect, their impact was visible immediately. The price of emission allowances started to climb, quickly doubled, increased fivefold within a few years, and by the end of 2021 it was nearly 90 euros per ton, an increase of more than tenfold. About half of the coal-fired power plants in Europe were shut down during the same period, and the coal mines that Swedish power company Vattenfall had sold when I entered as Green Party leader in the spring of 2016 had either never been opened or had become unprofitable for their buyers, because their whole business model was based on a low emissions price.

And what about the "Emission Brakes", the 300 million kronor per year Sweden was going to use to buy up and scrap emission allowances? Obviously that investment was pretty meaningless now that we'd implemented a system that would scrap surplus emission allowances automatically. But the money in the budget was still "ours," the Green Party's winnings, or rather a sort of consolation for the Vattenfall affair. So, I asked the civil servants to produce another proposal directed at industry, to further facilitate a transition. And thus was born the so-called *Industriklivet*, The Industry Leap, a budget allocation for state co-financing of pilot projects and research for heavy industries needing to make technological shifts to reach the goals in the climate law.

The steel industry uses coal in blast furnaces based on a medieval technique that hasn't changed in a thousand years,

POLITICAL CRAFTMANSHIP

and cement also releases carbon dioxide through various processes in its manufacture and can't be streamlined down to zero emissions. The Industry Leap soon became incredibly popular with industry, which was more than happy to invest in making new technological leaps. Before I stepped down as climate minister, The Industry Leap had more than doubled and had a total budget of several billion kronor, and steel company SSAB, mining company LKAB, and Vattenfall had built the world's first major pilot plant for manufacturing steel without coal in Luleå, northern Sweden, in the joint project "Hybrit," where the coal is replaced by hydrogen gas produced with renewable electricity. SSAB is Sweden's largest emitter, and when the company can fully move to green hydrogen technology Sweden's emissions will drop by 10 percent. LKAB has even greater potential through its large exports of iron ore.

As a result, the eyes of the world are on Sweden. The Secretary General of the United Nations had asked us to head up a group called the Leadership Group for Industry Transition (LeadIT) together with India, with the Stockholm Environment Institute and the World Economic Forum as secretariat. The Swedish steel industry now tours the world, puncturing the arguments of steel industries that are stuck in the old ways and that demand free emission allocation for their industry, which they claim must emit. Globally, the steel industry represents around 6 percent of Co2 emissions. The Swedish steel industry is now telling the world that through a technology shift from coal to green hydrogen, these emissions, earlier thought to be impossible to avoid, can actually be eliminated.

Today, many conservatives in Sweden highlight Hybrit and fossil-free Swedish steel as examples of "the industry", "the market" and Swedish technology taking their own leadership in the climate transition, but that's not quite the whole truth. Mårten Görnerup, the first CEO of Hybrit, told me there were three political reforms that made Hybrit possible: the climate law, the substantial direct financial aid via the Industry Leap, and the parliamentary energy agreement with the commitment to one hundred percent renewable energy by 2040, which is expected to give large surpluses of electricity that can be used to produce the green hydrogen needed for steel manufacturing (new nuclear power is much more expensive and immediately breaks the cost calculations). I'm proud that the initiative for all three reforms bears the Green Party's signature.

In the 2014 campaign, when the Green Party held up a piece of coal in each debate and demanded the closure of state-owned Vattenfall's German coal mines, this of course was rooted in a genuine frustration and anger that a government company – our property – would be engaged in activities that worsen the climate crisis. It was also a clear communicative message. But it didn't work in the real world; we couldn't intervene in a state company's operations in that way, or control another country's energy and labor market policies. To actually close coal-fired power plants and get the industry's climate transition and technological advances going, we'd need something more than clear, direct communication – namely, what few journalists write about and too few voters are aware of or seem willing to reward: political craftmanship. Politics, for real.

CHAPTER 10

Hate, Threats and Democracy

AT MY HOME, beside my mailbox, someone has hung a picture of me and the prime minister. Apparently we're traitors. Threatening, anonymous text messages show up on my phone, even on my husband's. For an entire summer I flinch whenever I see something in our backyard out of the corner of my eye. I go get the binoculars. Earnestly I study flocks of birds, the cat on the lawn, a neighbor walking by, worried that the person who's obviously been to our home, taken photos and uploaded them to the internet might be sneaking around. The Swedish Security Service is called and does a thorough investigation; but there doesn't seem to be any connection between the different incidents. It's partly my imagination, a few trolls, carelessness with my phone and the usual online hate – nothing to worry about. I have the support of a psychologist through my job, but it's gone so far now: letters to my home, my phone, my private sphere. I'm a person who tends to just keep going and not let things get to me, and I've never in my life imagined anyone would wish me harm. Now I keep having to remind myself that it's quite possible they do. It comes with the position; it's not about me – and yet it is. It is about me. But it's also about our democracy.

sd2022, #sd2022, countrymen, bullshit,
retard, harpy, muppet, resign, hypocrite,
murderer, idiot, extremist, extremism,
environmental nazi, environmental
hypocrite, heavy rocks, finspång, asylum
fraud, arab countries, fucking arab,
fatherland, traitor, fool, cult, hypocrisy,
hypocritical, scum, moron, halfwit,
radical, mass immigration, islamicize,
islamist, bullshit party, clown party,
clowns, gold diggers, age fraud, shame,
rape, freeloader, shit party, vermin,
parasites, parrasites, whore, ugly
feminist, cunt, feminist hag, witch, slut,
slutt, bitch

When I step down as party leader and minister in early 2021, I discover this list of words and phrases my staff has autoblocked in the comments on my social media accounts. I'm grateful. The amount of crap I avoided. The party platforms have hundreds of thousands of followers and attract trolls like flies around a sugar cube. No to anyone's surprise, after all, they get to spread their hate, all free of charge and with very little effort. Our local chapters of the Greens have the same problem. Some have grown tired of purging the comment threads and have instead closed them for any comments, which means cutting off dialogue with the local community. Some leave social media altogether because they can't stand the hateful tone. Still other active Green party members have left politics themselves. In all of these cases, the trolls have won and democracy has lost.

Populist parties, primarily on the far right, have grown like weeds in recent years. They use classic tricks to mobilize their support. Identify an enemy. Sow division and stoke strong emotions. Create an "us and them," a polarized society where dialogue is no longer the way to resolve conflicts, where one side instead must win and the other be defeated.

In Sweden, one of the more extreme expressions of this strategy has been the "Finspång" meme – a code word used by radical-right sympathizers that refers to the idea of a sort of Nuremberg trial that would take place in the town of Finspång, Sweden, where so-called traitors would be hanged from lampposts. They show up on social media from time to time: pictures of lampposts or strange references to Finspång, often portrayed as a joke. But their purpose isn't to make people laugh; it's to frighten them, crank up the tone of the discussion, pit person against person and ultimately dehumanize the opponent – basic tactics of those who want power and won't hesitate to use violence.

Are online threats and hate harmless? How far is the step between calling someone a traitor on social media and actually wanting to hang someone from a lamppost? This question didn't quite get its answer on January 6, 2021, when a mob stormed the US Capitol and people erected an actual gallows outside the building, with some in the mob chanting "Hang Mike Pence!" The main reason was that the vice president, whom Donald Trump had branded a traitor for doing his duty and communicating the result of the election to Congress, was whisked away by the Secret Service and was never seized by the mob. But what if they had found him?

In Sweden, established right-wing columnist Ivar Arpi tried for a long time to minimize the incident, which he described it as "a bunch of people in sweatpants taking selfies" in Congress – as if it were a practical joke, a group of visitors to the Capitol Building horsing around a bit in the corridors. We now know that wasn't the case. Five people died, members of Congress called their loved ones during the attack to say goodbye, several traumatized police officers who defended Congress against the mob later took their own lives, and the threat to elected officials remains in the US, where a significant portion of Trump voters still hold the false belief that President Joe Biden came to power through election fraud – and where people have increasingly been purchasing firearms since the election.

The right-wing populist recipe for success is about polarizing society. Create suspicion and animosity toward another group, divide society into the ordinary people – *the* people – and the elite. The honest and the corrupt. The deceived and the deceivers.

Strangely enough, it's often extremely wealthy people like Silvio Berlusconi, Donald Trump or Andrej Babiš who appoint themselves as the voice for "ordinary people," and who successfully gain the approval of many. "I'm already rich, I can't be corrupted" seems to work well as an explanatory model. But it might not make much difference *who* claims to be the "voice of the people"; it's *what* they say that matters, and how they say it. After years of frustration in their lives, many people seem to experience almost a sort of catharsis when a so-called leader suddenly "tells it like it is": points to immigrants, Jews, Muslims, the media, the global elite, environmentalists, feminists, scientists, intellectuals, the whole kit and caboodle, as the enemy. The language may be shocking at first, then it becomes titillating to shatter old taboos, and soon it's normalized.

When did this happen in Sweden? Or is it just about to happen?

"This government should never have taken office." "Sweden is governed by parties that are trying to circumvent the will of the people." In the spring of 2021, the Moderate party and the Christian Democrats started what appeared to be a joint attack on the legitimacy of the then Swedish government. The "January Agreement" – an agreement between four parties in the political center, published online, which had been negotiated after a record-high number of talks between the party leaders and the Speaker of parliament in the most transparent and protracted formation of government in Sweden's history – was called a "backroom deal" and "political gamesmanship" by the leader of the Christian Democrats, Ebba Busch. The leader of the Moderates, Ulf Kristersson, who'd been unable to get what he himself called "the mathematics" to work to form a government, that is, did not have a majority, said in an interview in the daily newspaper *Svenska Dagbladet* that the January Agreement was "tampering with democracy." Ebba Busch continued to claim that the policies pursued by the government "circumvented the will of the people," and Jimmie Åkesson of the Sweden Democrats joined the chorus, calling the cooperation between the more centrist parties "undemocratic." The potshots at the legitimacy of the red-green government were like a faint but eerie echo of the allegations of election fraud on the other side of the Atlantic some months earlier.

The attack culminated in the summer of 2021, when parties from both the far right and far left brought down the sitting government with a vote of no confidence. The reason for the lack of confidence was highly peculiar. The Left Party was critical of a market rent reform and launched the vote of no confidence. The parties on the right basically liked the reform in question, but what did that matter when they had the chance to show that the government "didn't have the parliament behind it"? Thus, the left and right happily threw out the sitting government without having their own alternative basis for government. This was a fact they wanted to sweep under the carpet as quickly as possible; opposition leader Ulf Kristersson quietly announced after a single day's renewed calculations of the numbers in parliament that he didn't have a basis to form a government, though this didn't stop him from maintaining that the red-green government was "absurd" and should never have been allowed to take office. Meanwhile, the real absurdity was to remove a government because it wanted to implement a policy you actually support.

The result of this circus was anyway that a new red-green minority government soon took office again, with the same prime minister, Stefan Löfven, and many Swedes must have wondered how this was possible after all the upset talk about how this government had cheated its way into power.

For democracy to survive, two things are indispensable: the citizens must trust in the democratic system, and there must be people willing to assume the role of elected representative. Unfortunately, both of these pillars now show serious signs of erosion.

Being elected nowadays doesn't just mean you have to endure mockery and harassment on the internet; you might also have to deal with direct death threats and harassment of your family. Being politically active can also make it harder to get the job you've trained for. I was deeply upset after speaking with a young person with a Master of Science in Engineering who'd done heroic work representing the Green Party in northern Sweden, and who'd had to make a living as a high school teacher for several years despite the desperate need for qualified engineers in the region. Being someone who keeps the local democracy running isn't a merit when job-hunting; it's a shackle. With such a high price to pay for the privilege of devoting weeknights and weekends to attending meetings and perusing documents about bike lanes, waste, and snow removal, it's not surprising that the Green Party has a hard time finding people willing to take on this role, especially in many northern Swedish counties, where the aggressive tone against the party is especially high (with the notable exceptions of Gällivare and Jokkmokk municipalities, where the party is doing well).

Between 2018 and 2020 more local politicians left the Green Party than any other party. The party has also become one of the least popular parties in Sweden, compared with 2014 when it was among the most popular, and, like our sister parties in Europe, has become a target of intensive campaigns and false rumormongering by the alt-right on social media. Leading up to the 2021 federal election in Germany, the Greens spokesperson, Annalena Baerbock, was subjected to twice as much fake news as any of the other candidates for chancellor. A favorite tall tale was the bogus claim that the Greens wanted to ban household pets due to their carbon dioxide emissions. Other false claims flourished as well, including that the party wanted to disarm the police, ban barbecues and mandate the teaching of the Koran in schools. In Sweden, too, outraged grassroots campaigns have arisen against fake news, for example that the Green Party wants to ban horse riding schools or wood stoves. Every time the world market price of oil goes up, and with it the price of gasoline and diesel, the anger on social media has exploded – not toward Saudi Arabia, Russia or the OPEC countries but toward the Green Party. In an op-ed in September 2021, Thomas Morell, the Sweden Democrats' representative on the parliamentary Committee on Transport and Communications, wrote: "The idea that sky-high fuel prices would force a climate-smart lifestyle onto people who live far beyond the subway stations of Södermalm, Stockholm, is a bizarre Green Party fever dream. The Green Party's vision of the future is a return to living in mud huts with stomped earthen floors. No electricity, no infrastructure, no cars and no domestic industry. The Green Party's policies constitute not only a danger to society but a threat to civilization as a whole."

Unfortunately, Morell's imagery isn't uncommon enough to laugh at. The traditional right-wing parties have increasingly adopted similar spin tactics, of course with the stated goal of making sure the shrinking Green Party isn't represented in Sweden's parliament – which would enable the opposition leader Ulf Kristersson and others to "get the math together" for a basis for a conservative government. In the winter of 2021 I see a symbol circulating on social media, even among people I know aren't trolls, showing a black stick figure kicking a crumpled wad into a wastebasket with the text: "Greens out of the Parliament 2022!"

There was a similar campaign ahead of the 2018 election. Even then, the online hatred and contempt for the Green Party knew know bounds, and we in the party had received ever stronger signals that people had started speaking in hushed tones about the fact they were Green Party members or were considering voting for the party. I remember so well the party board meeting where we got the numbers on this, and we set a new goal, not to try to win over new voters but to try to get the circles – the families, husbands, and co-workers – of our core voters, women in early middle age, to "at least not hate us," so we wouldn't lose them, too.

Contempt for politicians is not a new phenomenon. And of course, it isn't directed solely at the Green Party. According to the Swedish National Council for Crime Prevention, one out of three elected regional and municipal council members have received threatening text messages, telephone calls, emails or visits, or have been shamed online in some way, which can lead to self-censorship or resignation from their post. Still, the Green Party stands out: In 2021 we became the party with the highest proportion of parliament members subjected to hate and threats, a position previously held by the Sweden Democrats. Female representatives are particularly targeted, and they also receive the most personally offensive types of hate and threats, with comments on their appearance, sexual innuendos and general misogyny. This has been going on for so long that many Green Party members now say they've become jaded. They've given up reporting the attacks and violations; they're now part of everyday life.

So, what's the basis for this hate? The party's support for the right of asylum during the refugee crisis in 2015 is definitely one thing that sparks strong emotions, and the other is our policies for moving away from fossil fuels. When the party left government in the winter of 2021, because the opposition's budget had been passed with massive environmental spending cuts and a gasoline tax decrease, many people were happy. Peder Blohm Bokenhielm, leader of the so-called Bränsleupproret (the Fuel Rebellion), a Facebook group with 600,000 members, rejoiced in an interview in *Dagens Nyheter*: "The greatest validation I've ever received was when the Green Party left government because the gas tax was lowered. We don't deserve all the credit, but we've worked hard to shape public opinion for two and a half years, and now we're reaping the rewards."

It's not easy for me to write about the negative image that's been created of the Green Party, because it feels like whatever I say might come off as self-pity. But I'm doing it anyway, fully aware that we, like all other parties, have made mistakes and deserve criticism – but we Greens have a problem that sets us apart in Swedish politics, which is that we have no external "co-communicators": organizations, newspapers, trade unions or similar institutions with Green Party allegiances to defend us. The conservative opinion pages in newspapers from north to south praise conservative parties on a daily basis and routinely heap scathing criticism on us. The Social Democratic opinion writers make no mention of us at all in the best case; in the worst, they blame all of the much larger party's problems on us. Svenskt Näringsliv (the Confederation of Swedish Enterprise) and Lantbrukarnas Riksförbund (the Federation of Swedish Farmers) have close ties with certain parties and large trade unions with others, while environmental organizations, which many believe are our allies, keep us strictly at arm's length and regularly criticize the government, which we've been part of for seven years – which is their role. To make matters worse, we have outspoken Green Party members, including former party spokespersons, scolding us, which the media loves to pick up on. No business organizations, civil society organizations or major think tanks have our back. It's pretty lonely being a Green these days, especially for those who stand in the square in a small town with their green banners as passersby openly show their hostility.

With contempt for politicians thriving, it's no wonder confidence in democracy is crumbling. This is a global trend, especially among young people, according to a large-scale survey by the Centre for the Future of Democracy at the University of Cambridge. The center has analyzed the largest-ever data set, based on 4.8 million responses in 160 countries between 1973 and 2020, and found that the younger generation, the so-called millennials, everywhere in the world, both in the West and in developing countries, has significantly lower "satisfaction" with democracy as a system of governance than the three preceding generations. However, in places where a populist leader has been elected, the younger generation is, remarkably enough, significantly more satisfied with democracy than in other countries – with one interesting exception, namely young people in the United States under Trump.

The Cambridge center draws several conclusions. One is that the younger generation has fallen behind economically and blames its discontent on an elected leadership they see as failed and as benefitting only certain groups, which makes them more open to a populist leader's message. Another is that young people, both in the West and in many developing countries, have less personal experience living under authoritarian regimes or having to fight for democracy. This means they haven't seen the downsides of authoritarian leadership, but they have seen the weaknesses of democracy.

A 2017 Swedish survey conducted by Novus and commissioned by Studieförbunden (the Swedish Adult Education Association) shows similar results. Alarmingly, one out of ten people, regardless of age, responded that it would be good or fairly good if Sweden were run by a leader who didn't have to worry about parliament or general elections. And four out of ten thought it would be good or fairly good if experts, not the government, made decisions about what's best for the country. Among young people, the preference for "expert rule" was even higher: almost half thought it was preferable.

In professor and philosopher Åsa Wikforss' thought-provoking book *Alternativa fakta: Om kunskapen och dess fiender* (Alternative Facts: On Knowledge and Its Enemies) she explores in depth how we humans assimilate knowledge. We do it partly the way every other living creature on earth does it – through experiencing, feeling, seeing, tasting and verifying what the world around us looks like, where the food is, where the chair is – and partly through learning certain skills, like how to ride a bicycle, sew, dance, or repair an engine. Then there's the knowledge we can't verify for ourselves, which we learn through relying on other people to recount or explain something. The teacher at school, the journalist who writes an article, the neighbor who tells us what he's been through. Through this reliance on others, humanity has built a shared knowledge bank that's constantly being filled. So there's no need for each person to reinvent the wheel; we can, as Isaac Newton said, stand on the shoulders of giants and see further into the distance generation by generation. This is humanity's strength. It's how we've built our extremely complex social systems.

But, as Wikforss so pedagogically explains: this strategy of learning from each other and trusting each other as sources of knowledge, while evolutionarily quite advantageous, has a surprisingly weak point, particularly in a globalized information society where people are divided into so many different groups, and where so much knowledge is impossible for an individual to verify for themselves. That is that in order to absorb knowledge we must *trust* the person conveying it. We can't singlehandedly verify election results or research vaccines or climate change. Our entire complex society is based on division of labor and the transfer of knowledge from experts to others. But if we no longer trust each other, we don't assimilate the knowledge that's conveyed. That's why it's so frighteningly simple to create fact resistance. Once the narrative of "us and them," "ordinary people and elites," "patriots and traitors" has taken hold, the susceptibility to outright lies, alternative narratives and conspiracy theories is extremely high. Joe Biden won because of election fraud, Barack Obama is a Muslim, vaccines control people's brains, evil pedophile rings are running the world – anything goes.

When the newly elected President Donald Trump started calling the New York Times, CNN and pretty much all traditional media "fake news," it seems to have been quite deliberate. At first it came as such a surprise and was so bizarre that hardly anyone took it seriously. But once a claim is repeated enough times, it starts to take on a life of its own, and soon the goal was achieved: the voter base was immune to any revelation or criticism presented by any serious media outlet. Instead, "alternative" sources of truth like Breitbart News and the online oracle "Q" started to gain legitimacy and credibility among Trump's voter base – of course, with the willing assistance of foreign powers whose professional troll armies fuel the division in Western democracies. Eccentric media moguls and multibillionaires such as Rupert Murdoch and Robert Mercer have also done their part by funding bullhorns that ramp up the tone of the discussion. And the internet giants have done the same with algorithms that steer users toward more traffic, custom-tailored opinion bubbles and emotionally charged posts. Never has such a diverse range of overlapping interests had such a cheap and simple means to influence so many. The realization that "truth is the first casualty of war" is chilling.

But it's not just that. In her book, Åsa Wikforss explores whether we can even think about values, ethics and morals in a world where basic facts are called into question, where the legitimacy of established knowledge brokers is questioned, where everything is relative and nothing is filtered.

"Fact nihilism," she writes, is nothing but "philosophy's weapon of mass destruction."

Where are we headed, then? I can understand young people amid this confusion thinking and hoping there are "experts" or "scientists" who can make objectively correct decisions. I can also understand many people thinking a good dictator with common sense is the only solution for this world, which "everyone knows" needs to be brought under control. I believe we're in a dangerous place if we don't see how these opinions are spreading, don't discuss them in a serious way or treat them with respect. If we don't explain why it's better that an elected official with overall responsibility makes decisions than experts who are blind to consequences in areas other than their own. Discuss what democracy is and explain how its institutions are peaceful life insurance policies in our communities. Discuss why dictatorships always end in bloodshed, oppression and corruption.

The discussions must be held with new generations in the

West who've grown up in a consumption culture where the citizen identity is completely overshadowed by the customer identity. Where fewer and fewer people even think of joining a political party to do their stint of democratic service. Where more and more people select parties on election day as if they were goods or services, instead of seeing the parties as citizens who have joined together to pull society in a direction they believe is the right one.

This is democracy. This is how fragile it is. If no one participates, it dies.

And they know it: all the interests that offer to take over when no one else can be bothered, the ones that stoke contempt for politicians, the ones that intimidate with lampposts, call elected officials traitors and spit on democracy and its slow processes. The ones who lie willfully.

They know what they're doing.

We can't let them win.

CHAPTER 11

The Corporations

IT'S EASY TO be overwhelmed by the complexity of the world. Poor countries, rich countries. Huge countries, tiny countries. International organizations, multinational corporations. Banks, pension funds, cities, individuals. A handful of individuals richer than billions of others combined. Who has the power when it comes to the big, border-transcending global issues? Who should be held accountable for the climate crisis and the dramatic loss of species and ecosystems? Is it the governments or the corporations? The democracies or the dictatorships? The investors, the asset managers, or maybe the exorbitantly rich?

The media isn't doing much to enlighten us, either. The camera constantly shifts to a new angle. One day, aviation is the greatest threat to the climate. The next day it's deforestation. The third day we're told pension funds must divest, and the fourth day everything else is pointless if China won't stop burning coal... The bread can be sliced in so many different ways. Emissions can be broken down to the national level, the industry sector level, or per capita. The same emissions can show up in different calculations, one time as transportation, the next time as consumption emissions and another time as the environmental impact of the fashion industry.

But there's another way to slice the bread that sharpens our focus almost uncannily. That is to stop looking at who consumes fossil fuels and instead look at who produces them.

First and foremost: emissions from fossil fuels are the single biggest cause of climate change. Deforestation, live-stock farming and other greenhouse gases represent about a third of the so-called anthropogenic (human-created) emissions; the rest comes from coal, oil and fossil gas. That's why the Carbon Majors Report from the organization CDP (formerly known as the Carbon Disclosure Project) is extremely illuminating reading. CDP has compiled a database of producers of fossil fuels and has found that as few as one hundred companies have produced around half of the total global emissions since the start of industri-alization in the 1750s. Using the base year of 1988, when the UN Intergovernmental Panel on Climate Change was formed and there was no longer any doubt that anthropo-genic carbon dioxide contributed to global warming, the one hundred largest fossil fuel companies have produced 71 percent of emissions, and just twenty-five companies have produced half! These include publicly owned companies such as ExxonMobil, Shell, BP, Chevron, Peabody, Total and BHP Billiton, as well as state-owned companies such as Saudi Aramco, Gazprom, National Iranian Oil Company, Coal India, Pemex, China National Petroleum Corporation, Shenhua Group and China National Coal Group.

Even more striking is that these fossil fuel companies have, since 1988 – when leaders like Margaret Thatcher and George H.W. Bush were in agreement that global warming must be stopped – emitted *more* carbon dioxide into the atmosphere than they had over the previous two hundred-plus years (to be exact: 833 $GtCO_2$ between 1988 and 2017 versus 820 $GtCO_2$ between 1751 and 1988). As a result, earth's atmosphere now contains the highest level of carbon dioxide in 800,000 years.

The Climate Accountability Institute (CAI) carried out a

different exercise. Their base year is not 1988, when the IPCC was formed, but 1965, when President Lyndon B. Johnson declared before Congress that his generation had changed the composition of the atmosphere on a global scale. CAI compared the total emissions of the largest fossil fuel companies since 1965, and at the top of the list is Saudi Aramco, which alone is responsible for 4.33 percent of emissions, followed by the Russian company Gazprom at 3.17 percent, then American companies Chevron and ExxonMobil at just over 3 percent each, the National Iranian Oil Company at 2.62, British company BP at 2.45, Dutch company Shell at 2.30, Coal India at 1.73, Mexican company Pemex at 1.63 and China National Petroleum at 1.17 percent.

The list continues, but it's not overly long. Most of the companies, 60 percent, are state-owned, more than 30 percent are publicly owned, and fewer than 10 percent are privately owned.

So, despite everything the global community knows about the climate crisis, a very small number of companies have continued to thrive on making it much worse. The company responsible for the most emissions in the world overall, Saudi Aramco, had 2018 revenues of 356 billion dollars – more than any other company on earth. The company went public in 2019 as part of Saudi Crown Prince Mohammed bin Salman's plan to decrease the country's oil dependency. It was given an extremely high value: 1.7 trillion dollars, and the shares have continued increasing ever since.

There's also no indication that the fossil fuel industry in general is bracing for financial losses as a result of the Paris Agreement. The Stockholm Environment Institute's 2021 *Production Gap Report* showed that the industry is continuing to plan for more than double the fossil fuel production in 2030 than what would be consistent with the 1.5-degree target.

But it's not just the fossil resources that are concentrated in the hands of a small number of companies. In an article in *Nature Ecology & Evolution*, researchers Carl Folke, Henrik Österblom and others report their calculations of how much of the planet's nonrenewable resources, as well as certain important crops, are controlled by the largest corporations within each sector.

It turns out a substantial portion of the "production capacity" of earth's biosphere is owned by a very small number of companies. For example, just five companies control over 90 percent of the market for palm oil, five companies produce nearly half of all farmed salmon, three companies control 60 percent of the seeds, five companies control 62 percent of the cobalt, ten companies control 72 percent of the oil, ten companies control 40 percent of the coffee and ten companies control 30 percent of the world's cement. Wild fish stocks, soybeans, bananas, cacao, gas, gold, silver, platinum, iron, paper and fertilizer are also concentrated in remarkably few hands.

The article by Folke and Österblom raises many questions, most importantly the question of democratic influence and just how much power countries and governments have to affect these transnational megacorporations, especially smaller countries. In Sweden we have clear examples of how hard this can be. In 2021 the world's largest cement manufacturer, Heidelberg Cement, applied for continued limestone mining on the Swedish island of Gotland but repeatedly ignored requests by the Land and Environment Court to supplement the application with an adequate environmental impact assessment – perhaps because they felt confident the permit would be issued in any case, because otherwise Sweden would have essentially no cement manufacturing. And sure enough, the court's principled rejection of the incomplete application led immediately to sheer panic in parliament. The news that all construction work in Sweden would need to be halted spread in the media, and soon a unanimous parliament – from far-right to far-left – passed emergency legislation designed specifically to grant an exception to this one company. This act was so extraordinary that the Council on Legislation directed sharp criticism toward the government and parliament afterwards, saying it undermined the judiciary and contravened the Constitution.

And this was in Sweden, a rich, democratic, constitutional state with rule of law and freedom of the press. But what does it look like in developing countries, where transnational mining giants own the concession rights? What leverage do poor island states with weak institutions, and whose national economy depends on revenues from fisheries agreements, have against transnational fishing giants? Can a country whose entire GDP is far below the revenues of a global megacorporation ever be expected to impose demands on such corporations?

I don't even have to try to answer these questions; we can all see the results everywhere, all over the world. Even the EU can't always put proper reins on its companies, despite requirements for transparency and respect for human rights in trade and foreign investments.

*

But what actually is a corporation? What drives it?

When the idea of a "legal person," not made of flesh and blood, started to become established and accepted in the Netherlands and England in the 1600s, it was a quantum leap in human development. Suddenly, the personal responsibility that previously rested on the owner of a business could be lifted and instead placed on an impersonal, faceless corporation. Ownership could be spread out, and the worst that could happen was that the corporation went bankrupt and lost its assets, while the owners could keep their house and home and make a fresh start.

The concept, which we take for granted today, is based completely on a human idea. This has undeniably led to enormous progress and development in our societies and much greater appetite for risk and inclination to invest capital. But in the twenty-first century, with the knowledge that a small number of corporations have now taken over a vast share of the planet's natural resources and biospheres, isn't it time to slow down and take a good look at the innermost objectives, motivations and, yes, even the *souls* of these corporations?

The discussion isn't new. When the corporate business structure was debated in the British House of Lords in the late 1700s, the speaker, Lord Chancellor Edward Thurlow, warned emphatically against this unnatural concept, which would make it impossible to hold anyone accountable for a business. "Did you ever expect a corporation to have a conscience, when it has no soul to be damned, or no body to be kicked?" he asked his collegues, adding: "Corporations have neither bodies to be punished, nor souls to be condemned, they therefore do as they like."

So, here we are three hundred years later, with a handful of megacorporations controlling a considerable portion of the earth's resources, corporations we know have had the opportunity to save the planet for a long time and could have done so if they'd had such a conscience. As already noted, automobile manufacturers could have invested in electric cars long ago, and energy companies could have transitioned to renewable energy long ago. But they haven't.

How, then, should the world deal with these behemoths without souls, without human bodies, whose only real motivation seems to be constant growth? It's a growing discussion, not least among many talented employees of large corporations, themselves. Many use the UN Agenda 2030 as a framework for their activities, based on the mandate signed by the world stating that the agenda applies not only to countries but to all key players, not least corporations. Many also realize that if the world can't solve extreme poverty and climate change and prevent pandemics and wars, neither countries, the planet, customers, employees nor global corporations will fare well.

So why don't the companies' leaders simply change their activities and make it their objective to work for the greater good? Does the answer lie in corporate law, which obliges CEOs to constantly generate profits for shareholders? This is an interesting question. Many experts in corporate law object strongly to the interpretation that CEOs must deliver quarterly profits at the expense of long-term sustainability. In her book *The Shareholder Value Myth*, corporate law professor Lynn Stout writes that this isn't the case, but that it's mainly "activist hedge funds," which deliberately misinterpret corporate law and "harass boards" to make them adopt strategies that lead to short-term increases in stock prices. Many business leaders agree with her. A few years ago, Larry Fink, CEO of BlackRock, the world's largest asset manager, urged the Business Roundtable (the leaders of the 180 largest companies in the United States) to change its Statement on the Purpose of a Corporation, which had long declared that a corporation's primary duty was to deliver profit to its shareholders, to instead be about serving society at large. They did this in 2018. The founder of the World Economic Forum (WEF), Klaus Schwab, has long promoted the idea of "stakeholder capitalism," something he's written many books about, an idea of doing business with a clear conscience, a capitalism that cares about both employees and customers, both local communities and the planet. Jack Welch, who for twenty years was CEO of

General Electric, minced no words, calling the pretense that corporations should first and foremost work to maximize shareholder profits "the dumbest idea in the world."

But how do we help the forces for good within the corporate world who really do want corporations to contribute to sustainable development? And how do we rein in those who don't?

Before the 2021 UN Climate Change Conference in Glasgow, an interesting announcement came totally out of the blue from the International Corporate Governance Network (ICGN), an association of the world's largest investors, capital owners and pension funds. The same year, ICGN members were responsible for managing two-thirds of the world's GDP ($59 of $94 trillion), and if the ICGN's motto, "Inspiring good governance and stewardship," were actually reflected in each dollar in its member's portfolios, ICGN would undoubtedly be able to change the whole world for the better.

The ICGN's Statement of Shared Climate Change Responsibilities included ambitious appeals to all corporations to adopt science-based targets for reducing emissions, develop plans for a just transition, and much more. It also supported setting a price on emissions, banning subsidies for fossil fuel companies, phasing out coal-based electricity and introducing financial support for renewable energy. But what most captured my interest was something entirely different: an extraordinary call to the world's governments to establish a new international crime: ecocide.

Large-scale destruction of the environment, ecocide, as a crime against humanity was an idea launched back in the 1970s by the American bioethics professor Arthur W. Galston. At the first UN environmental conference, held in Stockholm in 1972, Swedish Prime Minister Olof Palme mentioned the concept, perhaps the first to do so in a UN context. The idea was later picked up by British lawyer and activist Polly Higgins, who started the campaign "End Ecocide on Earth," which has been the driving force behind a proposal to make ecocide a fifth "most serious crime of concern to the international community as a whole" according to Article 5 of the Rome Statute of the International Criminal Court in The Hague, joining genocide, crimes against humanity, war crimes and crimes of aggression.

That the world's largest investors want to introduce an international crime of this kind is pretty sensational, and it provides real food for thought. Today's corporations operate globally; money moves across borders while legislation stops at borders, and the majority of countries are too weak to stand up to the large corporations. At the same time, the air we breathe doesn't belong to any one country, and the oceans aren't separated by national borders; these are the common property of all of us.

So there's clearly a need for something new, a threat of prosecution across national borders, and ecocide in that context could be a real game changer, particularly when it comes to how the world views the global commons of ocean and atmosphere and what responsibility could be placed on those who today can dump carbon dioxide, poisons and plastic into them without penalty. Naturally, establishing this crime would also lead corporate analysts to place red warning flags on companies that were in danger of being prosecuted for ecocide. Asset managers' money would move at lightning speed. The private and state-owned companies would risk paying major damages, and no company, regardless of ownership, would be able to duck the moral normative pressure of the world community agreeing that large-scale or long-lasting environmental degradation is a crime against humanity.

Voluntarism is a concept we should think seriously about if we expect change from global corporations. So is the lack of a body and soul, and factors such as herd mentality and the tragedy of the commons. I often think about the curse that seems to afflict so many people when they see others grabbing all they can for themselves, and they realize that their only reward for abstaining from the grabbing is to watch others take more and more of the pie. This can apply to the fish in the ocean, or to the lucrative extraction of coal and oil that can be dumped free of charge into the common atmosphere. Is ecocide the crime that could change the view of the commons as something you'd be stupid not to take for yourself? Could it make participation in environmental destruction no longer a "victimless crime" but something that could actually lead to a trial in The Hague?

I sometimes think about a passage in the book *Den nödvändiga olydnaden* (The Necessary Disobedience) by Swedish social psychologist Maria Modig. In it, she describes psychologist Stanley Milgram's famous experiment in which subjects were tricked into believing they were giving electric shocks to people on the other side of a wall when they answered a question incorrectly. The subject was encouraged by a white-coated experimenter to continue the experiment at higher and higher voltage, even as the "victim" (who was an actor) complained more and more about their faked pain and, eventually, said they had a heart condition and might die. As long as the experimenter in the background assumed the responsibility and urged the subject to keep giving the electric shocks, nearly two-thirds of the subjects did, despite being told about the heart condition. The experiment has been repeated many times in different variations and in different countries, and unfortunately the results have been similar each time.

In her book, Maria Modig interviews an older Stanley Milgram about the concepts of obedience and authority, and about what he thought could have made the experimental subjects halt the experiment, which was clearly distressing them. Milgram said that in retrospect he'd come to wonder what would have happened if the "victim," instead of wailing, had referred to a higher authority, someone outside the room? If they'd said "If you don't stop, I'll sue you" or "I'll report you to the police and bring you to justice"? Milgram lamented that he hadn't thought of this variation of the experiment earlier, as he was convinced it could have made the difference. That it could have broken the logic in the closed room and reminded the subject of the society outside, of the authority of law that trumps the authority of the man in the white coat. And of what the subject actually knew deep down was wrong.

So, what bearing do Milgram's ideas about higher authorities have on the business world and the global problems we see today? Well, considering that the people in the closed system that is a corporation act according to the logic that prevails in that closed system, and that they are "only following orders" when they put shareholder profits before the earth's climate despite being told the climate is being destroyed, the experiment has a perfect bearing on today's problems.

For the experimental subject, pushing the electric shock button is part of the rules of the game. For the CEO, it's delivering profits. The fundamental goal of creating value for shareholders is even written into the Swedish Companies Act (Chapter 3, Paragraph 3), and only if specifically provided for in the company's articles of association can leadership compromise this principle. That is, it's not self-evident that the CEO of a corporation can knowingly decrease the company's profits to invest in a less profitable but more human- or environment-friendly way and still keep their job, even if many CEOs can argue successfully that sustainability efforts will result in good returns in the longer term. But there's no duty to invest in sustainability. Animal species and ecosystems have no legal rights, but corporations and their shareholders do. They're the normative signals in the boardroom, and the nods from the man in the white coat as he encourages the subject to continue giving electric shocks.

So what is needed? New objectives in the company laws? New international legislation that brings an external authority into corporate boardrooms? Or can the corporate giants, unlike Milgram's experimental subjects, take voluntary responsibility and stop when they hear the pain, the cries and the warnings? Can good stewardship, public service and "stakeholder capitalism" really become a corporate culture that is rewarded, that isn't just on the surface but permeates the whole operation, and might even become its goal? Can economists develop new norms and theories better suited to a fragile, sick planet that can't tolerate more blind exploitation and profit maximizing? Can it become a given that corporations support environmental legislation instead of trying to skirt it, strengthen small countries' institutions instead of trying to exploit their weaknesses, support the uncorrupted forces in poor countries instead of taking shortcuts that cause deep wounds and mistrust in countries in the global south?

The answer is that it *must* be possible, because we have no time to lose; the climate crisis and the ecological crisis are already here. We need all hands on deck.

But it won't happen on its own. Corporations need governments in order to succeed. And in many cases, governments also need corporations. But the basis, the rationale for doing it also must be formulated. We need a new ethical value system in relation to nature, to replace the human-centered one that's all about dominance, exploitation and growth for growth's sake. We need to reboot our relationship to nature, we need to repair it, and to do that, we need a new narrative.

CHAPTER 12

The Narrative

WE ARE ALL in the same canoe.

It doesn't sound quite as spot-on coming from a Swede, this metaphor my colleagues from the small island nations in the Pacific use routinely in their speeches. But I say it anyway. And I mean it. We are all in the same canoe. We are. And of course, in a way, we're not. The people of the island nations really are at the mercy of their canoes. Many of the atolls are just two meters above sea level at their highest point, and once the ocean has risen by one meter, perhaps by the end of this century, their only option will be to flee to their boats, their canoes.

But we on the other side of the world, bound together by the same ocean, are sitting in that same canoe in the sense that we must work together to deal with the climate crisis, which impacts us all. We can't see it as charity to help the small island nations, to fund adaptation efforts or share our technology. If the whole world can't make the leap, we all lose. Rugged individualism won't get us there. We only have one canoe, and it's called Earth.

*

It's World Oceans Day, June 8, 2016, and I'm in New York representing Sweden in the UN General Assembly. As always, I feel the solemnity of being here. The gold emblem with the world map and olive branches gleams against green marble at the front of the room, the ceiling is endlessly high, around me are people from literally every country in the world.

I greet many familiar faces. Since becoming Minister for International Development Cooperation I've made countless trips all over the world, and I regularly meet ministers from many of the world's poorest countries. A number of them are Sweden's allies on ocean- and climate-related issues. The small Pacific states are inarguably among the most important and most influential on both issues – and they were the countries that, through mobilizing a High Ambition Coalition, were able to influence the world in the Paris climate negotiations so that the goal became 1.5 degrees instead of 2 degrees – which wouldn't have been possible if they hadn't joined forces with the very poorest countries and the most ambitious rich ones, including Sweden. Now we work together to push for more emphasis on oceans in climate negotiations and to unite the world around Agenda 2030's Sustainable Development Goal 14, the goal of healthy oceans.

On the stage in the General Assembly stands Nainoa Thompson, a Hawaiian sailor who learned from the world's last traditional Polynesian navigator to use know-how passed down through generations to navigate the world's oceans without any modern instruments, only by observing nature and the starry sky.

Nainoa is in his sixties, with hair the color of steel wool, a weather-beaten face, a thoughtful, almost mournful voice and a presence that fills the whole General Assembly Hall. He's spent the last twenty-five months at sea on a traditional double-hulled sailing canoe called Hōkūleʻa, and has just arrived in New York on the boat that is now moored down by the East River. He looks around the darkened room in a dazed squint, speaks haltingly, without notes, and tells us about his father and what he learned from him. That a good society is a society where we care about each other. Where we give each other training and education. Where everyone has a role. Simple words, but filled with meaning. Everyone is listening. Next, he talks about the sailing voyage he's made on Hōkūleʻa with his crew from the Polynesian Voyaging Society to gather testimony from people on how the ocean has changed. Tragic stories of overfishing, eutrophication, plastic waste, dying coral reefs, and rising sea levels, the same stories everywhere, from people all around the world's oceans.

"Behind Hōkūleʻa is a movement of millions of people, a movement coming from what is good inside every person", he says with a gesture towards his heart. "And what they are saying, the message coming out from the depth of their despair is this: you leaders, need to cooperate to save our planet!"

He continues by showing photographs from the canoe, the waves and the ocean, and finally the large wall is covered by a powerful image of the blue side of planet Earth, taken through the window of a space station by the Hawaiian astronaut Lacy Veach.

Nainoa lets the image glow in the darkened Assembly for a moment before he continues.

"When Lacy saw Hawaii out in the middle of the Pacific Ocean, he thought about his family down there on the islands, and he also thought about our ancestors who navigated by the stars in their canoes, out in the immense blue ocean, without maps or charts, and then it struck him that they were the astronauts of their time."

Nainoa squints out at the Assembly again.

"Now Lacy is not with us anymore But he said to us: prepare your starship. Go to the United Nations. Talk to the people. And tell the leaders that Earth is our only canoe in an infinite sea of dark and empty space. Tell them we have nowhere else to go."

*

There will soon be eight billion people on earth. Eleven billion by the end of this century. The age we live in is called the Anthropocene because humans are the defining factor on our planet, from the outer reaches of the atmosphere to the deepest point in the ocean. We've achieved this in a minimal span of time, geologically speaking. We humans. Not the Chinese, the Chileans, or Swedes. Not the Christians, Buddhists, or Muslims – but one single species out of millions on earth, the one with two legs, two arms, and a large brain in relation to its strangely upright, naked body. *Homo sapiens*. You and I.

How often do we identify this way? As human beings? It's not something we're taught as children, something that gives us a sense of pride or belonging. Instead, we learn our national anthems, go to church or mosque, and focus on the characteristics that differentiate our specific group of people from all others. The typical flute, food dish, folk costume or lore that we've preserved through the centuries and that makes us "us" and the others "them." We learn to ignore other people's problems and focus on our own – and forget about the ones we have in common. The ones that aren't part of our own specific narrative.

"Those who tell the stories run the world," writes British journalist George Monbiot in his book *Out of the Wreckage – A new Politics for an Age of Crisis*. What he means is that stories are humanity's way of sorting out the world and understanding it. Stories put borders on the map, leave out what doesn't fit, depict heroes and enemies, explain motivations, and describe a direction and a goal. Our way of thinking is driven completely by our tendency to create stories, and once a coherent story is in place it's almost impossible to dislodge. Facts and figures dangle in loose threads if they don't fit; anything that contradicts the story is rejected reflexively, and the more invested people are in the story, the more categorical the rejection. Entire life stories, the meaning of life for generations of people can hinge on a particular story being true. Family members may have died for it, you may have gone to war for it yourself and raised your children in it. This is why demonstrating that a story is false or harmful isn't enough to erase the story. There's only one way to get rid of a story, Monbiot says, and that is to replace it with another story.

In his book *Identity and Violence*, Indian political economist and Nobel laureate Amartya Sen illustrates the spiral of violence in identity politics and sectarianism. How quickly and unexpectedly the hate can flare up when it is fueled by what Sen describes as "the magical power of some allegedly predominant identity that drowns other affiliations, and in a conveniently bellicose form can also overpower any human sympathy natural kindness that we may normally have."

Amartya Sen recalls being eleven years old during the Hindu-Muslim riots of the 1940s and seeing a poor, Muslim laborer named Kader Mia stabbed while walking along his street, most likely by people who'd never seen him before. The young Amartya had held the bleeding man's head in his lap, unable to save his life, and he remembers how, as an eleven-year-old child, it was not only a frightening but also a deeply confusing experience. "Why should someone suddenly be killed? And why by people who did not even know the victim, who could not have done any harm to the killers? That Kader Mia would be seen as having only one identity – that of being a member of the 'enemy' community who 'should' be assaulted and if possible killed – seemed altogether incredible. For a bewildered child, the violence of identity was extraordinarily hard to grasp. It is not particularly easy even for a still bewildered elderly adult."

In his book, he describes the incomprehensible course of events, the speed in which "the broad human beings of January were suddenly transformed into the ruthless Hindus and fierce Muslims of July" because political agitators called for the killing on behalf of "our people." The same unimaginable experience is described by people from Rwanda, Burundi, Myanmar, Iraq, Somalia, Bosnia, Ukraine, Israel and Palestine.

One of the most emotionally trying visits I made as minister was to Sarajevo, where the wounds from the Bosnian War are still essentially wide open. The stories were grim and hit uncomfortably close to home. The people who told them were around my age, with clothing and skin color similar to mine, and they spoke with darkness in their eyes of horrors that had happened such a short time ago, such a short distance from the safe, secure European Union. The Srebrenica massacre. The mass graves. Sniper attacks from the slopes around Sarajevo that killed children in playgrounds, mothers blown up on their way to the store. The inhuman violence flared up almost overnight, and people who'd never even thought about their religious or ethnic affiliations were suddenly murdering each other, even their own neighbors, based on what is perceived as an overarching identity, more important than that of neighbor, friend, colleague, or human being.

But why should our nationality, religion, or ethnicity be our predominant identity? Why should circumstances that in most cases we can't even control, like where we're born, our skin color, or our religion, trump all other attributes a person can have: class, sex, political views, profession, or the multitude of other identities every one of us has, from being a parent, a child, young, old, rural, urban, member of a choir, football fan, homeowner, globetrotter, union representative, queer person, allergy sufferer, handyperson, intellectual, birdwatcher, or human? Why should my affinity with other Swedes be more important to me than my affinity with other women around the world? Why should "Christian" be more important to me than, for example, "animal lover"? Likely for no other reason than that people have told the stories that way for generations, and in so doing have made it all too easy for those who aspire to power to dehumanize "the others," thereby creating the will to fight and justifying invasions, purges and genocides.

But there's actually another story, about a united humanity. It's incredibly interesting, and important, because it's been written by humanity itself, and has quite recently been adopted by the UN General Assembly.

On September 25, 2015, after three years of intense negotiations and a consultation process involving millions of people and thousands of organizations – the most comprehensive in the history of the UN! – the gavel fell, and the whole General Assembly stood up and applauded for several minutes. The story established that day is about where humanity wants to be in 2030. Unlike previous strategies and goals negotiated within the UN, this time the world community didn't limit itself to identifying one or a few problems at a time, but instead did the exact opposite. For the first time, Agenda 2030 depicts the larger goal, what a sustainable, *interconnected* world must look like. All the relevant areas and dimensions of humans' needs and living conditions are identified and are woven into a single sustainability agenda, where the goals within the environmental, economic and social dimensions enhance each other and are mutually dependent.

The initiative for the agenda came from the conclusion of the big sustainability conference I attended in Rio in 2012. It was truly a great victory for civil society. To get the world to chisel out a holistic approach and realize that without it, the world can't eliminate poverty, create peace or save the planet. Realize that all the injustices and all the important areas need to be on the table at once, and all countries, rich and poor, must work together toward the same goals.

When all the important areas for the global community had been identified through the long consultation process, the result was no fewer than 17 Sustainable Development Goals (SDGs) – everything from full access to health care, education, and clean energy to protecting oceans, nature, and the climate, as well as gender equality and freedom from violence – with 169 associated targets that were all considered indispensable and often interconnected. Without living oceans, there could be no stable climate. Without equality and decreased disparities, no peaceful development. Without a stable climate, no food security.

Many synergies were also identified: gender equality leads to economic and social development, clean water to better health, protection of biological diversity to better climate resilience, food security and wellbeing. And so on.

What was negotiated was not the product of a clever consulting firm or political strategist looking for clear targets they knew could be reached within fifteen years so they could then declare progress; from that perspective, Agenda 2030 is clearly mission impossible. Nothing less than peace on earth, an end to poverty, gender equality, and sustainable management of the major planetary ecosystems is what must be achieved by 2030. But this is also the greatness in the agenda. That the world, despite all the pressure from the less ambitious, "realistic" member states, resisted the idea of decreasing the number of SDGs and whittling the targets down to a manageable number that could be committed to memory. Maybe it would have been easier to communicate about, say, ten goals – but the story isn't about the number of goals but the total package. Where we want to go as humanity, from a common perspective.

Most of Agenda 2030 is nothing new, though – values such as peace on earth, clean oceans and a healthy nature have long been recognized in other contexts, in conventions and resolutions. What's new is that the world now agrees that we must take a comprehensive approach and broaden our perspective, not narrow it, and that all countries are developing countries. Not everything is good in the rich countries and bad in the poor; all countries have a long way to go. And time is running short. We can't afford to take one problem at a time. Neither we humans nor the planet have the time or resources to continue destroying nature or trust between people.

So, what impact has the agenda made on the consciousness of humanity as a whole, halfway to its designated completion date? The short answer: very little. The slightly longer answer is that the agenda actually is used by governments, cities and companies all over the world to measure progress in sustainability and to decide what measures are needed to accomplish it. So, in practice, the agenda is an important tool. But the amazing potential in the shared *story* of the agenda, and about humanity's common understanding, is barely utilized at all, by any government, anywhere. In fact, it's used more commonly by forces trying to sow division and suspicion in the world, than by those that want to create a sense of community and collaboration. On the internet you can find a proliferation of conspiracy theories about what Agenda 2030 "actually" means and who is behind it, peppered with lies about what the agenda is meant to achieve: things like globalists taking over the world, forcibly vaccinating people and confiscating all private property.

But could Agenda 2030 even be established as a global story, a course of history that we believe in? Do we even have it in us as humans to believe in a common story? Has it ever happened before at a global level?

From a Western perspective, I can think of at least two clear stories that have characterized our view of the direction, purpose and meaning of global history and have included all of humanity. Both stories are linear and have a finish line we've already crossed. The first is the story of conquering, "discovering" and "civilizing" the whole planet. For centuries, this view of the world has driven history forward and affected all countries and cultures, whether or not they wanted it to. In this overarching story of human destiny, every blank spot on the map would be inventoried and claimed, every tiny component of its materials investigated – and its people, too, down to the smallest psychological nook and cranny. Science, reason and Western religious ideas would spread around the world, until goodness and reason had triumphed and wild, unbridled nature had been forced into submission to fulfill humankind's every need. Something like that.

The second global story of human civilization is the one that took place throughout the 1900s: the battle between major political ideologies. Which system would win? Large parts of the world took different sides in a worldwide struggle. There were world wars, there were intense debates, there were economic theories, the false doctrine of "racial biology," women's struggle for rights, revolutions; an avalanche of different currents gained leeway when science opened the door to human nature and thinkers all over the world started questioning established authorities like emperors, kings, nobility and the clergy. Fascism and Nazism lost the battle after several decades of horrific genocide and war, and most socialist and communist countries imploded a few centuries later from the pressure of their appalling crimes against their own people as well as shortages of goods and the lack of freedom of speech. In 1989 the Berlin Wall fell, and the Cold War was over. The Chinese communist state started to embrace a market economy, and author Francis Fukuyama declared in a famous book that humanity had now reached "the end of history."

So, presumably we've reached our goal – but which one? A democratic free-market system of government that in certain countries, including those in Scandinavia, had a strong welfare state at its core; in others, less strong. But the assumption was that the material wealth and peaceful development that had arisen through democratic free-market economics in Europe and the United States without serious competition from other ideologies would, slowly but surely, spread around the world and, with a little help from institutions such as the IMF, the World Bank and the World Trade Organization, abolish poverty and create peace.

Thirty years later, however, we have a world that looks totally different from what we might have expected based on this story. According to democracy index measurements, democracy in the world has been going backwards, not forwards, for a number of years. The free-market economy has not succeeded in abolishing poverty in the world; to the contrary, in many cases it has concentrated wealth and increased the disparities. It has also failed utterly to replace harmful goods and consumption patterns with others in a self-regulated way, not even when there is a demand for emission-free technology, and not even when the harm is so serious it jeopardizes the life-support system of the whole planet. And despite foreign aid and world trade, states continue to crumble in ethnic or religious conflicts that go on for generations – the most obvious being Afghanistan,

Palestine, Somalia, South Sudan, Liberia, Sierra Leone, the Democratic Republic of Congo, the Central African Republic, Mali, Myanmar, Yemen, Libya, Lebanon, Syria and Iraq – and young people in too many states can't plan for their future without either anticipating violence and atrocities or having to leave their own country. At the same time, entirely new players that weren't on the map when "the end of history" was declared have been established in the form of tech giants that own a staggering abundance of digital information and "big data," which in the wrong hands could, at any time, create a surveillance society that is virtually impossible to elude for any citizen, dissident or opposition figure. Artificial Intelligence is creating new dangers and possibilities that were not even imaginable just a few years ago. We seem to be approaching a perfect storm of global vulnerability: from pandemics to the climate crisis, economic crisis, crisis of democracy and crisis of values.

When history ended, the free market had won, most of earth had been discovered and we were linked together in global networks, what happened to our common story then? Did we get a new one, or are we still living in the same old one? Do we have the perfect society, where nothing needs to be changed? Do we still believe democracy will eventually triumph around the world, that global market liberalization and consumer empowerment will end poverty and stem the climate crisis, and that individualism will continue to liberate and fulfill humankind? And if we do believe this, how should we deal with the fact that even in countries where we have democracy and wealth, people aren't satisfied? When there are even many signs that *precisely* in countries where we've achieved the goals the common global story led us too, the mental illness, depression, loneliness and Seinfeldian neurotic discontent are greatest. Is this it? What happens now? Is this the end of the journey, the end of history: an endless series of workdays, vacations, and shopping sprees as the planet slowly dies?

The absence of a new, meaningful global story has also left the door wide open for other, backward-looking narratives that only grow stronger, told by leader after leader, from Erdoğan to Putin to el-Sisi in Egypt. A narrative that Trump, two years after Agenda 2030 was adopted, stood in the same General Assembly and unabashedly argued for. I was seated in the Swedish bench with PM Stefan Löfven as the world's leaders listened with growing astonishment to Trump's message to the UN, a message of "America First!" Not a word about Agenda 2030 or the importance of multilateral cooperation, but the more about what Trump believed every country should do: to put itself first, just like the US! *"You should do that too!"* He also announced that the US would no longer take any position regarding other countries' governance or traditions, as long as they didn't bother the US, which was a strong signal to the world's dictators and human rights abusers. "Strong, sovereign nations let their people take ownership of the future and control their own destiny," Trump summed it up confidently, as if walls and arms races could control climate crises, pandemics, or the spiral of conflicts and terrorism.

Once again, this question: "Why is it so difficult to do something, when everyone knows what needs to be done?" The answer can be sliced and diced any number of ways. We can find economic explanations, political, psychological, historical; these are all pieces of the puzzle. But I believe an extremely important part of the explanation is the story we tell about ourselves. The self-image we humans have. Do we see ourselves as egoistic by nature, competition-driven creatures, born with original sin, who must constantly wage a war of each against all – or do we see ourselves as empathetic, cooperative, social creatures with a desire to do good? Judging by the state of the world, we're capable of both, but judging by how we function in our daily lives, the vast majority of us, the vast majority of the time, without even thinking about it, seem to be decent, cooperative, empathetic, social citizens. But the predominant story of ourselves at the end of history is a totally different one.

Science has given us an extremely fragmented image of ourselves; different disciplines have broken humans down to the smallest cell and reptile brain and have placed us in evolution with the ultimate goal of spreading our own genes. Freud's theory that we are forced to socialize away from our inborn dark urges is still alive, as is the concept of a *Homo economicus* by definition driven by economic egoistic maximalist reasoning, and that civilization is moved forward by competition, that it's every man for himself and material wealth is the main motivation. Look out for number one. Rich equals happy.

At the same time, there is very little scientific evidence for any of the above. Hundreds of factors other than rational thinking steer our economic choices for example; otherwise advertising and branding would be a complete waste. And through modern psychology we know there's nothing to indicate that we're born as egoists, or that children naturally behave as in *Lord of the Flies* or that Freud's claim that the primary drivers of humankind are libido and the death instinct is true. To the contrary, the drive to be part of social communities and serve a purpose seems to be very strong and our capacity for love, empathy, and altruism very large. Innumerable humans have sacrificed their lives for a higher cause, be it a nation, a god, or their own children. Humans have what psychologists call a "hive switch," an ability to, like a bee in a beehive, rise above self-interest to a larger context together with others, a quality that has inarguably been far more important to our evolutionary survival than egoism, aggression, and competition. We would never have come this far as a species without cooperation and empathy, no matter how smart we were.

But our herd instincts can also lead to fatal missteps, and this is what the significant philosophical, scientific and psychological advancements of the past century have illustrated, which has given us tools to deal with and understand them. The era of major scientific and geographic discovery was necessary so that we could move beyond what were in many cases feudal societies dominated by dictators and religious leaders. The liberal political movement and focus on the individual gave us the tools to resist and question collectivist oppression. But today it's clear we need a new story of humanity to give our situation meaning and map out our next steps. So, how could it be formulated?

UN General Secretary António Guterres got a similar question from the UN member states in 2021, and in his response, "Our Common Agenda," he writes that humanity is at in inflection point and must choose "a breakdown or a breakthrough." Those are dramatic words, but everything science can tell us about our situation on this wonderful little blue planet, with its thin cloak of water and fragile potential for life, proves him absolutely right. Either we step up now, or the world breaks down. The story of ourselves can't be backward-looking, nor can it continue down the path we know is wrong; we need to take the next evolutionary step for human civilization. The journey we've taken as humanity so far is astonishing. Our social constructions and exploration of reality have brought us extremely far, but we have in no way reached an endpoint. In the best case, there is no end to history, but if we're going to make it to the next stage, we need to reassess both who we are and what it means to us to be here on earth.

Individualism and the free market economy have liberated the world from brutal dictatorships and collective terrors, but they've also made people lonely and unhappy and haven't given us the answer to how to solve the global problems that threaten the existence of the whole planet. To solve them we need to get rid of destructive conceptions of humans themselves, not only the played-out psychological theories about humans' "animal" instincts, or the market-economy postulations of a human as a *Homo economicus* who seeks to maximize personal benefit, but also equally strange religious ideas that focus on an inherited original sin and a paradise beyond life, something that diverts attention from life here and now and undermines our will to act and to care about *this* world.

In other words, we're in need of a serious revision of what we regard as "normal." Just as the eleven-year-old Amartya Sen asked himself how it can be possible for people to kill each other without cause, we must all go to our inner eleven-year-old and question the premises underlying our society, the ones that have steered us so terribly wrong. Most of us have a gut feeling when something is wrong. Destroying our planet, killing our neighbors. What would happen, then, if we simply stopped accepting the premise, in politics or in our everyday lives, that egoistic actions by states or individuals is part of our human nature? If instead we started from humanity's overwhelming capacity for empathy, including toward animals and nature, and our hardwired instinct to cooperate and take responsibility for future generations? Could we start to build a new sense of togetherness, both in local society and in the global community, in the knowledge that the only way we can weather the storm is together? Guterres puts it simply: "Humanity's welfare – and indeed, humanity's very future – depend on solidarity and working together as a global family to achieve common goals."

*

The word "trust" is often repeated in international contexts. So hard, and so easy, actually. As long as trust is there, we can reach agreement on all the difficult things. That we should help each other, that we should ban what is bad, that our interests are essentially the same, that we're all in the same boat – or canoe, if you like. With a new self-image, based on what we now know about ourselves, trust is simply there for the taking. It's human nature to be true to our word, to work together, to have goodwill. Not to betray each other. To be ashamed when we hurt the weak.

When selfishness is no longer the accepted starting point in either international policy or psychology and can't be excused – not even by those who claim it's a virtue – then trust will be self-evident.

Is what I'm describing a sacrifice for the world's richest countries? I really don't think so. I think people have such a strong yearning for meaning, for a goal that's bigger than ourselves. To end poverty, to let the earth heal, to grow as a person – these goals go a long way.

But the sustainable society isn't just global, abstract, far away. It's also about local influence and community. It's very much about living here and now, building a local societal culture where everyone participates, about filling the word "solidarity" with a meaning that doesn't exclude those who don't have a job to go to, and that doesn't burn out those who do. A society where people have roles to fill and can develop and find happiness and pride in contributing to a community, without being reduced to passive consumers.

As soon as we accept and incorporate two simple premises, the possibilities will be wide open. The first is that we are good, not evil. The second is that it is cooperation, not competition, that gives us the power we so desperately need right now. The power to save the planet, and ourselves.

*

Another story is much shorter. Also this one I heard in the UN General Assembly, this time from a female astronaut who spoke about her experiences seeing Earth from space, without national borders, vibrating, spinning, living, impossibly beautiful, all alone in empty space. She said: "It became so clear. Earth is our spaceship. But we, humans, are not the passengers. We are the crew."

CHAPTER 13

The Oceanic Feeling

WHAT AN INCREDIBLE privilege it's been to participate in democracy as an elected politician. It's been tough
at times, but it's also been thrilling to be included in a
human-created system that actually spans the globe. Where
we meet each other, help each other, debate, reach agreement.
Where we discover that we are more alike than different.

I remember the women I met on the mountainside
outside La Paz, Bolivia. With their children on their backs,
their characteristic and striking black bowler hats, their
colorful striped shawls. In the background was the retreating
Illimani glacier, which within a few decades might disappear, taking with it the drinking-water supply for millions of
people. The women proudly showed me the crops they were
growing, always addressing me in the same way. *Hermana
ministra*, look at this; *hermana ministra*, listen to this. If the
glacier disappears, we won't be able to live here anymore.

Sister minister.

I remember the thousands of internally displaced people
in the camp outside Juba in the world's youngest country,
South Sudan, who had fled their homes due to conflicts
created by the pursuit of natural resources, primarily oil.
People who had hoped independence would give them
freedom and prosperity but who had only fallen prey to
more violence. When I told them I had just met their pres-

ident, Salva Kiir, the weathered old guerrilla leader with the cowboy hat and the heavy, gold wristwatch, the appointed leader of the refugees said, "He's not our leader! Our leaders are you, the UN. The UN must help us!"

I remember the children in blue UNICEF t-shirts in the world's largest refugee camp, Dadaab, in Kenya near the Somali border, chanting a rhyme they'd learned in school: "Education, education, education! Gives freedom to generations, generations, generations!"

So happy, so full of hope. Their homes were UNHCR tarps reinforced by sticks in the middle of the desert. Every one of them dreamed of becoming a doctor, teacher or police officer.

I remember the girl in the construction program in Somalia's capital, Mogadishu, who was so proud to be learning a trade to literally rebuild the war-ravaged country. I remember the desperate Syrian refugees in Beirut who weren't allowed to find work because Lebanon didn't want them to stay. I remember the hands that clung to mine when I had to leave the internal camp for female victims of violence within the larger refugee camp in Kenya. One, named Mary, was orphaned; her mother had died when she was fourteen just as my mom died when I was fourteen, but while I lived in security, she was unprotected in every sense: a refugee born in a refugee camp, without family, without anywhere to call her home or her country, shunned, branded by other refugees for various reasons. She was no one. She had no one. She ran after the UN car, knocked on the window. She really wanted me to take her out of there. What if I could have? What if she could've become someone else, been given another chance, the same chance I had?

All those meetings with the leaders of poor countries, all the political messages I'd delivered as Minister for International Development Cooperation, all the handshakes, all the dark wood and gold-embellished chairs in rooms with fluorescent lighting and frigid air conditioning where I'd sat and said that Sweden is happy to be your partner, but that we want environmentally sustainable development, we want women to have a seat at the table, we want corruption to end and rule of law to be established, we want an end to the persecution of dissenters and an end to tribal conflicts. All those meetings, when the answer was always, without fail: Yes, absolutely, but we need more help. Invest in our country. Help us!

Swedish aid is important and saves lives, but at the same time I know, obviously, that the sliver of resources we supply can effect only marginal change if at the same time a constant flood of money, investments and interests, with no conditions other than self-interest, gushes forth from countries, corporations and corrupt leaders enriching themselves. How can citizens ever take control of their own destiny, then? Without education, without a functioning constitutional state, without food on the table? It's a vicious cycle, and this vicious cycle stretches all the way to us. We are all impacted by war and conflict, even if it is far away. The destruction of our ocean and damage to our climate aren't confined to any country. And our gasoline at the pump, and our savings invested in Swedish oil companies, feed the conflicts in South Sudan. We can't ignore that it's all interconnected. That we all impact each other.

*

The oceanic feeling. I feel it when a calling woodpecker suddenly flies overhead with its red-and-white belly and dark wings against the blue sky, I feel it when the moon hangs vast and orange on the horizon, I feel it in a cat's soft paw, in the rainbow glint of snow crystals in the sun, in the beauty of a butterfly, in the tenacious twisting of an old pine to withstand the ocean strong winds. The oceanic feeling is everywhere. It's the exhilaration, the humility, the connection, the feeling of being a part of the living world.

The oceanic feeling spreads out in all directions, but perhaps especially in three dimensions. One between all living things and creation, that exhilarating feeling of our own boundaries dissolving when we make contact with animals, with nature. One between humans when we work toward the same goal, when we become part of a community, when we forget our own egos in the service of something greater than ourselves. And a third exists in time. When the present, past and future are united in a single now, a single moment where we're carried forward by what came before us, and where we're the key to what comes after us. When we meet our grandchild's gaze, or decipher messages from the past, things engraved, things thought by someone like us thousands of years ago. The oceanic feeling runs through the world, and through us, in all of these directions, and our selves are a part of all of this, a part of the universe, no more, and certainly no less.

Nobel laureate and author Romain Rolland wrote a letter in 1927 to the founder of psychoanalysis, Sigmund Freud, and commented on Freud's book about the origin of religion, *Die Zukunft einer Illusion* (The Future of an Illusion). Rolland agreed with the substance of Freud's criticism of the Abrahamic religions, but there was one thing missing. Freud hadn't mentioned the spontaneous religious feeling in humans, the feeling of contact with something bigger, something eternal, without limits: what Rolland calls an "oceanic feeling". And he describes how he himself, with no need for church dogma or holy texts, constantly feels the oceanic feeling "like a sheet of water which I feel flushing under the bark." But, as he also points out, "without affecting in any way my critical faculties and my freedom to exercise them"! "I think you will classify it also under the Zwangsneurosen (obsessional neurosis)," he suggests to Freud, but the oceanic feeling is always a "rich and beneficent power," a "source of vital renewal," a true "religious energy."

Freud replies to Rolland's letter in his book *Civilization and its Discontents*. In his characteristically authoritative tone, Freud doesn't rule out the existence of such a thing as an oceanic feeling, nor does he think it "has to be pathological." But if it exists he relegates it to a memory of the "narcissistic" stage of infancy in which the child sees the external world and its mother as extensions of itself. Freud himself had never felt an oceanic feeling. But by all means, he is not going to deny it, and could acknowledge that the feeling could be commonly occurring, as Rolland claimed.

But Freud did not go on to analyze the oceanic feeling, which was what Rolland had asked him to do, but instead continued to put forward his theories of humans as a basically sexually neurotic creatures driven by primarily the death drive and the Oedipus complex, ideas that have made an enormous impact on the human self-image in the Western world for more than a hundred years, through psychology as well as through story-telling in literature and film. If the oceanic feeling, as Rolland described it, had instead become an established concept in modern humanity's understanding of itself, maybe the world would look different today. Maybe reverence for nature would be an accepted feeling, as well as connection to something greater. Maybe the three solidarities the Green movement is based on – solidarity with animals and nature, solidarity with all humans in the world, and solidarity with future generations – would have an easier time asserting themselves as a natural basis for economics, policy, and human relations. Maybe cynicism and egoism based on prevailing notions of humanity's inborn destructive nature wouldn't be quite as socially acceptable. Maybe it would be easier for us to reach each other?

*

A few months after I became minister, the Ministry of Foreign Affairs was contacted by Kiribati, a small island nation on the international date line in the Pacific Ocean, on the other side of the globe. Their president, Anote Tong, wanted to come to Sweden and meet with me. He'd read my book *Silent Seas - The Fish Race to the Bottom* and wanted to discuss a cooperation between Sweden and Kiribati in the areas of ocean and climate.

And so, in March 2015, he made the first-ever official visit from Kiribati to Sweden. President Tong turned out to be a warm, wise and charismatic person with an urgent problem. He told me he was watching his country disappear. That the slowly rising sea level is eating its way into the atolls centimeter by centimeter, that salt water is entering the precious drinking water supply, that topsoil is being destroyed. That the main island, Tarawa, whose highest point is only two meters above sea level, is struck by increasingly frequent, violent hurricanes with tidal waves washing inland, and that there is now an evacuation plan for the whole island. The 120,000 residents will have nowhere to go when the time comes, so the government has purchased land on the mountainous neighboring island nation, Fiji. Kiribati's strategy, which is already underway, is to encourage its young population to leave the islands, using the motto "Migration with Dignity." The country is also studying the international legal implications when the islands disappear beneath the ocean's surface. Who will have the rights to the fishing grounds and the economic zone that belongs to citizens of Kiribati? The

UN Convention on the Law of the Sea did not anticipate this situation.

President Tong was understandably extremely concerned, but also determined to do what he could for future generations. He asked me to look at different concrete projects to combat rising sea levels, such as digging up sand from the bottom of the lagoon and placing it on land, building flood barriers, or planting mangroves. It was heartbreaking to hear. The rising sea levels his people must plan for are already carved in calving Antarctic glaciers. And the residents of Kiribati didn't put themselves in this position, we did. My country, and other countries like mine. All of us who, thanks to many decades of unchecked consumption of the earth's resources and emissions of greenhouse gases, are doing well. He didn't need to convince me of this, I already knew it. Oceans separated us, both geographically and culturally, but as human beings we both knew that what's been allowed to happen is wrong – very wrong.

President Tong traveled on to other countries in Europe, but our meeting left me no peace. That this gray-haired man had come to Sweden, to me, to tell me about his country – I couldn't just let it go. When I started my term as Minister for International Development Cooperation, Sweden had bilateral development cooperation with more than thirty countries and regional development strategies for Africa, Latin America and Asia, but none that extended to Oceania and all of the small, vulnerable island nations that are in the same situation as Kiribati. And so my meeting with President Tong was the start of what would become a new Swedish aid strategy that included ocean and climate issues in the Pacific, and for Sweden's initiative, together with Fiji, to organize the first UN Ocean conference around SDG 14 (UNOC) in 2017.

The year after my meeting with Tong in Sweden, I had

the opportunity to reciprocate his visit. Sweden supported a regional oceans conference for countries in the South Pacific, and I was invited as guest of honor. The conference took place in Tonga's capital city, Nuku'alofa, and when it was over I would travel on to Kiribati.

At first it was a bewildering experience, meeting at the conference with leaders of the Pacific Island nations in Melanesia, Polynesia, and Micronesia and discussing what we had in common: overfishing, plastic marine litter and the climate crisis. I had a lei placed around my neck as did all the other leaders, and I was surprisingly moved when the Bishop of Tonga eloquently and engagingly blessed the conference, saying it clearly had a special meaning. The mood prevailed throughout the discussions; the bishop struck a sort of tone rarely found in politics. He talked about purpose. He gave the impression that the participants had a mission, a job to do.

Afterwards I spoke with the Tongan fisheries minister, Semisi Fakahau, a friendly, white-bearded man dressed in a navy blazer and the black skirt often worn by men in the Pacific Islands, with its accompanying arrangement of braided bast fiber around the waist. I told him about the problems in the Baltic Sea, and he told me about the problems in the Pacific Ocean. He said that when he was a child, the adults used to bring a dolphin or a sea turtle or some large fish and shut them inside a small lagoon so the children could play with them. Several children at a time could climb onto the dolphin's back and play all day long. Then the animals were released. Fakahau also remembered how the turtles that were caught for food were laid out on their backs on the beach, and that when he walked past them on the way to school he could see them crying, tears falling from their eyes. I listened, fascinated, and suddenly he started talking about what the ocean means to him today. One day he'd realized he was depressed, and his grandmother, who was still living, told him he needed to go down to the ocean. So he did. He lay under a palm tree for a few days. And the ocean washed away his worries, gave him back his energy.

"I love the ocean," Fakahau said with the gentle dignity that characterizes Pacific Island leaders. "But I'm afraid the ocean is not a comfort to younger people anymore. Our beloved ocean is now raising because of climate change, threatening us, our islands and cultures."

*

We approach Kiribati after several hours in the air with nothing out the window but sky and ocean. Suddenly we begin to descend, and at first I can't see the island where the plane is going to land, but then I discover a very narrow strip of land in the middle of the blue. It's the densely populated main island, Tarawa, surrounded by water in all directions. The vast, pulsating Pacific Ocean in one direction, the still, turquoise lagoon on the other.

I'm the first Swedish minister to visit the country. But thanks to President Tong's active outreach, ministers from several other countries have been here, as has UN Secretary General Ban Ki-moon. Surprisingly enough, the car that picks me up has Swedish flags provisionally attached to the rearview mirrors, and because I know that only two flights arrive here each week, I understand how much effort must have gone into such a welcoming detail.

The road through Tarawa is easily the worst road I've ever driven on. It takes almost longer to drive one or two kilometers than to walk, because the driver is constantly dodging meter-deep, water-filled potholes. After a long, unspeakably bumpy drive we suddenly came to an excellent asphalt road. It turns out that the Japanese had built it in exchange for fishing rights. And that when they couldn't agree on terms for continued fishing rights, Japan had stopped building the road after a few kilometers. It's been this way for many years now.

Tarawa is very poor, and while it may have a blue lagoon and palm trees, it's far from the Pacific paradise it could be. Slummy development sprawls into every available area of this narrow piece of land. Walls and sandbags line the beaches, and out in the lagoon, which is heavily polluted by untreated sewage, I see barges with excavators on them, digging up sand to be placed on land in an attempt to protect the island from floods.

My visit to Kiribati is earthshaking. Nowhere else have I come across such a concrete image of a whole culture threatened by climate change. In Bolivia and Bangladesh, which I've also visited, many more people will be forced to move due to the climate crisis, but very few currently have plans to leave their country. Here, they do.

I meet school children and young people who all talk about Australia, Fiji or New Zealand as their future, all according to the country's strategy to migrate with dignity. I visit the new, modern fish processing plant that was built with the help of foreign aid but has never really gotten up and running. The distance is too great to transport fresh fish to the market in California, and the Japanese are much quicker and drive the prices down. The fish are caught in Kiribati waters, but the profits flow elsewhere.

We visit some of the other islands by boat and have amazing encounters with people. Kiribati traditions are part of the people's daily lives. We see that the culture here is alive, the dance performances aren't for tourists – there are no tourists to speak of here – but for the islanders themselves. There's nothing artificial in our hosts expecting us to take part in both the dancing and the ceremonies. And time never seems to be a scarce commodity. I have to brush aside my Western stress and ministerial rigidity a few times, like the time I'm earnestly instructed to ask the god of the ocean for permission to visit an island, and it turns out the god of the ocean is hanging out at least an hour's walk away through rough terrain. But all I can do is follow, do what people do here, what they've always done here but, incomprehensibly as it seems, may not be doing for many decades longer.

On one of the islands we visit a white, weather-beaten church along the beach, and we can see it's bound to vanish into the ocean. Inside it's basically just four walls with a stained glass window and flaking paint. The villagers' attempt to protect it by building a wall along the shoreline seems to have come to a halt. The wall has eroded, and when the storms come the church is flooded. I walk down to the water's edge and take a picture of this man's futile battle against the ocean, so full of symbolism.

On the final evening, we're starting to prepare ourselves to return home to a completely different reality, but the residents of the village we're visiting don't let themselves be stressed by our watching the clock and wanting to get going. By now we've learned that it's common courtesy and showing of respect in this country to never go against your host's wishes, not even if you're a minister. It's getting dark and we're getting more and more stressed when the village leader finally accepts that we're leaving, after a lot of food that needed sampling, a lot of dancing, and some disappointment. Tradition actually dictates that strangers should sleep over, which there obviously wasn't time for.

With some relief we hurry toward our boat, which is moored a long way out in the shallow lagoon. I and the whole Swedish delegation take off our shoes, roll up our pants and start wading out as the stars light up one by one. Soon we find ourselves in a surreally illumined, shimmering disk of sea under a cupola of cloud-strewn starry sky. The moon is at its zenith as we wade through warm, translucent water. Hundreds of meters along the coral sand seafloor; bits of hard coral stick up here and there, but they're sparse enough that you can feel your way along with your toes and keep gazing at the sky. Orion's Belt, the Southern Cross – four stars with one star in the middle – shine above our heads, the water splashes around our legs, otherwise the silence is absolute. Not one electric light, not one sign of civilization anywhere, only us in this place in the middle of the blue side of the planet, with nothing but horizon in all directions, thousands of kilometers from any continent. The oceanic feeling surges through my body. It's like a space walk on earth.

*

On July 5–9, 2017, Sweden and Fiji hosted the largest UN oceans conference ever, the first conference to focus on one of the UN's Sustainable Development Goals. We worked in partnership throughout the process and received a lot of recognition for our ability to cooperate and be generous with what our respective countries could contribute. The conference had thousands of attendees, from governments as well as industry, civil society and the scientific community. Partnership dialogues were conducted throughout the week at the United Nations Headquarters in New York regarding all the important problem areas listed in UN Sustainable Development Goal 14, which is about saving the oceans.

The conference resulted in more than a thousand voluntary committments from different stakeholders, from adopting marine protected areas to allocating money to various efforts. The conference also decided to have a follow-up process, and the baton was passed to Portugal and Kenya to organize the next major oceans conference in 2022, where the measures would be followed up along with each of the targets adopted under UN Sustainable Development Goal 14. Another result of the conference was the appointment of Peter Thomson as the UN Secretary Generals Special Envoy for the Ocean. The oceans conference also resulted in a negotiated document – "Our Ocean, Our Future: Call for Action" – which identifies everything the ocean requires of us: cross-border cooperation and cross-sectorial approaches; a holistic approach, which is so much harder to achieve than working on one small detail at a time as global marine policies do today, with responsibilities for fisheries, pollution, the climate, shipping, the ocean floor, social responsibility and research are all held by different organizations with different mandates: the FAO, UNEP, IMO, ISA, RFMOs, UNFCCC and UNESCO. And issues involving the Arctic and Antarctic and everything that happens on land that affects our oceans are handled by still other organizations. The ocean is one water body, but humanity's efforts to take care of it, utilize it and try to manage it are myriad and fragmented and have thus far been ineffective.

Yet everyone knows how important the ocean is to life on earth. In the final resolution, which I had the great honor of gaveling through from the high podium in the UN General Assembly together with Fijian Prime Minister Frank Bainimarama, the world agreed on the following sentence. "We recognise that the wellbeing of present and future generations is inextricably linked to the health and productivity of our ocean."

The ocean is the rule, the earth the exception. The ocean gives us all life, and has no national borders. The ocean demands something of us, and we can do it, as long as the political will is there. Cooperate. Prioritize what's most important. What is self-evident, if we just let the oceanic feeling guide us.

Thanks

THIS BOOK TOOK many years to write, and it's impossible to thank everyone who's helped me in various ways. Still, I want to extend a special thank you to those of you who read texts and offered your opinions during the final stages, and to those of you who quickly answered factual questions by email, especially Eva Svedling, Lasse Nilsson, Gunnar Harrius, Martin Linton, Fredrik Hannerz, Martin Visbeck, Callum Roberts, Sam Dupont and Beatrice Gorez. I'm so grateful for your time, without you, the book wouldn't have been possible. I also want to extend a very big thank you to my Swedish publisher Richard Herold for all the trust and work he put in me and this book.

But above all, I want to thank my wise, dedicated staff and collaborators over the years, a few of them already mentioned above. I also want to mention the super-team Ulrika Ekfeldt, Michael Earle, Staffan Danielsson, Eva Winqvist and Axel Naver in the European Parliament. And the other super teams at the Ministry of Foreign Affairs and the Ministry of Environment Ulrika Modéer, Gunvor G Ericson, Annika Jacobson, Sven Elander, Alev Nybladh, Annika Flensburg, Gabriel Liljenström, Jakob Lundgren, Liza Pettersson, Anders Mankler, Mikaela Kotschack, Katarina Hellström, Magda Rasmusson, Julia Finnsiö, Maud Larsen plus a few other excellent collaborators that worked shorter terms with me. The brilliant civil servants at the different ministries I can't mention, because they are just too many, I will just mention two names, because they were brave enough to participate in the photo on the signing of the climate law: Julia Hector and Alexandra von Linde. Thank you for your courage and generosity. All these teams have made magic things happen – including some amazing successes described in this book, and I want to thank you all from the bottom of my heart. A huge thanks also to all the other party members, elected or not, in the party board and in the Swedish parliament and environmentalists at all levels who has fought with me, from grassroots to party spokespersons. You are the foundation of democracy; without you, the whole building teeters. I'm proud to be a part of your community.

Finally, I want to thank all the wise people who have written books and articles that have widened my horizons and deepened my knowledge, many of them mentioned among the sources in the following pages. And of course a great thanks to everyone that I have worked with internationally, many of which are doing a tremendously important jobs at the EU or in the UN without much public recognition. Thank you, we trust in you.

And also, thank you to the voters. Without you – nothing.

Sources

Chapter 1: The Ocean

Brittle stars affected by ocean acidification:

Sam Dupont et al: "Near-future level of CO2-driven ocean acidification radically affects larval survival and development in the brittlestar *Ophiothrix fragilis*," *Marine Ecology Progress Series*, vol. 373, p. 285– 294, 2008.

Mussel larvae affected:

Alexander Ventura et al: "Maintained larval growth in mussel larvae exposed to acidified under-saturated seawater," *Scientific Reports*, vol. 6, article 23728, 2016.

Ocean acidification thresholds:

Narimane Dorey et al: "Assessing physiological tipping point of sea urchin larvae exposed to a broad range of pH," *Global Change Biology*, vol.19, nr 11, p. 3355–3367, 2013.

Tjalling Jager et al: "Near-future ocean acidification impacts maintenance costs in sea-urchin larvae: Identification of stress factors and tipping points using a DEB modelling approach," *Journal of Experimental Marine Biology and Ecology*, vol. 474, p. 11–17, 2016.

Acidic shrimp taste worse:

Sam Dupont et al: "First evidence of altered sensory quality in shellfish exposed to decreased pH relevant to ocean acidification," *Journal of Shellfish Research*, vol. 33, no. 3, p. 857–861, 2014.

Living space in the ocean:

https://science.nasa.gov/earth-science/oceanography/living-ocean
https://ocean.si.edu/planet-ocean/seafloor/just-how-big-ocean

Ocean relative to the size of the Earth:

US Geological Survey: https://www.usgs.gov/special-topics/water-science-school/science/how-much-water-there-earth

Microbes in seawater:

https://ocean.si.edu/ocean-life/microbes/marine-microbes

Combined length of viruses:

Curtis A. Suttle: "Viruses in the sea," *Nature*, vol. 437, no. 15, p. 356–361, 2005.

Expeditions of Thor and Olav Heyerdahl:

Thor Heyerdahl: *Kon-Tiki*, trans. F.H. Lyon, Rand McNally, 1950.

Håvard Jenssen, Anders Berg: *The Tangaroa Expedition*, 2007.

Thor Heyerdahl's speech at UNEP, 1982:

Sylvia A. Earle: *The World Is Blue – How Our Fate and the Ocean's Are One*, National Geographic, p. 157, 2009.

Global thermohaline conveyor belt:

World Ocean Review 2010, Maribus, Future Oceans Kiel Marine Sciences p. 18–22, 2010: https://oceanrep.geomar.de/22086/

Overfishing and ecosystem flips:

Daniel Pauly: *Vanishing Fish: Shifting Baselines and the Future of Global Fisheries*, Greystone Books, 2019.

Daniel Pauly: *In a Perfect Ocean: The State of Fisheries and Ecosystems in the North Atlantic Ocean*, Island Press, 2003.

"After almost 3 decades, cod are still not back off N.L. Scientists worry it may never happen," The Canadian Press, CBC News, 19 April 2021.

Carbon binding in the ocean:

United Nations Environment Programme (UNEP): *Blue Carbon: The Role of Healthy Oceans in Binding Carbon*, 2009.

Ralph Chami et al.: "Nature's Solution to Climate Change – A strategy to protect whales can limit greenhouse gases and global warming," *Finance & Development*, vol. 56, no. 4, December 2019.

Daniele Bianchi et al: "Estimating global biomass and biogeochemical cycling of marine fish with and without fishing," *Science Advances*, vol. 7, no. 41, 2021.

"How whales help cool the Earth," BBC/Future Planet, 20 January 2021: https://www.bbc.com/future/article/20210119-why-saving-whales-can-help-fight-climate-change

"Bottom trawling releases as much carbon as air travel, landmark study finds," *The Guardian*, 17 March 2021: https://www.theguardian.com/environment/2021/mar/17/trawling-for-fish-releases-as-much-carbon-as-air-travel-report-finds-climate-crisis

Enric Sala et al: "Protecting the global ocean for biodiversity, food and climate,"

Nature 592, p. 397–402, 2021: https://www.nature.com/articles/
s41586-021-03371-z

Ocean acidification; coral reefs dying:
IPCC: *Special Report on the Oceans and Cryosphere in a Changing Climate*, 2019.

Impact on calcareous marine algae:
World Ocean Review 2010, Maribus, Future Oceans Kiel Marine Sciences,
p. 36–43, 2010.
Callum Roberts: *Ocean of Life: How our Seas are Changing*, p. 96–108, Allen Lane,
2012.
Andrea Niemi et al. "Biological Impact of Ocean Acidification in the Canadian
Arctic: Widespread Severe Pteropod Shell Dissolution in Amundsen
Gulf," *Frontiers in Marine Science*, vol. 8, article 600184, March 2021.
Lisette Mekkes et al.: "Effects of Ocean Acidification on Calcification of the
Sub-Antarctic Pteropod *Limacina retroversa*," *Frontiers in Marine
Science*, vol. 8, article 581432, March 2021.

Gulf Stream weakening:
Levke Caesar et al: "Current Atlantic Meridional Overturning Circulation
weakest in last millennium," *Nature Geoscience*, 14, 118–120, 2021.
"Ny forskning: Golfströmmen har mattats av upp emot 20 procent," SVT, 21
February 2021: https://www.svt.se/nyheter/utrikes/varningen-golf-
strommen-kan-stanna-helt-1

Joanie Kleypas reaction:
"Ocean of life: How Our Seas Are Changing by Callum Roberts," *The Times*, 20
May 2012: https://www.thetimes.co.uk/article/ocean-of-life-how-our-
seas-are-changing-by-callum-roberts-m8zj3wcb6bq
"Saving the oceans: 'Mission Possible'," Environmental News Network, 25
February 2009: https://www.enn.com/articles/39367-saving-the-
oceans--mission-possible
Adam McKay: *Don't Look Up*, Netflix, 2021.

Chapter 2: Political Communication

**Sweden highest ranked by Climate Action Network and Germanwatch *Climate
Performance Index* (2018, 2019, 2020 and 2021):**
https://ccpi.org/wp-content/uploads/climate_change_performance_
index_2018_20503.pdf
https://ccpi.org/download/the-climate-change-performance-index-2019/
https://newclimate.org/wp-content/uploads/2019/12/CCPI-2020-Results_Web_
Version.pdf

https://www.germanwatch.org/en/19552

Left Party's priorities in budget negotiations for parliamentary term 2014–2018:

"Reformer för välfärd och jämlikhet," Vänsterpartiet, 2018: https://www.vansterpartiet.se/app/uploads/2018/04/reformer-budget-18.pdf

Resource consumption if everyone lived as Swedes live, compared with other countries:

https://www.overshootday.org/newsroom/country-overshoot-days/

Total carbon emissions from countries with less than 2 percent of global emissions greater than China's and India's combined:

"When it comes to emissions, the 'too small to matter' argument is absurd, reckless and morally bankrupt," *The Guardian*, 9 January 2020: https://www.theguardian.com/australia-news/2020/jan/09/when-it-comes-to-emissions-the-too-small-to-matter-argument-is-absurd-reckless-and-morally-bankrupt

"This Interactive Chart Shows Changes in the World's Top 10 Emitters," World Resources Institute: https://www.wri.org/insights/interactive-chart-shows-changes-worlds-top-10-emitters

Moderates against raising ambitions in EU:

"Klimathotet: M:s EU-röst överraskar – valde lägst ambitionsnivå," *Svenska Dagbladet*, 7 October 2020: https://www.svd.se/ms-eu-rost-overraskar--valde-lagst-ambitionsniva

"Europaparlamentet: EU måste införa koldioxidtullar på importvaror," *Europaportalen*, 11 March 2021: https://www.europaportalen.se/2021/03/europaparlamentet-eu-maste-infora-koldioxidtullar-pa-importvaror

Sweden's climate law and climate policy framework:

"Ett klimatpolitiskt ramverk för Sverige," Government's proposition, 2016/17:146, 9 March 2017: https://www.regeringen.se/rattsliga-dokument/proposition/2017/03/prop.-201617146

Establishment of *Industriklivet* and large budget allocations:

"Den största investeringen någonsin för ett grönt samhällsbygge," Ministry of the Environment and Energy, Fakta-PM, 4 September 2017: https://mb.cision.com/Public/4172/2338743/bba2908c3f667fc6.pdf

Fossil-Free Sweden established, 2016:

"Så ska företagen bli fossilfria," press release, Swedish government, 8 July 2016: https://www.regeringen.se/pressreleasen/2016/07/sa-ska-foreta-gen-bli-fossilfria/

Fossil-Free Sweden's 22 roadmaps:

"Färdplaner för fossilfri konkurrenskraft – uppföljningsrapport 2021," Fossilfritt Sverige, 2021: https://fossilfrittsverige.se/wp-content/uploads/2021/10/Fardplaner_for_fossilfrikonkurrenskraft_uppfo%CC%88ljningsrapport_2021.pdf

EU Emissions Trading System reform:

"Svenska förslaget vände allt: 'Det har varit helt galna år'," *Svenska Dagbladet*, 9 October 2021: https://www.svd.se/svenska-forslaget-vande-allt-varit-helt-galna-ar

Swedish government: "Svenskt initiativ minskar utsläppsutrymmet inom EU ETS," 3 September 2020: https://mb.cision.com/Main/4172/3188158/1302025.pdf

Sale of Vattenfall coal mines, introduction of "Emission Brakes":

"Köp av utsläppsrätter ska göra brunkolen mindre lönsam," Isabella Lövin and Karolina Skog in DN Debatt, *Dagens Nyheter*, 2 July 2016: https://www.dn.se/debatt/kop-av-utslappsratter-ska-gora-brunkolen-mindre-lonsam/

Best in party leader debate on SVT's "Agenda," 8 May 2018, according to SVT/ Novus survey:

"De var bäst i SVT:s partiledardebatt i Agenda – enligt tittarna," svt.se, 6 May 2018: https://www.svt.se/nyheter/inrikes/de-var-bast-i-debatten-enligt-tittarna

Fact-checking of Arctic ice melt:

"Mestadels fel av Isabella Lövin om isavsmältningen i Arktis," *Dagens Nyheter*, 9 May 2018: https://www.dn.se/nyheter/politik/mestadels-fel-av-isabella-lovin-om-isavsmaltningen-i-arktis/

Chapter 3: The Glacier

Landownership in Greenland:

https://www.businessingreenland.gl/da/Planl%C3%A6gning-og-Arealanvendelse/Arealtildeling-og-byggetilladelse

https://www.norden.org/sv/info-norden/bostad-pa-gronland

"Trump Is Thinking of Buying a Giant Socialist Island," *The Atlantic*, 16 August 2019: https://www.theatlantic.com/science/archive/2019/08/trump-wants-buy-greenland-apparently/596263/

Distribution of Kiattuut Sermiat (Døde Bræ) glacier:

https://mapcarta.com/19190620

Sea level rise if entirety of Greenland's (7.4 meters) and Antarctica's (57.9 meters) ice cover melted:

https://climate.copernicus.eu/climate-indicators/ice-sheets

Jakobshavns Isbræ (aka Ilulissat Glacier or Sermeq Kujalleq) melting, 2014:

"Nytt världsrekord i glaciärsmältning," svt.se, 3 February 2014: https://www.svt.se/nyheter/vetenskap/nytt-varldsrekord-i-glaciarsmaltning

"Greenland's fastest glacier reaches record speeds," press release, European Geosciences Union, 3 February 2014: https://www.egu.eu/news/100/greenlands-fastest-glacier-reaches-record-speeds/

Western Antarctic glacier melt has passed threshold:

"West Antarctic Ice Sheet collapse is under way," press release, University of Washington, 12 May 2014: https://www.washington.edu/news/2014/05/12/west-antarctic-ice-sheet-collapse-is-under-way/

"The 'Unstable' West Antarctic Ice Sheet: A Primer," NASA News, 12 May 2014: https://www.nasa.gov/jpl/news/antarctic-ice-sheet-20140512/

Appeal from 23 cryosphere researchers, 2021:

"Loss Irreversible on Human Time Scales," International Cryosphere Climate Initiative: 9 December 2021: https://iccinet.org/wp-content/uploads/2015/11/Thresholds-Guardian-Dec-9.pdf

Threshold effects in the cryosphere:

"State of the Cryosphere Report 2021: A needed Decade of Urgent Action," International Cryosphere Climate Initiative, 2021.

"Thresholds and Closing Windows – Risks of Irreversible Cryosphere Climate Change," International Cryosphere Climate Initiative, December 2015.

Plastic is everywhere on the planet:

"Plastic Bag Found at the Bottom of World's Deepest Ocean Trench," *National Geographic Society*, 3 July 2019: https://www.nationalgeographic.org/article/plastic-bag-found-bottom-worlds-deepest-ocean-trench/

"Microplastics found near Everest's peak, highest ever detected in the world," *National Geographic*, 20 November 2020: https://www.nationalgeographic.com/environment/article/microplastics-found-near-everests-peak-highest-ever-detected-world-perpetual-planet

Karin Kvale et al: "Zooplankton grazing of microplastic can accelerate global loss of ocean oxygen," *Nature Communication*, vol. 12, article 2358, April 2021.

"Microplastics found in human blood for the first time," *The Guardian*, 24 March 2022: https://www.theguardian.com/environment/2022/mar/24/microplastics-found-in-human-blood-for-first-time

Proportion of biomass represented by domesticated birds, humans och livestock:

"Humans just 0.01% of all life but have destroyed 83% of wild mammals – study," *The Guardian*, 21 May 2018: https://www.theguardian.com/environment/2018/may/21/human-race-just-001-of-all-life-but-has-destroyed-over-80-of-wild-mammals-study

Gus Speth quote:

https://en.wikiquote.org/wiki/James_Gustave_Speth

Chapter 4: Reaching Agreement

The Global Legislators Organization (GLOBE):

https://globelegislators.org/about-globe
http://rio20.net/en/iniciativas/world-summit-of-legislators/

UN Conference on Sustainable Development, 20–22 June 2012, Rio de Janeiro:

https://www.un.org/en/conferences/environment/rio2012

Speakers at Global Ocean Forum on World Oceans Day at Rio+20:

https://www.icriforum.org/wp-content/uploads/2019/12/Rio20-OceansDay-Program.pdf

Overview of fragmented global ocean governance:

"Oceans governance in a wide arena," World Ocean Review, fig 3.8: https://worldoceanreview.com/en/wor-4/politics-and-the-oceans/on-the-difficulty-of-governing-the-sea/ocean-governance-in-a-wide-arena/

"83 countries are more Ocean than Land," World Economic Forum:

https://www.weforum.org/agenda/2017/10/global-ocean-governance-all-at-sea/?utm_content=buffer4a5cd&utm_medium=social&utm_source=twitter.com&utm_campaign=buffer

10 percent of ocean protected by 2020:

"Global marine protected area target of 10% to be achieved by 2020," press release, Convention on Biological Diversity, 5 June 2017: https://www.cbd.int/doc/press/2017/pr-2017-06-05-mpa-pub-en.pdf

30 percent of ocean protected by 2030:

"The Drive to Protect 30% of the Ocean by 2030," PEW, 14 October 2021: https://www.gov.uk/government/topical-events/global-ocean-alliance-30by30-initiative/about

Long way to a binding agreement on ocean outside national jurisdiction:

Glen Wright, Julien Rochette, Kristina Gjerde, Isabel Seeger: "The long and winding road: negotiating a treaty for the conservation and sustainable use of marine biodiversity in areas beyond national jurisdiction," IDDRI Report, Institut du développement durable et des relations internationales, no. 08/18, August 2018.

"The UN BBNJ Negotiations for a legally binding instrument," 2020: http://www.highseas-abidjanconvention.org/un-bbnj-negotiations-legally-binding-instrument?language_content_entity=en

"High seas treaty talks fail to reach a deal," France24, 19 March 2022: https://www.france24.com/en/live-news/20220319-high-seas-treaty-talks-fail-to-reach-a-deal

UNCLOS, one of world's most important agreements for peace and security:

Myron H. Nordquist, Ronán Long: "Marine Biodiversity in Areas Beyond National Jurisdiction," *Center for Oceans Law and Policy*, vol. 24, chapter 2 (by Hans Corell): "The United Nations Convention on the Law of the Sea in the Present Geo-Political Situation," 2021.

Campaign against President Obama's support for UNCLOS:

U.N. Treaty That Redistributes Drilling Revenues," *Forbes*, 20 May 2012: https://www.forbes.com/sites/larrybell/2012/05/20/will-u-s-sovereignty-be-lost-at-sea-obama-signs-u-n-treaty-that-redistributes-drilling-revenues/?sh=6b-8f7bea7af3

"Obama officials press Senate to ratify sea treaty," Reuters, 24 May 2012: https://www.reuters.com/article/usa-treaty-seas-idUSL1E8GN-GJX20120523

The Future We Want, Rio+20 Outcome Document, United Nations, 2012: https://www.un.org/disabilities/documents/rio20_outcome_document_complete.pdf

Chapter 5: Political Will

Fisheries agreement between EU and Republic of Guinea, with attached protocol:

http://extwprlegs1.fao.org/docs/pdf/bi-88309.pdf

Massacre in Conakry, 28 September 2009:

"Human Rights Watch says Sept. 28 massacre was premeditated," France24, 28 October 2009: https://www.france24.com/en/20091028-human-rights-watch-says-sept-28-massacre-was-premeditated

Fisheries Committee votes no on fisheries agreement for first time:

"EU backar efter kritik mot fiskeavtal," Europaportalen, 22 October 2009:

https://www.europaportalen.se/2009/10/eu-backar-efter-kritik-mot-fiskeavtal-0

Commission withdraws the agreement:

EU skrotar fiskeavtal med Guinea, *Aktuell Hållbarhet*, 21 October 2009: https://www.aktuellhallbarhet.se/

Fisheries Agreement with Morocco terminated based on Western Sahara:

"Oväntat fiskestopp," *Svenska Dagbladet*, 21 December 2011: https://www.svd.se/ovantat-fiskestopp

End to shark finning:

"Stopp för hajfening," SVT Nyheter, 21 November 2012: https://www.svt.se/nyheter/utrikes/stopp-for-hejfening

CFPReformwatch.eu – website with information about the process of the EU's reform of Common Fisheries Policy (CFP), now defunct. Facebook page with cursory overview of content:

https://sv-se.facebook.com/pages/category/News---Media-Website/CFP-Reform-Watch-114867715217300/

Historic reform of reform of the EU Common Fisheries Policy:

"Stoppa överfisket – ledamöterna röstar för en ambitiös reform," Europaparlamentet Nyheter, 6 February 2013: https://www.europarl.europa.eu/news/sv/press-room/20130201IPR05571/stoppa-overfisket-ledamoterna-rostar-for-ambitios-reform

"Euro MPs back large-scale fishing reform to save stocks," BBC News, 6 February 2013: https://www.bbc.com/news/world-europe-21352617

"MEPs vote to ban discards in historic reform of fishing policy," *The Guardian*, 6 February 2013: https://www.theguardian.com/environment/2013/feb/06/meps-back-fishing-policy-reform

"EU agrees to end decades of overfishing," *Financial Times*, 30 May 2013: https://www.ft.com/content/05c56eba-c8fa-11e2-bb56-00144feab7de

"Hummingbirds," London's electric taxicabs:

"The surprisingly old story of London's first ever electric taxi," Science Museum, 9 July 2012: https://blog.sciencemuseum.org.uk/the-surprisingly-old-story-of-londons-first-ever-electric-taxi/

History of the electric car, see e.g.:

"Worth the Watt: A Brief History of the Electric Car, 1830 to Present: EVs weren't born yesterday," *Car and Driver*, 15 March 2018: https://www.caranddriver.com/features/g15378765/worth-the-watt-a-brief-history-of-the-electric-car-1830-to-present/

Henry Ford's plans for an electric Model-T:

"Ford, Edison and the Cheap EV That Almost Was," *Wired*, 18 June 2010:
https://www.wired.com/2010/06/henry-ford-thomas-edison-ev/

California's Zero Emissions Vehicle Program, background and development:

"About Zero Emissions Vehicle Program," California Air Resources Board:
https://ww2.arb.ca.gov/our-work/programs/zero-emission-vehicle-program/about

Chris Paine: *Who Killed the Electric Car? A Lack of Consumer Confidence…or Conspiracy?* Sony Pictures Classics, 2006, available full-length on YouTube: https://www.youtube.com/watch?v=GJ9e0okuEpY

Examples of 1990s arguments against e-cars:

Peter Gordon, Harry W. Richardson: "The Case against Electric Vehicle Mandates in California," *Reason Foundation Policy Study*, no. 189, May 1995: https://development.reason.org/wp-content/uploads/1995/05/89cec443d302f97d88cb10ae0473fac4.pdf

George W. Bush introduces $100,000 tax credit for purchase of heavy vehicle:

"Fed Tax Break Encourages SUV Purchases," ABC News, 7 January 2006:
https://abcnews.go.com/Technology/Hybrid/story?id=97505&page=1

Emissions from SUVs increasing more than emissions from industry globally:

"Global SUV sales set another record in 2021, setting back efforts to reduce emissions," International Energy Agency, December 2021:
https://www.iea.org/commentaries/global-suv-sales-set-another-record-in-2021-setting-back-efforts-to-reduce-emissions

Volvo's investment in e-cars, 2011:

"Volvo C30 Electric – full körglädje och så gott som fri från koldioxid-utsläpp," press release, Volvo, 1 April 2011:
https://www.media.volvocars.com/se/sv-se/media/pressreleases/37345
https://carup.se/carup-avslojar-darfor-tvingas-volvo-masskrota-elbilen-c30-electric/

Coalition government removes green car premium:

Miljöbilspremien väck, Vi Bilägare, July 2009:
https://www.vibilagare.se/nyheter/miljobilspremien-vack-2659

Coalition government's new definition of "green car" benefits heavier cars, 2013:

"Så blir nya miljöbilsreglerna 2013," *Vi Bilägare*, September 2012:
https://www.vibilagare.se/nyheter/sa-blir-nya-miljobilsreglerna-2013-39849

Preem withdraws application for increased emissions:

"Regeringen prövar tillåtligheten av Preems planerade verksamhet i Lysekil," press release, Swedish government, 23 August 2019:

https://www.regeringen.se/pressreleasen/2019/08/regeringen-provar-tillatligheten-av-preems-planerade-verksamhet-i-lysekil/

"Regeringen tar över ärendet om Preems utbyggnad," *Dagens Nyheter*, 23 August 2019: https://www.dn.se/ekonomi/regeringen-tar-over-aren-det-om-preems-utbyggnad/

"Preem drar tillbaka ansökan om nytt miljötillstånd för Lysekil," press release, Preem, 28 September 2020: https://www.preem.se/om-preem/press/rapporter--publikationer/preem drar-tillbaka-ansokan-om-nytt-miljotillstand-for-lysekil/

Energy agreement between Social Democrats, Moderates, Center Party, Green Party and Christian Democrats, 2016:

"Överenskommelse om den svenska energipolitiken," press release, Swedish government, 10 June 2016: https://www.regeringen.se/artiklar/2016/06/overenskommelse-om-den-svenska-energipolitiken/

Wind power:

"Ny statistik över installerad vindkraft 2020," Swedish Energy Agency, 2021: https://www.energimyndigheten.se/nyhetsarkiv/2021/ny-statistik-over-installerad-vindkraft-2020/

Climate law and goals of a fossil-free welfare state, freed-up investments:

https://www.hybritdevelopment.se/en-fossilfri-framtid/; https://www.h2greensteel.com; https://northvolt.com; https://www.pitea.se/invanare/Kommun-politik/hallbar-samhallsutveckling/alla-projekt-samhallsutveckling/aktuella-projekt-landsbygdsutveckling/storsta-vinkraftsparken-i-europa---markbygden/

"400 miljarder satsas av LKAB – Sveriges största industrisatsning någonsin," SVT Nyheter, 23 November 2020: https://www.svt.se/nyheter/lokalt/norrbotten/400-miljarder-satsas-nar-lkab-slopar-pellets-for-svamp

Marginal additional costs in relation to necessary infrastructure investments:

"Better Growth, better climate," *The New Climate Economy Report*, Global Commission on the Economy and Climate: 2014: https://sustainabledevelopment.un.org/content/documents/1595TheNewClimateEconomyReport.pdf

The New Climate Economy Report, chapter 6: http://newclimateeconomy.report/2014/wp-content/uploads/sites/2/2014/08/NCE_Chapter6_Finance.pdf

Examples of forest lobbying and criticism from EU Commission:

"Skogsbolagens berättelse om skogen – lobby för 150 miljoner," *Dagens Nyheter*, 14 March 2021: https://www.dn.se/sverige/skogsbolagens-berattelse-om-skogen-lobby-for-150-miljoner/

Magnus Nilsson blog: https://www.nilssonproduktion.se/slu-kolinlagringen-och-den-akademiska-integriteten/

Parliament on Taxonomy Regulation:

"Riksdagsnej till EU-taxonomi för hållbarhet," *TT*, 22 June 2021: https://www.svd.se/riksdagsnej-till-eu-taxonomi-for-hallbarhet

"Sverige säger nej till EU:s omstridda taxonomiförslag," *Dagens ETC*, 22 June 2021: https://www.etc.se/klimat-miljo/sverige-sager-nej-till-omstritt-taxonomiforslag

Ebba Busch Thor's "new message" on nuclear power during live broadcast:

Expressen and *Dagens Industri* party leader debate, 15 August 2018, 44 minutes in: https://www.expressen.se/tv/politik/debatten-2018-se-hela-expressens-partiledardebatt/

Christian Democrats' spokesperson for energy policy surprised:

"Kaos i KD efter Busch Thors kärnkraftskrav," *Expressen*, 15 August 2018: https://www.expressen.se/nyheter/val-2018/kds-forvaning-over-busch-thors-utspel/

"KD öppnar för mer kärnkraft – får mothugg inom egna partiet," *Ny Teknik*, 15 August 2018: https://www.nyteknik.se/energi/kd-oppnar-for-mer-karnkraft-far-mothugg-inom-egna-partiet-6926064

Climate-denying Australian parliament member Craig Kelly's impact:

"As Australia Burns, a Climate-Change Denier Rallies the Troops," *New York Times*, 22 January 2020: https://www.nytimes.com/2020/01/22/world/australia/fires-craig-kelly-climate-denial.html

Dietrich Bonhoeffer quote:

From Bodil Jönsson, *Tio tankar om arbete*, p. 74, Brombergs förlag, 2016.

Chapter 6: Leaving No One Behind

More than three million children in Somalia don't attend school:

UNICEF: https://www.unicef.org/somalia/education

Median age in Somalia is 16.7 years (2020):

https://www.worldometers.info/world-population/somalia-population/

70 percent of all fish eaten in EU doesn't come from EU:

European Commission: *The EU Fish Market*, 2020 edition, p. 31: https://www.eumofa.eu/documents/20178/415635/EN_ The+EU+fish+market_2020.pdf

Indira Gandhi's speech at Stockholm environmental conference, 1972:

"Climate change and poverty: why Indira Gandhi's speech matters," *The Guardian*, 6 May 2014: https://www.theguardian.com/global-development-professionals-network/2014/may/06/indira-gandhi-india-climate-change

"Man and Environment," Indira Gandhi's speech at the Stockholm Conference in 1972: http://lasulawsenvironmental.blogspot.com/2012/07/indira-gandhis-speech-at-stockholm.html

Information on the world's refugees from UN refugee agency UNHCR:

https://www.unhcr.org/en-us/figures-at-a-glance.html

Sweden's first contribution to the Green Climate Fund:

"4 svenska miljarder till Gröna fonden," *Svenska Dagbladet*, 20 October 2014: https://www.svd.se/4-svenska-miljarder-till-grona-fonden

"Sverige får ärorik plats i gröna klimatfonden," *Supermiljöbloggen*, 31 August 2015: https://supermiljobloggen.se/nyheter/sverige-far-arorik-plats-i-grona-klimatfonden/

How tax havens affect the world:

Oliver Bullough: *Moneyland: Why Thieves & Crooks Now Rule the World & How to Take it Back*, Profile Books, 2019.

Global Financial Integrity Report: *Trade-Related Illicit Financial Flows in 134 Developing Countries 2009–2018*, December 2021.

Nicholas Shaxson: "Tackling Tax Havens," *Finance and Development*, vol. 56, no. 3, 2019.

"Inequality and poverty: the hidden costs of tax dodging," Oxfam: https://www.oxfam.org/en/inequality-and-poverty-hidden-costs-tax-dodging

Tax havens in Europe:

https://www.visualcapitalist.com/worlds-biggest-private-tax-havens/

Promise to "leave no one behind": https://sustainabledevelopment.un.org/content/documents/2754713_July_PM_2_Leaving_no_one_behind_Summary_from_UN_Committee_for_Development_Policy.pdf

Chapter 7: Political Unwillingness

Brazil withdraws offer to host COP25:

"Brazil withdraws offer to host UN conference on climate change," *Al Jazeera*, 28 November 2018: https://www.aljazeera.com/news/2018/11/28/brazil-withdraws-offer-to-host-un-conference-on-climate-change

United States holds big "clean coal" event:

"Protesters disrupt US panel's fossil fuel pitch at climate talks," *The Guardian*, 10 December 2018: https://www.theguardian.com/environment/2018/dec/10/protesters-disrupt-us-panels-fossil-fuels-pitch-at-climate-talks

Four countries refuse to "welcome" IPCC report on 1.5-degree warming:

"Climate change: COP24 fails to adopt key scientific report," com/news/science-environment-46496967

Poland air quality worst in EU:

European Environment Agency: *Air Quality in Europe Report 2021*: https://www.eea.europa.eu/publications/air-quality-in-europe-2021/

"Over 47,000 Polish deaths due to air pollution: report," TVP World, 29 October 2018: https://tvpworld.com/39699663/over-47000-polish-deaths-due-to-air-pollution-report

World's most air-polluted cities:

https://www.iqair.com/world-most-polluted-cities?page=1&perPage=50&-cities=

Number of coal workers in Poland decreasing:

https://euracoal.eu/info/country-profiles/poland/

Todd Stern's remark in Durban:

Jonathan Pickering et al: "'If Equity's In, We're Out': Scope for Fairness in the Next Global Climate Agreement," *Ethics & International Affairs*, vol. 26, article 4, p. 423–443, 21 December 2012.

Groupings of countries in climate negotiations:

https://www.carbonbrief.org/interactive-the-negotiating-alliances-at-the-paris-climate-conference

"The Carbon Brief Interview: Saudi Arabia's Ayman Shasly," *Carbon Brief*, 12 December 2018: https://www.carbonbrief.org/the-carbon-brief-interview-saudi-arabias-ayman-shasly

"Saudi Arabia's Ayman Shasly on why he dislikes figure SPM.4 in the IPCC's 1.5C report, Carbon Brief," YouTube: https://www.youtube.com/watch?v=vGzSmMEIJz4

"Ödesdag för klimatet – riskerar kidnappas av ordval," *Aftonbladet*, 14 December 2018: https://www.aftonbladet.se/nyheter/samhalle/a/1kAvGQ/ odesdag-for-klimatmotet--riskerar-att-kidnappas-av-ordval

Greta Thunberg's speech at COP24 plenary meeting, Katowice, 15 December 2018:
https://www.youtube.com/watch?v=VFkQSGyeCWg

Greta Thunberg on mental illness and other topics:
"'I was kind of a troublemaker': How Greta Thunberg became a climate activist," *Democracy Now!* 11 September 2019, YouTube: https://www.youtube. com/watch?v=tEChhzDbLdo

On the formation of a transitional government budget, November 2018:
https://www.regeringen.se/artiklar/2018/11/om-utformningen-av-en- overgangsregeringsbudget/
"SD säkrade seger åt M-KD-budgeten," Sveriges Radio, 12 December 2018: https://sverigesradio.se/artikel/7112964

Impact of Moderates' and Christian Democrats' budget motion on environmental and climate work, 2019:
"Sveriges nya budget – ett slag mot klimatet," *Supermiljöbloggen* 12 December 2018: https://supermiljobloggen.se/nyheter/sveriges-nya-budget-ett- slag-mot-klimatet/
"M och KDs budget innebär kraftiga nedskärningar i miljöbudgeten," Natursidan, 11 December 2018: https://www.natursidan.se/nyheter/m-och-kds- budget-innebar-kraftiga-nedskarningar-i-miljobudgeten/

Final decision at COP24:
https://unfccc.int/process-and-meetings/the-paris-agreement/the-katowice- climate-package/katowice-climate-package

Chapter 8: The Knowledge

Brannon Report, 1957:
Johan von Mirbach: *Smoke and Fumes: The Climate Change Cover-Up* – A&O Buero, 2017: https://www.dailymotion.com/video/x7pcqkv; https:// javafilms.fr/film/smoke-and-fumes-the-climate-change-cover-up/
"Dokumentär: Oljeindustrin har tystat ned klimatförändringarna i sextio år," SVT, 22 November 2018: https://www.svt.se/nyheter/utrikes/dokumentar- oljeindustrin-har-tystat-ned-globala-uppvarmningen-i-sextio-ar

Svante Arrhenius' first article about the Green House Effect:
Svante Arrhenius: "Ueber den Einfluss des atmosphärischen Kohlensäuregehalts

auf die Temperatur der Erdoberfläche," Royal Swedish Academy of Sciences, 1896.

Lyndon B. Johnson: Special Message to Congress, 1965:

Naomi Oreskes, Erik M. Conway: *Merchants of Doubt: How a Handful of Scientists obscured the Truth on issues from Tobacco Smoke to Global Warming*, p. 171, Bloomsbury, 2011.

Roger Revelle's early conclusions on fossil fuels and climate:

Roger Revelle, Hans E. Suess: *Carbon Dioxide Exchange Between Atmosphere and Ocean and the Question of an Increase of Atmospheric CO2 during the Past Decades*, Scripps Institution on Oceanography, 1957: https://onlinelibrary.wiley.com/doi/10.1111/j.2153-3490.1957.tb01849.x

Exxon knew:

Article series in nine parts: *The Road not Taken*, Inside Climate News, 2015: https://insideclimatenews.org/project/exxon-the-road-not-taken/

James Hansen's testimony before the US Senate:

"Global Warming Has Begun, Expert Tells Senate," *New York Times*, 24 June 1988: https://www.nytimes.com/1988/06/24/us/global-warming-has-begun-expert-tells-senate.html

Margaret Thatcher:

Speech to UN General Assembly – Global Environment, 8 November 1989: https://www.margaretthatcher.org/document/107817; https://www.youtube.com/watch?v=VnAzoDtwCBg

Members of "Climate Change Coalition":

James Hoggan, Richard Littlemore: *Climate Cover-up: The Crusade to Deny Global Warming*, p. 16, Greystone Books, 2009.

George E. Marcus (ed.): *Paranoia Within Reason: A Casebook on Conspiracy as Explanation*, University of Chicago Press, 1999 (chapter 5, Myanna Lahsen: "The detection and attribution on of conspiracies: The controversy Over Chapter 8)".

Formation of the Marshall Institute:

Naomi Oreskes, Erik M. Conway: *Merchants of Doubt: How a Handful of Scientists Obscured the Truth on Issues from Tobacco Smoke to Global Warming*, p. 36–65, Bloomsbury, 2011.

Contents of Jastrow, Nierenberg and Seitz paper "What does science tell us?":

Naomi Oreskes, Erik M. Conway: *Merchants of Doubt: How a Handful of Scientists Obscured the Truth on Issues from Tobacco Smoke to Global Warming*, p. 186–190, Bloomsbury, 2011.

Attacks on Roger Revelle:

Naomi Oreskes, Erik M. Conway: *Merchants of Doubt: How a Handful of Scientists Obscured the Truth on Issues from Tobacco Smoke to Global Warming*, p. 190–197, Bloomsbury, 2011.

Al Gore: *Earth in the Balance: Ecology and the Human Spirit*, Houghton Mifflin, 1992.

Attacks on Ben Santer and accusations of "scientific cleansing":

Maths Nilsson: *Spelet om klimatet: Vem kan man lita på i klimatdebatten?* p. 41–51, Roos & Tegnér, 2021.

Naomi Oreskes, Erik M. Conway: *Merchants of Doubt: How a Handful of Scientists Obscured the Truth on Issues from Tobacco Smoke to Global Warming*, p. 197–215, Bloomsbury, 2011.

Rohrabacher's remarks:

Naomi Oreskes, Erik M. Conway: *Merchants of Doubt: How a Handful of Scientists Obscured the Truth on Issues from Tobacco Smoke to Global Warming*, p. 213, Bloomsbury, 2011.

Fuel lobby's 1998 "Global Science Communication Plan":

https://www.sourcewatch.org/index.php/Global_Climate_Science_Communications_Plan_(1998)

Early consensus within climate science:

Naomi Oreskes: "The Scientific Consensus on Climate Change," *Science*, vol. 306, no. 5702, 3 December 2004.

Half of all Republicans in Congress are climate skeptics:

Center for American Progress: "Climate deniers in the 117th Congress," 30 March 2021: https://www.americanprogress.org/issues/green/news/2021/03/30/497685/climate-deniers-117th-congress/

Financing of the Climate Change CounterMovement Organizations:

Robert J. Brulle: "Institutionalizing delay: foundation funding and the creation of U.S. climate change counter-movement organizations," *Springer Link*, 21 December 2013: https://link.springer.com/article/10.1007/s10584-013-1018-7; updated 2021: https://www.researchsquare.com/article/rs-178750/v1

European and Swedish think tanks that opposed the Kyoto Protocol and have spread climate skepticism. Connections to Gunnar Hökmark, Maria Rankka och Jonas Petterson:

Maths Nilsson: *Spelet om klimatet: Vem kan man lita på i klimatdebatten?* p. 100–104, Roos & Tegnér, 2021.

"Korten på bordet, M," *Aftonbladet*, 12 December 2005: https://www.aftonbladet.
se/ledare/a/0EV0OE/korten-pa-bordet-m

"How America plotted to stop Kyoto deal," *The Independent*, 8 December 2005:
https://www.independent.co.uk/climate-change/news/how-america-
plotted-to-stop-kyoto-deal-518575.html

"Skeptikerna rasar mot miljödebatten," *Veckans Affärer*, 6 December, 2006:
https://web.archive.org/web/20081008002406/http:/www.va.se/
magasinet/2006/48/skeptikerna_rasar/index.xml

"Bluff om klimatet," *Aftonbladet*, op-ed, 20 August 2006: https://www.aftonbladet.
se/debatt/a/kaw21a/bluff-om-klimatet

"Pressekreterare åt näringsminister Annie Lööf," Swedish government,
press release, 25 October 2011: https://www.mynewsdesk.com/
se/naringsdepartementet/pressreleases/pressekreterare-aat-
naeringsminister-annie-loeoef-697788

"Tankesmedjan som fördröjer Sveriges klimatomställning," *Supermiljöbloggen*,
22 January 2022: https://supermiljobloggen.se/nyheter/tankesmedjan-
som-fordrojer-sveriges-klimatomstallning/

"Timbro, Bryssel och klimatet," *Supermiljöbloggen*, 30 January 2022: https://
supermiljobloggen.se/nyheter/timbro-bryssel-och-klimatet/

"Svenskt Näringslivs inflytande i media – vilseleder om klimatet,"
Supermiljöbloggen, 16 February 2022: https://supermiljobloggen.
se/nyheter/svenskt-naringslivs-inflytande-i-media-vilseleder-om-
klimatet/

Greenfreeze, the Freon-free refrigerator:

"Protest mot freoner. Electrolux blockerades av gamla kylskåp," *Dagens Nyheter*,
2 October 1992: https://www.dn.se/arkiv/inrikes/protest-mot-freoner-
electrolux-blockerades-av-gamla-kylskap/

https://www.ecomall.com/greenshopping/greenfreeze.htm

https://www.electroluxgroup.com/wp-content/uploads/sites/2/2000/04/
ELECTROLUX-ÅRSREDOVISNING-1992-SVENSKA.pdf

Reduction of climate emissions due to COVID19 pandemic:

"Covid-19 caused only a temporary reduction in carbon emissions – UN report,"
press release, UNEP, 16 September 2021: https://www.unep.org/news-
and-stories/press-release/covid-19-caused-only-temporary-reduction-
carbon-emissions-un-report

Potentially reduced emissions through individual choices:

"Individens eget ansvar: Så skapas och sprids lögner i klimatfrågan," *Dagens
Nyheter*, 23 August 2021: https://www.dn.se/kultur/sa-skapas-och-
sprids-logner-i-klimatfragan/

Annika Carlsson Kanyama et al: "Shifting expenditure on food, holidays and

furnishings could lower greenhouse gas emissions by almost 40 %,"
Journal of Industrial Ecology, vol. 25, no. 6, 19 July 2021.

Kristian S. Nielsen et al: "How Behavioral Interventions Can Reduce the Climate
Impact of Energy Use," *Joule*, vol. 4, no. 8, 19 August 2020.

Six percent of Swedes are climate skeptics:

Henrik Oscarsson et al: *Ingen anledning till oro (?)*, chapter "Svenska
klimatförnekare", p. 245–248, SOM-institutet, June 2021:
https://www.researchgate.net/publication/352679959_Svenska_
klimatfornekare

Bjørn Lomborg on the scope of his columns:

https://www.copenhagenconsensus.com/our-impact

Copenhagen Consensus' summary of the "smartest" development goals in Agenda
2030, with graphic: https://www.copenhagenconsensus.com/sites/
default/files/post2015brochure_m.pdf

Bjørn Lomborg's Australia controversy:

"Still no consensus for Bjorn Lomborg, the climate change refugee," *The
Conversation*, 30 July 2015: https://theconversation.com/still-no-
consensus-for-bjorn-lomborg-the-climate-change-refugee-45423

"Australian university pulls plug on climate skeptic's center," *Science*, 12 May 2015:
https://www.science.org/content/article/australian-university-pulls-
plug-climate-skeptics-center

"Bjorn Lomborg's WSJ Response to Nixing of Australian Project," *Scienceblogs*,
14 May 2015: https://scienceblogs.com/gregladen/2015/05/14/bjorn-
lomborgs-wsj-response-to-nixing-of-australian-project

"Copenhagen Consensus Centre's Bjorn Lomborg unfazed by criticisms and
setbacks," *Sydney Morning Herald*, 22 May 2015: https://www.smh.
com.au/national/copenhagen-consensus-centres-bjorn-lomborg-
unfazed-by-criticisms-and-setbacks-20150521-gh6h2g.html

Lomborg reported for misconduct in research:

Maths Nilsson: *Spelet om klimatet: Vem kan man lita på i klimatdebatten?* p. 62–63,
72–75, Roos & Tegnér, 2021.

Lomborg's video on Bill Gates' blog, 2014:

"How Bill Gates and Peabody Energy Share Vision For Coal Powered Future
Through Views of Bjorn Lomborg," *DeSmog*, 28 October 2014:
https://www.desmog.com/2014/10/28/how-bill-gates-and-peabody-
energy-share-vision-coal-powered-future-through-views-bjorn-
lomborg/

"Bjorn Lomborg sheds light on energy poverty in these two videos," GatesNotes,
the blog of Bill Gates, 25 June 2014: https://www.gatesnotes.com/

Energy/Two-Videos-Illuminate-Energy-Poverty-Bjorn-Lomborg

William D. Nordhaus' "wait and see" advice to the White House in 1979 and Nobel Prize-winning DICE model:

Naomi Oreskes, Erik M. Conway: *Merchants of Doubt: How a Handful of Scientists Obscured the Truth on Issues from Tobacco Smoke to Global Warming*, p. 177–183, Bloomsbury, 2011.

The Sveriges Riksbanks Prize in Economic Sciences in Memory of Alfred Nobel Lecture 2018: *Climate Change: The Ultimate Challenge for Economics*: https://www.nobelprize.org/prizes/economic-sciences/2018/nordhaus/lecture/

Martin Weitzman's death:

"Martin Weitzman, Virtuoso Climate Change Economist, Dies at 77," *New York Times*, 4 September 2019: https://www.nytimes.com/2019/09/04/business/energy-environment/martin-weitzman-dead.html

"Martin Weitzman, environmental economist who emphasized uncertainty, dies at 77," *Washington Post*, 4 September 2019: https://www.washingtonpost.com/local/obituaries/martin-weitzman-environmental-economist-who-emphasized-uncertainty-dies-at-77/2019/09/04/3562dd64-cf20-11e9-8c1c-7c8ee785b855_story.html

Costs to the world economy of different global warming scenarios:

Risks associated with global warming of 1.5 or 2 degrees, Tyndall Centre for Climate Change Research, Briefing Note, May 2018: https://tyndall.ac.uk/wp-content/uploads/2021/11/briefing_note_risks_warren_r1-1.pdf

Chapter 9: Political Craftmanship

Donald Trump signs "Global Gag Rule"/"Mexico City Policy":

"Trump Revives Ban on Foreign Aid to Groups That Give Abortion Counseling," *New York Times*, 23 January 2017: https://www.nytimes.com/2017/01/23/world/trump-ban-foreign-aid-abortions.html

"How Trump signed a global death warrant for women," *The Guardian*, 21 July 2017: https://www.theguardian.com/global-development/2017/jul/21/trump-global-death-warrant-women-family-planning-population-reproductive-rights-mexico-city-policy

"Donald Trump: 'I could shoot somebody and I wouldn't lose any voters'," *The Guardian*, 24 January 2016: https://www.theguardian.com/us-news/2016/jan/24/donald-trump-says-he-could-shoot-somebody-and-still-not-lose-voters

Signing of Swedish climate law goes viral:

"Did Sweden's deputy PM just troll Trump with a women-only parody picture?"

The Local, 3 February 2017: https://www.thelocal.se/20170203/
swedens-deputy-pm-trolls-trump-in-abortion-order-image-parody/

"Some people seem to think this picture of Sweden's deputy leader is
trolling Trump," *Washington Post*, 3 February 2017: https://www.
washingtonpost.com/news/worldviews/wp/2017/02/03/some-people-
seem-to-think-this-picture-of-swedens-deputy-leader-is-trolling-
trump/

"Swedish Politicians Troll Trump Administration While Signing Climate Change
Law," *Huffington Post*, 3 February 2017: https://www.huffpost.com/
entry/swedish-politicians-troll-trump-administration-while-signing-
climate-change-law_n_58948c3be4b0c1284f2558ca?ncid=fcbklnkus
hpmg00000063

"Swedish climate minister appears to mock Trump administration with
all-women photo," *The Hill*, 3 February 2017: https://thehill.com/
homenews/news/317758-swedish-climate-minister-appears-to-mock-
trump-administration-with-all-woman

"Swedish deputy PM mocks Trump with all-female photo," *Arab News*,
3 February 2017: https://www.arabnews.com/node/1048671/offbeat

"Sweden's deputy PM trolls Donald Trump by posting an all-woman picture
signing a bill," *Indian Express*, 3 February 2017: https://indianexpress.
com/article/trending/trending-globally/sweden-deputy-pm-trolls-
donald-trump-by-posting-an-all-womens-picture-signing-new-
climate-law-bill-4507565/

"Suède: la ministre de l'Environnement se paye la tête de Trump," *Le Point* (AFP),
3 February 2017: https://www.lepoint.fr/monde/suede-la-ministre-de-l-
environnement-se-paye-la-tete-de-trump-03-02-2017-2102287_24.php

"El Gobierno sueco 'responde' a Trump con una foto de mujeres del gabinete," *El
País*, 3 February 2017: https://elpais.com/internacional/2017/02/03/
actualidad/1486138306_245675.html

"The Swedish deputy prime minister is expertly trolling Donald Trump with
one picture," *indy100*, 3 February 2017: https://www.indy100.com/
celebrities/swedish-deputy-prime-minister-isabella-lovin-trolling-
president-donald-trump-one-pic-7561381

"Is Sweden's deputy PM trolling Donald Trump in Facebook photo?" BBC News,
3 February 2017: https://www.bbc.com/news/world-europe-38853399

"Swedish government pokes fun at Trump with all-female photo," *Politico*,
3 February 2017: https://www.politico.eu/article/swedish-government-
pokes-fun-at-trump-with-all-female-photo/

"Meet Isabella Lövin, the Swedish politician who 'trolled Donald Trump'," *Inews*,
4 February 2017: https://inews.co.uk/news/politics/isabella-lovin-
trolled-donald-trump-45370

"Swedish Deputy PM trolls Trump," *Gulf Times*, 5 February 2015: https://www.
gulf-times.com/story/531699/Swedish-deputy-PM-trolls-Trump

"Här hyllar Miley Cyrus svensk jämställdhet och Isabella Lövins parodi på
        Donald Trump," *Metro*, 6 February 2017: https://metromode.se/noje/
        har-hyllar-miley-cyrus-svensk-jamstalldhet-och-isabella-lovins-bild-
        som-driver-med-donald-trump/

"Last Night in Sweden":

"'Last Night in Sweden'? Trump's remark baffles a nation," *New York Times*,
        19 February 2017: https://www.nytimes.com/2017/02/19/world/
        europe/last-night-in-sweden-trumps-remark-baffles-a-nation.html?

Green Party's long-term work for a Swedish climate law:

Ordning och reda i klimatpolitiken, motion to Swedish parliament 2012/13:MJ481
        by Åsa Romson et al. (Green Party): https://www.riksdagen.
        se/sv/dokument-lagar/dokument/motion/ordning-och-reda-i-
        klimatpolitiken_H002MJ481/html

Green Party platform, 2014–2018:

https://www.mp.se/politik/valmanifest2014#1.
"Miljömålsberedningen föreslår ett klimatpolitiskt ramverk med klimatmål till
        2045 och en klimatlag som reglerar former för arbete," press release,
        Ministry of the Environment, Swedish government,
        9 March 2016: https://news.cision.com/se/miljodepartementet/r/
        miljomalsberedningen-foreslar-ett-klimatpolitiskt-ramverk-med-
        klimatmal-till-2045-och-en-klimatlag-s,c9931718

Ett klimatpolitiskt ramverk för Sverige, interim report from the Swedish
        parliamentary Committee on Environmental Goals, SOU 2016:21:
        https://www.regeringen.se/rattsliga-dokument/statens-offentliga-
        utredningar/2016/03/sou-201621/

Juncker quote:

"We all know what to do, but we don't know how to get re-elected once we
        have done it." Jean-Claude Juncker, "The Quest for Prosperity," *The
        Economist*, 15 March 2007.

**Verhofstadt reveals that Nigel Farage doesn't participate in fisheries committee
        work:**

"Time to Expose UKIP MEPs for what they really are – Lazy & Unprincipled,"
        GMB, 13 August 2013: https://www.gmbnorthwest.co.uk/news/
        time-expose-ukip-meps-what-they-really-are-%E2%80%93-lazy-
        unprincipled

"Farage called out for never attending Fishery committee," *Metro*, 21 March 2018:
        https://metro.co.uk/video/farage-called-never-attending-fishery-
        committee-1653402/

Reform of EU Emissions Trading System and the Swedish Proposal:

"Sweden proposes measures to strengthen carbon prices," Reuters, 17 October 2016: https://www.reuters.com/article/us-europe-carbon-idUSKB-N12H1N2

"Sweden floats options to strengthen EU's ailing carbon market," *Bloomberg*, 17 October 2016: https://www.bloomberg.com/news/articles/2016-10-17/sweden-floats-options-to-strengthen-eu-s-ailing-carbon-market

Statsrådet Isabella Lövins agerande i samband med EU-nämndens sammanträde inför möte i rådet (miljö- och klimat) och efterföljande möten i Luxemburg, report to the Swedish parliamentary Committee on the Constitution, KU-anmälan 2016/17:20 (371-2016/17) by Jesper Skalberg Karlsson (Moderates): https://www.riksdagen.se/sv/dokument-lagar/dokument/ku-anmalan/statsradet-isabella-lovins-agerande-i-samband-med_H4A1dnr371

Uppteckningar vid EU-nämndens sammanträden 2016/17:26, Swedish parliament, 24 February 2017: https://data.riksdagen.se/fil/A52C23A5-3BD1-4707-9E6D-591D85F21B0D

EU Environment Council, public session, video, morning discussion, 28 February 2017: https://video.consilium.europa.eu/event/en/22540?-start_time=0

EU Environment Council, public session, video, afternoon discussion (16.55–17.30), 28 February 2017: https://video.consilium.europa.eu/event/en/22541

EU Member States agreed on future of EU Emissions Trading System, press release, Ministry of the Environment, Swedish government, 1 March 2017: https://www.government.se/press-releases/2017/03/eu-member-states-agreed-on-future-of-eu-emissions-trading-system/

EU ETS Reform: European countries outbid the Parliament, giving hope for the long-term future of the ETS, Ember, 1 March 2017: https://ember-climate.org/commentary/2017/03/01/eu-ets-reform-european-countries-outbid-parliament-proposals-tighten-flagship-eu-climate-policy-giving-hope-long-term-future/

Reform of the EU emissions trading system – Council endorses deal with European Parliament, press release, EU Council of Ministers, 22 November 2017: https://www.consilium.europa.eu/en/press/press-releases/2017/11/22/reform-of-the-eu-emissions-trading-system-council-endorses-deal-with-european-parliament/

"Storartad kollaps för kolkraften – Sverige ligger bakom," *Svenska Dagbladet*, 5 February 2020: https://www.svd.se/storartad-kollaps-for-kolkraften--pa-grund-av-sverige

"Svenska förslaget vände allt: 'Det har varit helt galna år'," *Svenska Dagbladet*, 9 October 2021: https://www.svd.se/svenska-forslaget-vande-allt-varit-helt-galna-ar

"Svenskt initiativ minskar utsläppsutrymmet inom EU ETS," press release,

Swedish government, 3 September 2020: https://www.regeringen.se/
pressreleasen/2020/09/svenskt-initiativ-minskar-utslappsutrymmet-
inom-eu-ets/

Reformen av EU:s utsläppshandel – konsekvenser för svensk klimatpolitik, Westander
Klimat och Energi, 2018: https://www.westander.se/wp-content/
uploads/2018/09/reformen-av-eus-utslappshandel-konsekvenser-for-
svensk-klimatpolitik.pdf

Criticism of EU Commissioner for Climate Action Miguel Arias Cañete:

"Spanish politician claims he had to hold back in Europe debate with woman,"
The Guardian, 18 May 2014: https://www.theguardian.com/
world/2014/may/18/spainish-politician-miguel-arias-sexism-debate

"MEPs say Cañete's family still has ties to oil industry," *Politico*, 25 September
2014: https://www.politico.eu/article/canetes-family-still-has-ties-to-
oil-and-agriculture-industries/

"Panama Papers: EU's Canete implicated in leak," *EUobserver*, 4 April 2016:
https://euobserver.com/justice/132897

UN initiative on industry transition, led by Sweden and India: "Lead IT":

"Agreement on higher ambitions and increased international collaboration at
LeadIT Summit," press release, Ministry of the Environment, Swedish
government, 1 December 2020: https://www.government.se/press-
releases/2020/12/agreement-on-higher-ambitions-and-increased-
international-collaboration-at-leadit-summit/

"Sweden, India re-affirm commitment to LeadIT at virtual summit," Leadership
Group for Industry Transition, 9 March 2021: https://www.
industrytransition.org/insights/sweden-india-re-affirm-commitment-
to-leadership-group-for-industry-transition-leadit/

**Three Green Party-initiated reforms that enabled world-unique investment
green steel:**

Klimatlagen: *Ordning och reda i klimatpolitiken*, motion to Swedish parliament
2012/13:MJ481 by Åsa Romson et al. (Green Party): https://www.
riksdagen.se/sv/dokument-lagar/dokument/motion/ordning-och-reda-
i-klimatpolitiken_H002MJ481/html

Energiöverenskommelsen: *100 procent förnybar energi*, motion to parliament
2013/14:N352 by Lise Nordin et al. (Green Party): https://data.
riksdagen.se/fil/3BE7AEDD-9714-485C-AABD-3A9F0C2F39BE

Establishment of *Industriklivet*: "Långsiktig satsning för att minska industrins
utsläpp av växthusgaser," press release, Ministry of the Environment,
Swedish government, 26 August 2017: https://www.regeringen.se/
pressreleasen/2017/08/langsiktig-satsning-for-att-minska-industrins-
utslapp-av-vaxthusgaser/

Chapter 10: Hate, Threats and Democracy

Use of language and more:

"Så sprids nazisternas mordfantasier," *Expo*, 21 June 2018: https://expo. se/2018/06/sa-sprids-nazisternas-mordfantasier

"Trump defended Jan. 6 Capitol rioters chanting 'hang Mike Pence,' called anger over Biden election result 'common sense'," *CNBC*, 12 November 2021: https://www.cnbc.com/2021/11/12/trump-defended-jan-6-capitol-rioters-chanting-hang-mike-pence.html

Ivar Arpi on Twitter 6 January 2021 (later deleted): "Men för guds skull, sluta kalla det ett kuppförsök! Det är uselt ändå och ska givetvis fördömas, men ingen, absolut ingen, kan tro att detta leder till att några arga killar i mjukisbyxor som tar selfies snart tar makten i USA."

"Hur ofarliga är våra egna 20-åringar i mjukisbyxor?" *Magasinet Paragraf*, 7 January 2021: https://www.magasinetparagraf.se/nyheter/ kronikor/202585-hur-ofarliga-ar-vara-egna-20-aringar-i-mjukisbyxor/

Jamie Roberts: *Four Hours at the Capitol*, HBO Original, 2021: https://www.hbo. com/movies/four-hours-at-the-capitol

Januariavtalet (January Agreement): https://www.mp.se/januariavtalet

"Busch: Sverige har styrts av partier som trott att det går att runda folkviljan," *Omni*, 20 June 2021: https://omni.se/busch-sverige-har-styrts-av-partier-som-trott-att-det-gar-att-runda-folkviljan/a/1BmlJQ

"Alex Voronov: Mygel, sa kappvändaren," *Eskilstuna-Kuriren*, 22 June 2021: https://ekuriren.se/artikel/r91n1nzl

"Kristersson får hård kritik: 'Mycket farligt språkbruk'," *Svenska Dagbladet*, 4 September 2021: https://www.svd.se/partiledare-far-kritik-for-sprakbruk

"Åkesson: Att fälla Löfven viktigare än egen politik," *Svenska Dagbladet*, 1 February 2020: https://www.svd.se/akesson-viktigare-att-falla-regeringen-an-egen-politik

"Ohelig allians kan fälla Sveriges regering på måndag," *Hufvudstadsbladet*, 20 June 2021: https://www.hbl.fi/artikel/kommentar-ohelig-allians-kan-falla-sveriges-regering-pa-mandag/

Green Party has most dropouts in local politics:

"Två år efter valet: Så många politiker har lämnat," *Dagens Arena*, 6 October 2020: https://www.dagensarena.se/innehall/tva-ar-efter-valet/

"Avhopp från politiskt förtroendeuppdrag: Helt eller delvis på grund av hot och hat," Sveriges Kommuner och Regioner, 19 October 2020: https:// webbutik.skr.se/bilder/artiklar/pdf/7585-899-9.pdf

"Hot och hat påverkar: Intervjuer om förtroendevaldas situation," Sveriges
    Kommuner och Regioner, 8 November 2018: https://webbutik.skr.se/
    sv/artiklar/hot-och-hat-paverkar.html

Green Party least popular:

"SvD/Sifo: Så få accepterar Miljöpartiet i en regering," *Svenska Dagbladet*,
    21 February 2022: https://www.svd.se/svd-sifo-sa-fa-accepterar-
    miljopartiet-i-en-regering

Greens most targeted by fake news:

"Disinformation, fake news plague German election campaign," Deutsche Welle,
    6 September 2021: https://www.dw.com/en/disinformation-fake-
    news-plague-german-election-campaign/a-59104314

"German Greens' election hopeful targeted by fake news," France 24, 29 April
    2021: https://www.france24.com/en/live-news/20210429-german-
    greens-election-hopeful-targeted-by-fake-news

Green Party highest percentage of representatives receiving threats:

"MP Sveriges mest hotade parti: 'Man blir avtrubbad'," TV4, 28 October
    2021: https://www.tv4.se/artikel/1p8poGeyCAozuQBOHLnhHj/
    mp-sveriges-mest-hotade-parti-man-blir-avtrubbad

"Politikernas trygghetsundersökning," Brottsförebyggande rådet (Brå), 28 October
    2021: https://bra.se/statistik/statistiska-undersokningar/politikernas-
    trygghetsundersokning.html

"Hotet mot Amanda Lind: Jag skulle hängas i en snara av mitt eget hår,"
    Expressen, 21 February 2021: https://www.expressen.se/debatt/hotet-
    hanga-mig-i-en-snara-av-mitt-eget-har/

"Hoten mot Bromhed (MP) är ett hot mot vår demokrati," *Helahälsingland*,
    1 October 2021: https://www.helahalsingland.se/2021-10-01/
    demervall-hoten-mot-bromhed-mp-ar-ett-hot-mot-var-demokrati

Examples of anti-Green Party rhetoric:

"Morell (SD): 'Största hotet mot miljön är Miljöpartiet'," *Tidningen Proffs*,
    8 September 2021: https://www.tidningenproffs.se/asikter/2021/09/
    morell-sd-storsta-hotet-mot-miljon-ar-miljopartiet/

"Bränslechocken – därför pyr missnöjet med klimatpolitiken," *Dagens Nyheter*,
    9 February 2022: https://www.dn.se/sverige/branslechocken-darfor-
    pyr-missnojet-med-klimatpolitiken/

Decreased confidence in democracy:

Youth and Satisfaction with Democracy, Bennett Institute for Public Policy at
    the University of Cambridge, October 2020: https://www.bennett-
    institute.cam.ac.uk/media/uploads/files/Youth_and_Satisfaction_with_
    Democracy_lite.pdf

Tillståndet i demokratin. En opinionsundersökning av Studieförbunden, 2017:
http://docplayer.se/68532700-Tillstandet-i-demokratin-en-
opinionsundersokning-av-studieforbunden.html

Åsa Wikforss: *Alternativa fakta: Om kunskapen och dess fiender*, Fri Tanke Förlag,
2020.

Chapter 11: The Corporations

Updated "purpose" of corporations:

"Nearly 200 CEOs just agreed on an updated definition of 'the purpose of a
corporation'," *Quartz*, 19 August 2019: https://qz.com/work/1690439/
new-business-roundtable-statement-on-the-purpose-of-companies/

Klaus Schwab: *Shaping the Future of the Fourth Industrial Revolution: A guide to
building a better world*, Portfolio Penguin, 2018.

Klaus Schwab: *Stakeholder Capitalism: A Global Economy that Works for Progress,
People and Planet*, Wiley, 2021.

Proportion of total anthropogenic climate emissions from fossil fuels:

UNEP Emissions Gap 2021 report (chapter 2.2): https://www.unep.org/
resources/emissions-gap-report-2021

Small number of companies produce majority of emissions:

"New report shows just 100 companies are source of over 70% of emissions,"
Disclosure Insight Action, 10 July 2017: https://www.cdp.net/en/
articles/media/new-report-shows-just-100-companies-are-source-of-
over-70-of-emissions

"The Carbon Majors Database, CDP Carbon Majors Report 2017," CDP,
July 2017: https://cdn.cdp.net/cdp-production/cms/reports/
documents/000/002/327/original/Carbon-Majors-Report-2017.
pdf?1501833772

Paul Griffin et al., "The Carbon Majors Database: Methodology Report," CDP
Worldwide, July 2017.

"Update of Carbon Majors 1965–2018," press release, Climate Accountability
Institute (CAI), 9 December 2020: https://climateaccountability.org/
pdf/CAI%20PressRelease%20Dec20.pdf

"Saudiska oljejätten Aramco rusade under börsdebut," SVT Nyheter, 11
December 2019: https://www.svt.se/nyheter/saudiska-oljejatten-
aramco-debuterar-pa-borsen

Stockholm Environment Institute: *The Production Gap Report 2021*.

Concentration of ownership of the biosphere:

Carl Folke et al: "Transnational corporations and the challenge of biosphere stewardship," *Nature Ecology & Evolution*, vol. 3, October 2019, p. 1396–1403.

Sweden and Cementa's authorization:

"Lagrådet säger nej till undantagslag för Cementa," *Dagens Nyheter*, 16 September 2021: https://www.dn.se/ekonomi/lagradet-sager-nej-till-forslag-om-undantag-for-cementa/

"Enig riksdag röstade ja till fortsatt kalkbrytning," *Arbetaren*, no. 77, 2021: https://www.arbetaren.se/2021/09/30/enig-riksdag-rostade-ja-till-fortsatt-kalbrytning/

Thurlow quote:

Oliver Bullough: *Moneyland: Why Thieves & Crooks Now Rule the World & How to Take it Back*, p. 93, Profile Books, 2019.

Profit as purpose of corporations:

Lynn A. Stout: *The Shareholder Value Myth: How Putting Shareholders First Harms Investors, Corporations, and the Public*, BK Business Book, 2012.

Lynn A. Stout: "Corporations Don't Have to Maximize Profits," *New York Times*, 16 April 2015: https://www.nytimes.com/roomfordebate/2015/04/16/what-are-corporations-obligations-to-shareholders/corporations-dont-have-to-maximize-profits

"Does Jack Welch Think Shareholder Value is a Dumb Idea?" CBS News, 25 March 2009: https://www.cbsnews.com/news/does-jack-welch-think-shareholder-value-is-a-dumb-idea/

Aktiebolagslagen 2005:551: https://www.riksdagen.se/sv/dokument-lagar/dokument/svensk-forfattningssamling/aktiebolagslag-2005551_sfs-2005-551

ICGN (International Corporate Governance Network): *Statement of Shared Climate Change Responsibilities to the United Nations Climate Change Conference of the Parties 26*, 20 October 2021: https://www.icgn.org/statement-shared-climate-change-responsibilities-cop26

Polly Higgins: *Eradicating Ecocide: Exposing the Corporate and Political Practices Destroying the Planet and Proposing the Laws to Eradicate Ecocide*, Shepheard-Walwyn, 2010.

Maria Modig: *Den nödvändiga olydnaden*, Natur & Kultur, 1984.

Chapter 12: The Narrative

Defenders of Ambitious Climate Action: https://www.highambitioncoalition.org

Polynesian Voyaging Society: https://www.hokulea.com/moananuiakea/; http://

www.hokulea.com/hokulea-update-world-oceans-day/

George Monbiot: *Out of the Wreckage*: A new politics for an age of crisis, Verso, 2017.

Amartya Sen: *Identity and Violence*, Norton, 2006.

The Sustainable Development Agenda: 17 Goals for People, for Planet: https://www. un.org/sustainabledevelopment/development-agenda/

Francis Fukuyama: *The End of History and the Last Man*, Free Press, 1992.

"Full text: Trump's 2017 U.N. speech transcript," *Politico*, 19 September 2017: https://www.politico.com/story/2017/09/19/trump-un-speech-2017-full-text-transcript-242879

"The hive switch":

Jonathan Haidt: *The Righteous Mind: Why Good People Are Divided by Politics and Religion*, Vintage Books, 2013.

Our Common Agenda, United Nations Secretary-General's report, 2021: https://www.un.org/en/content/common-agenda-report/

Chapter 13: The Oceanic Feeling

Sigmund Freud: *The Future of an Illusion*, Institute of Psychoanalysis/Horace Liveright, 1928.

William. B. Parsons: "The Oceanic Feeling Revisited," including Romain Rolland's letter to Freud, *The Journal of Religion*, 78, p. 501–523, 1998.

Sigmund Freud: *Civilization and Its Discontents*, Institute of Psycho-analysis/ Hogarth Ltd., 1969.

Romain Rolland: *The Life of Ramakrishna*, Advaita Ashrama, 1929.

Jussi Saarinen: "The Oceanic Feeling: A Case Study in Existential Feeling," *Journal of Consciousness Studies*, vol. 21, no. 5–6, p. 196–217, 2014.

Grön ideologi – Solidaritet i handling, Miljöpartiets partiprogram i kortversion: https://www.mp.se/sites/default/files/partiprogram_kortversion_klarsprak_webbversion.pdf

"Climate change in focus when President Tong visited Sweden," press release, Swedish government, 11 March 2015: https://www.government.se/articles/2015/03/climate-change-in-focus-when-president-tong-visited-sweden/

"Sjunkande land vädjar om hjälp," *Svenska Dagbladet*, 9 March 2015: https://www.svd.se/sjunkande-land-vadjar-om-hjalp

"Minister for International Development Cooperation visits Tonga, Fiji and Kiribati," press release, Swedish government, 17 February 2016: https://www.government.se/articles/2016/02/minister-for-international-development-cooperation-visits-tonga-fiji-and-kiribati/

"Ny strategi för regionalt utvecklingssamarbete i Asien och Oceanien 2016–2021,"

Ministry for Foreign Affairs, June 2016: https://www.regeringen.se/land--och-regionsstrategier/2016/08/strategi-asien-oceanien/

UN Ocean Conference, 2017:

Official website: https://oceanconference.un.org/about

Our Ocean, Our Future: Call for Action, resolution adopted by UN General Assembly, 2017: https://digitallibrary.un.org/record/1291421?ln=en

"UN Ocean Conference Concludes with Call For Action and 1,300 Commitments," IISD/SDG Knowledge Hub, 13 June 2017: https://sdg.iisd.org/news/un-ocean-conference-concludes-with-call-for-action-and-1300-commitments/

Silent Seas - The Fish Race to the Bottom

ISBN 9781908341532